SHADOW OF DARKNESS, DAWNING OF LIGHT

The Awakening of Human Consciousness
in the 21st Century and Beyond

by

Paul Tice

The Book Tree
San Diego, California

© 2008, 2016
The Book Tree

All rights reserved. No part of this book, in part or in whole, may be reproduced, transmitted, or utilized, in any form or by any means, electronic or mechanical, including photocopying, recording, or by any information storage or retrieval system, without permission in writing from the author, except for brief quotations in articles, books and reviews.

Second edition 2016
Revised and Updated

ISBN 978-1-885395-99-3

Cover layout & design

Mike Sparrow

Editor

Tony Presser

Published by
The Book Tree
P O Box 16476
San Diego, CA 92176
www.thebooktree.com

We provide fascinating and educational products to help awaken the public to new ideas and information that would not be available otherwise.
Call 1 (800) 700-8733 for our *FREE BOOK TREE CATALOG*.

Consciousness is a singular for which there is no plural.
—Erwin Schrodinger

Also by Paul Tice

Triumph of the Human Spirit: The Greatest Achievements of the Human Soul and How Its Power Can Change Your Life

Life's Biggest Questions Workbook

THIS Is a Book: Why Real Books are Better

A Booklet of Meaningful Quotes

That Old-Time Religion: The Story of Religious Foundations, with Jordan Maxwell and Dr. Alan Albert Snow

Mysteries Explored: The Search for Human Origins, UFOs, and Religious Beginnings, with Jack Barranger

The Book No Pope Would Want You to Read, contributor

CONTENTS

Introduction 7
1) Identity 19
2) Education 29
3) Catalysts for Change 63
4) Deeper Levels of Reality 71
5) Greed, Conspiracies and the Meaning of Life 79
6) Mind Cages 93
7) Primitive Politics 107
8) Holistic World View 115
9) Control of the Soul 145
10) Astrological Ages 151
11) Paradigm Lost 159
12) New World Economics 179
13) Mutual Respect and Religion 199
14) The God Pact 209
15) Shifting the Paradigm 219
Bibliography and Recommended Reading 237
Index 240

Acknowledgments

Heartfelt thanks to Vicki Renee for her many years of love and support. She has expanded my spiritual horizons through her intuitive gifts, the depth of her poetry, and the love of all creatures. Thank you to Tony Presser for his sharp editing skills and suggestions made in the final draft. A special thank you to Rebecca Wadsworth for her continued help and support, and to my father, whose timely wisdom and advice over the years have been greatly appreciated. I am thankful to Jack Barranger for his years of friendship and the recommendation of many interesting books that have helped shape my thoughts. Also to Jordan Maxwell, who was the first person to open my eyes to the behind the scenes reality of world affairs and how to look more deeply for the truth. I am grateful to Janis Boles for the transcription of audiotape lectures connected to this work and especially to you, the reader, for your interest in this important subject and for whom this book was written.

INTRODUCTION

Evolution of consciousness is the central motive of terrestrial existence. —Sri Aurobindo

Humanity has been evolving on a conscious level and the pace of its transformation has quickened with time. We will soon find ourselves confronted with a situation that *requires* a mass awakening in order for us to survive, but with very few having experienced such a state. Therefore, we need an answer, or a course of action, that will bring us into a new form of thought better suited toward planetary survival. This means salvaging the planet's dwindling resources and its damaged eco-system, caused by the warped sense of reality of the main perpetrators, mankind itself.

We currently operate from within a form of consciousness that is so flawed that it is destroying the planet and ourselves. We lack the knowledge of our own identities—not even knowing who we are in relation to the rest of creation, so we fail to behave in a way that respects it. If the crisis we have created does not lead to our self-destruction, it can do only one other thing—awaken us, very quickly, to our own self-recognition. If we can experience that, then the rest of what needs to happen may fall into place.

In this section, I have outlined a four-point societal plan which, if implemented, can not only guide us into a new form of consciousness, but an entirely new paradigm altogether. It is a guideline for world change—through consciousness change. The remainder of the book will flow in and out of the four major areas that challenge our growth: the recognition of our true identity, a new educational approach, a holistic awareness (with its matching proper conduct), and the restructuring of global economics.

Since this *Introduction* serves as an overview, some parts do in fact repeat themselves later in the text. I opted to leave these later sections intact, however, due to their level of importance and because the work would otherwise lose its flow.

The Human Predicament

We believe ourselves to be in control of human destiny and the planet, but more and more each day, we find this control vanishing. Why? As far as consciousness is concerned, humanity is living in the dark ages. At some future point we will look back and be amazed at how ignorant we were during these times, while having remained so steadfast in our egotistical, narrow views.

We currently believe ourselves to be "advanced" from a conscious point of view—yet the vast majority of us, including world leaders, are living in a completely unconscious state—the exact opposite of how we perceive ourselves.

This earth is populated by ignorant sleepwalkers who continually fight and kill each other over the planet's resources. The "victor" that emerges with control of these valued resources has won the privilege to blindly pollute our home and ruin the fragile, natural balance of the earth. That balance has weakened to such an alarming level that we are in peril of losing our place on this planet should we not make immediate changes. In the past hundred years, we have managed to deplete and ruin millions of years' worth of the earth's precious resources, including much of its water and atmosphere, directly contributing to the extinction of a few hundred thousand species of plants and animals. From a collective level, very few seem to care, or have not bothered to notice. This situation is similar to the Titanic tragically hitting its deadly iceberg, followed by the captain announcing that it's time to take a nap.

We need to start acting quickly to reverse some gigantic trends, but it's not going to happen until more of us "wake up." This is no time to take a nap—or rather, to continue it. Survival is about awareness. And with a limited awareness, our priorities—as caretakers of the earth—have become scattered and confused. We can marvel at the incredible technology and amazing scientific advances we have achieved, and base our views of consciousness on that, but we have yet to place them into a larger framework that allows us to function holistically. Our best science and technology are most often used for warfare, the most divisive and damaging human endeavor ever conceived. And we call it progress.

Those few who are truly awake in today's world are considered "freaks" by those in the mainstream, and are often ridiculed by any media that could otherwise use them as role models to help awaken others. The "machine," at least at this point, does not allow such things. So these awakened ones, often teachers of great wisdom, only appear to students who are ready for their wisdom and the resulting personal changes that often follow.

Many of us do sense that something is wrong. The great thinkers of the 21st Century will be charting a completely new direction. It does not take a genius to see that the path we are on does not bode well for our future if it remains the same. If we should exhibit enough wisdom as a species, then this new direction should contain the following features.

1) Identity. Having an understanding of who we really are and why we are here in the physical world. Without this foundational starting point, it is unlikely that any of the other features will follow or, if they do, have much impact.

2) Education. A completely revised and updated educational system must be based on the revelation of identity. With a better understanding of exactly what a human being really is, we can then intelligently approach how to determine our values and future actions. This revelation of identity will not happen overnight, so we should have enough foresight to begin using spiritually based educational programs to serve as a catalyst for higher awareness.

3) Holistic Awareness. Requires us implementing what we have learned through this new educational process—first locally, then regionally, then throughout the world. This means achieving higher ethical standards, with compassion and mutual respect for other forms of life and belief systems. It also concerns a new ecological, green-based view of the environment, which is already here and beginning to strengthen.

4) Economic Restructuring. The final implementation of this new consciousness, on a worldly scale, involves using the fruits of this gradual awakening in local and world economics. Without such usage, we will remain as slaves. The vast majority in the world could still reach these three previously stated goals or realizations; but if those who control the economic purse-strings of the planet insist on continuing to impose their materialistic control on the rest of us, then positive change may remain difficult. It does not seem likely that the world economic system will change unless the first three points mentioned are successfully addressed. The first three are a prerequisite for the fourth; otherwise, a *successful* economic restructuring will likely never be achieved. We can, however, overcome each of these four challenges with clear focus and intent.

People often listen to ideas such as the four just listed, dwell on them briefly, and move on with their lives without doing anything. Unfortunately, when people move on with their lives without action they fall back asleep. Therefore, I will elaborate on each of these points to get the point driven home and keep you awake a little longer. The great sage Gurdjieff would often do outrageous things in the presence of his students just to snap them out of their daily stupor. Since I am not with you physically, I will instead try to "awaken" you with words rather than actions.

In the coming years, humanity's awareness will only increase in response to its discomfort. Yet the level of discomfort we already have spells out how late we are in the game. It is almost too late. What people will be wanting, more and more with each passing day, is a new paradigm to operate under to relieve us of the increasing discomfort that will continue to manifest. What we must understand, however, is that this new paradigm will never come to pass successfully *unless we do something now*. We must begin to bring structure to this new paradigm or path. How do we do it?

Identity

We must step back from this worldly dilemma and figure out who "we" are, first. It is essential to understand that it is not the *path* we must examine, which is what we've been doing all along. It is the traveler. Identifying what goes *on* the path, meaning us, needs to be determined before one can know whether or not it is proper for us to be there. We've been approaching things backwards and must now look from the inside out, instead of focusing on outer conditions first. In each individual case, this journey through life is being taken by a soul who is using a body. We are using this body to experience certain challenges and to learn from them.

Most of us believe that we are a physical body that may happen to have a soul. That is the extent of it, since no one can scientifically prove the existence of the soul right now. Although many of us can *feel* our souls, we place more importance on our bodies because they can be *seen*. If we don't know who we really are, then how are we going to figure out what this journey is all about?

We cannot change the world's structure overnight, but what we can change and what we have the power to change is ourselves. We can do this in a more appropriate way, based on how we view ourselves, who we really are and what we're doing here. After we experience this life, the world will be left behind. What we take with us when we leave is going to be important.

Far more is involved in grasping our true identities, but this is a start. At some future time, possibly in the coming century, we will more clearly identify a basic religious "structure" existing in the world and come to understand how it has served us in our spiritual infancy. Although we will begin to "see through" the various religions of the world, we will still respect them all in a mutual sense, rather than attacking those that differ from our views.

We will begin to understand how to transcend the inherent duality of the world while gaining an understanding of our own dualistic natures. Many will learn how to use our own spiritual powers to tap in and experience our true selves more deeply. Those entrenched in or strictly brought up within a strict religious dogma will be the very last ones to connect with their inner spiritual power—holding out instead for some outside power or "savior" to show up instead. When one examines the original teachings of the great masters like Jesus, Buddha, Mohammed and others, one will find that they preached such inner teachings from the very beginning. We have an inner power that should be used, not hidden away. Jesus taught in parables, often showing us how to use our spiritual gifts. His sayings, as found in the *Gospel of Thomas*, are magnificent examples.

During the next millennium, we will discover spiritual secrets through a deeper exploration of advanced science and quantum physics. We will gain a better understanding of how and why the cycles of both time and nature connect directly to each of us. So far, however, we know very little about our true selves. We have explored and conquered much of the visible world, but the inner world, which awaits, promises the greatest of treasures.

Transform yourself and walk away, at least a bit further, from the outer "you." There is no organization out there, outside of yourself, which has your truth. Including organized religions. Only you have your truth. And if you're not willing to look for it, then you will never be able to find it.

After you have been jarred from the path that this "system" wants you on, it's time to proceed with a new path—one that will actually get you somewhere. A number of methods are available to transform yourself, but you must choose something that feels right for you. With that said, meditation is a good choice because it has been proven successful for thousands of years and is the key component for those who have reached an enlightened state.

Various methods exist, but the first thing we need to do is to define meditation. What exactly is it? Meditation is a way to relax the mind so fully that an elevated state of consciousness can be achieved. Some will point out that this higher state of consciousness cannot actually be "achieved" because we already have it. It's just a matter of accessing it and knowing *how* to access it. Many other ways exist to wake us up, but consistent meditation is a good starting point.

The conscious mind, without being grounded in meditation, is often equated to having a chattering monkey in your head, sending you in unwanted directions and preventing a focused life. We are stumbling around without true wisdom because we have not developed it yet. We are mistreating each other and the planet to an incredible degree because we simply don't know any better. Because of this we are easily manipulated and treated like *sheeple*, by those who know how to exploit us. But with an awakened humanity, without a bunch of sleepwalkers responding blindly to whatever is dictated to them, a huge wave of compassion and mutual respect could crash down upon the face of the earth and transform it almost instantly. Since a mass awakening of this magnitude probably won't happen soon, or so suddenly, the next best thing is to start educating ourselves with this aim in mind.

Education

When we reach the point where we understand more about who we really are, an educational system should be in place that caters to us as spiritual beings rather than one that mainly grooms and conditions us to function as workers for corporations. A new educational approach, begun now, can serve as a catalyst for this new awareness. Humanity will advance faster when we can identify a proper life path for each individual and limit the exploitation that occurs for material gain only.

For now, it has gotten to the point where we have lost sight of our own values for the sake of materialistic gain. We chase the almighty dollar from an early age, being brainwashed into thinking that an abundance of money is the key to happiness. It is not, and the bulk of profits often goes to those at the very top, while the vast majority of us who do virtually all the work earn the "privilege" of working paycheck to paycheck, struggling to pay the bills and feed our families. This struggle and its resulting stress rips families and people apart. The worldwide economic system has become a huge, untamed monster that will be overcome only through concerted effort and mindful planning. Many of us deserve far more than we are getting, and should start planning now.

Becoming aware of our true selves does not mean that we will become instantly enlightened as a result. It means that we may be able to see a more beneficial path for humanity more clearly, so that we can begin to work toward something better. It will start with education.

Some groups have spiritually based, non-sectarian education programs in place that could lead the way in this regard. One of those is the Oak Grove School, fashioned after the spiritual teachings of Jiddu Krishnamurti, founded in 1975 and located in Ojai, California. Krishnamurti was a man of great wisdom who wanted to instill a sense of spirit in people above and beyond anything else. Of course many worldly and necessary things are taught at this school as well, but its main focus is the attempt to create a more fully rounded, conscious human being. As a society we are still lacking in educational programs that strive for the most full and complete development—spiritually, mentally, and physically—of students, so this is a good model for meaningful education that should be seriously explored.

Another well-tested, proven program was developed in 1919 by Rudolf Steiner, called Waldorf Education. It is geared primarily for children and the spiritual realities of the developing child. Its stated goal is "to produce individuals who are able, in and of themselves, to impart meaning to their lives." This is one of the fastest growing educational programs in the world, with about 900 schools worldwide in over 32 countries, with about 150 in North America. It has not being given much press, but there is a "Waldorf Movement" growing in the world. Although more spiritual than standardized education, some of the schools are fully accredited and recognized by governmental authorities.

The curriculum covers different religious viewpoints but is not religiously based in itself. This did not stop a lawsuit from being filed in California against two government school districts employing Waldorf methods, claiming that the schools violate the First Amendment's protection against the establishment of a state sponsored religion. The court quickly ruled in favor of Waldorf in the 2005 trial. It seems that some fundamentalist Christians are petrified that children are being taught to *think for themselves*. Concerned Christians protested at other Waldorf schools in California, claiming the schools were "rooted in a New Age, cult-like religious sect."

Everyone outside of a dogmatic fundamentalist mindset should be excited about Waldorf education. For example, according to the Wikipedia Internet information on Waldorf, the SAT scores of Waldorf students in the U.S. are usually above the national average, despite the fact that standardized testing is not used as much within its program. In Germany, Waldorf graduates as a group passed their college entrance exams at double and triple the rate of state-educated students. According to UNESCO, a Waldorf training college in South Africa was instrumental in the elimination of apartheid, and a Waldorf school in Israel employs both Arab and Jewish faculty for a student body of the same diversity. In 2005, the first Arab-Jewish kindergarten was founded near Haifa in Israel. An international study shows that Waldorf students are more creative than state-educated children. All in all, it has been shown that this type of program can make a positive difference in the world and is the next logical step for us to take in a spiritual direction.

As part of the program, Steiner developed something called *eurythmy* — taught in the schools and described as a new art of movement for the human form. It allows body, mind and spirit to be expressed as a functional unity, sometimes referred to as "visible speech." Steiner was brilliant. He founded the Anthroposophic Society, wrote dozens of books and had a profound understanding of the human spirit. He, like Krishnamurti, was considered to be ahead of his time.

Another interesting educational system worth mentioning has been developed by Daisaku Ikeda, who has devoted his life to promoting peace through education. Unlike the Oak Grove School and Waldorf, it is based on a religious framework, being Buddhist, but George David Miller, in his book *Peace, Value and Wisdom: The Educational Philosophy of Daisaku Ikeda*, puts forth in his Conclusion a number of creative applications of Ikeda's philosophy that could seemingly be applied in general terms without the need of a prerequisite religious mindset or having religious conversion as an aim. Certain spiritual truths cut across all religions and it might be possible to expand parts of Ikeda's brilliant spiritual program into a more secular framework.

There are other alternative systems that could be used, but these are the most proven and powerful ones this author has found. None are perfect, but as we learn more about ourselves, we may modify them as we progress. This will be a gradual process because none of these systems should be "imposed" on the masses. As more and more communities willingly test the methods and see the benefits, things will progress.

Holistic Awareness

The more spiritually aware we become, the more we understand that everything is connected. The divisions we have created between ourselves will gradually fall away—the most challenging one being religious in nature.

The fiercest and most barbaric human actions on this earth have resulted from the "my God can beat up your God" syndrome, with a non-stop history of incredibly dense and barbaric morons rushing headlong into any kind of fray they can find, just to prove that point. After centuries of this behavior, these people have failed to wipe each other out for the benefit of all others who have discovered a higher use for the brain. As we become more spiritually evolved, we will continue to move farther away from religion, as evidenced by the large number of people who have abandoned their faiths, which "seem to be missing something," during the last century. We will look back and see that religion was a tool, or a crutch, to help us along to a higher awareness. There is good in every religion, so taking its goodness can be a learning experience that we should embrace while we have the opportunity. Many have taken these lessons and moved on, "graduating," if you will, to a more spiritual, rather than dogmatic, point of view.

There's a distinction that should be made between religion and spirituality. Religion is for the masses, while spirituality is for the individual. There is nothing wrong with religion if you want to be part of the masses, but if you want to be an individual and search more deeply, then spirituality will come into play. Virtually all organized religion, from inception, has been in constant dispute among its own members and between all other organized religions. There have been more people killed in the history of this earth because of religion than for any other reason.

Then we have spirituality. With true spirituality, if it is recognized within one's self, there can be no dispute whatsoever. True spirituality transcends all religious boundaries. If we can learn to respect one another in a spiritual sense, without bringing man-made religions into it, then it would solve all kinds of problems that we've been experiencing throughout the world. If we ever want to make any progress, then spirituality is the answer as opposed to the divisive religions in this world. The sooner we realize that, the better off we will be.

We have begun to see the earth and its natural eco-system in a holistic way, but must act in ways that can truly make a difference. We must adopt a holistic view or continue to self-destruct. We are all one with each other, and with nature as well. We have started to understand this about nature, but not ourselves. That is because science can examine the natural world and clearly conclude how we have poisoned the earth. We cannot see so clearly our poisoned souls.

Economic Restructuring

A restructured world economy is the payoff point. There will be no new paradigm until the worldwide materialistic economic stranglehold is released from the suffering millions. We suffer at the expense of profit, while the vast majority never profit at all, in any way. Am I promoting socialism? No. I am promoting compassion and spiritual awareness—a mode of thought that goes beyond any "isms."

What we are finding in the early 21st Century, as far as compassionate, positive change is concerned, is that the governments of the world continue to fail and are making less of an impact. The worldwide economic system does not allow individual governments, locked within the financial clutches of their "system," to do anything except pay back (or try to pay back) the loans made from international banks, taken out just so these governments can continue to operate. In turn, most individuals are being financially squeezed in the same way, for the same reasons—but on a smaller scale.

How strong, or willing, is the world economic system when it comes to helping us, rather than bankers? When a major disaster occurs, as in the case of the huge tsunami in Indonesia in 2004, the New Orleans hurricane disaster of 2005, or the continuing Darfur genocide in Africa, we find famous actors and artists coming to the rescue more than governmental agencies, mostly through music. Concerts put on by caring musicians have raised enough funds—coming from *us*, rather than governments—to save many people from starvation, death and disease. This trend started in the late 20th Century with the Farm Aid concerts, meant to raise money for U.S. farmers who were having their farms repossessed by the banks.

If this trend continues, then in another century or two the world's most creative people will be running the world—after the current system has run everyone else into the ground. Beware of governments that offer to "work with" these artists. I would suspect this has already started to happen, and to the artists and musicians I say this: Trust your instincts, handle it yourselves, and steer clear of government-related "authorities."

A powerful reflection of our spiritual awareness can be seen in what we eat. In large part, what we consume controls the economy. Our choice in food, especially meat, plays a negative role in the world. Every year more than 40 million people die of starvation, many being children, because more than a third of the world's grain goes to feed livestock instead of people. Children who need this grain, and would otherwise get it, starve to death because Burger King and McDonalds need their Whoppers and double cheeseburgers. It is a proven fact that each time you eat a four-ounce hamburger made from rain forest beef, you are allowing approximately 55 square feet of rain forest to vanish, and you contribute to the starvation of children.

Our bodies are not compatible for eating meat, which, by the way, is almost always filled with hormones not meant for human consumption, but pumped into the animal to make it grow at a hideous rate. You want fries with that? Carnivores have a much shorter digestive system to pass meat through more quickly. The long digestive tract of humans allows meat to rot inside the body before being fully digested, releasing toxins that contribute to the huge rates of cancer found as a result, not to mention the dozens of other diseases related directly to the consumption of meat.

Millions worldwide have no clean water to drink, while each pound of beef generated requires over 2400 gallons of water to produce. This water could be diverted to save lives, but the powers that be would never allow it. In the U.S., about 70% of all grain produced is gobbled up by livestock and nearly half the water used goes to growing feed for cattle and other livestock. If we fed people instead of livestock, no one would be starving.

Because of skyrocketing oil prices the U.S. has now begun to use 20% of its grain to create a methanol additive for car fuel, and this percentage will undoubtedly increase. We have diverted so much of our food into non-edible purposes, for humans, by feeding cattle and creating alternative fuels, that a major food crisis has begun worldwide (termed a crisis by the United Nations), causing riots in a number of countries. According to *Time Magazine* (Apr. 8, 2008), the only existing biofuel that is cost effective is sugarcane, and the ethanol used to fill just one SUV with fuel could feed one person with the same grain for an entire year. These types of things have always been the concerns of "environmental extremists," and ignored by the general public, but it has now become abundantly clear that these are serious, legitimate concerns about things that will actually kill us—all or most of us—if we fail to act. This entire paradigm is on a crash course and we need to wake up and change it, on an individual or local level if necessary, using wind, solar, hydrogen and/or electric energy as alternatives.

As humanity awakens we will move further away from meat and the economic machinations that peddle it and waste our precious food and water resources in the process. The more intelligent you are, the more likely you will be vegetarian and join the ranks of Buddha, Plato, Pythagoras, Shakespeare, Socrates, Voltaire, Isaac Newton, Leonardo Da Vinci, Benjamin Franklin, Albert Einstein, Mahatma Gandhi, Albert Schweitzer, Bertrand Russell and Ralph Waldo Emerson, to name a few. Jesus might also be part of this list, which will be more fully explained later in the book. According to Sir Paul McCartney, legendary rock star and respected vegan activist, the best thing you can do to help save the planet is to become a vegan or vegetarian, echoing the same sentiments of Albert Einstein, the greatest mind of the 20th Century, from decades earlier.

On a personal level it is no coincidence that the greatest spiritual masters were, or are, vegetarian and require their students to be the same. Spiritual people don't normally allow their bodies to be a graveyard for the carcasses of other living beings. Stores and restaurants are now catering to vegetarianism to the point where you can find many great tasting and nutritious foods to eat while knowing that an innocent creature did not have to die a terrible death just so you could snack on it.

Those who control the worldwide economy have a vested interest in the things we purchase. We can choose otherwise. The agenda of such a system has nothing to do with spirituality, and that is what we're up against. But without a doubt, powerful economic systems always end up crashing. Self-sustaining, cooperative systems whereby everyone is more concerned with each other rather than themselves, stand a better chance at surviving over the long-term. This is not a plug for socialism or communism. A new paradigm is exactly that—new—and contains very little from the past in a foundational sense. A system based on spiritual values can thrive if it becomes a clear goal and we approach it intelligently.

Those who hold power of any kind should study Mahatma Gandhi's concept of *swadeshi*. This is a self-acting law requiring the volition of a person who strives to identify himself with the entire creation. This means being conscious enough to recognize a connection to all things; to see things holistically. According to Gandhi, the first duty of one with this mindset is to dedicate himself to his immediate neighbors. If prominent members in each community would focus in such a way, it would spread. A tremendous cohesion would result, along with local wealth, brotherly love, teamwork and a strong sense of community. This would create the fabric for a new economic paradigm, right within your home town—one that could replace the current paradigm that is destroying innocent lives and the environment. With such a system in place we would no longer feel helpless and would no longer *be* helpless. We would be proactive, with more direct control of our economic success. An amazing synergy would result and we would be far less dependent on unseen forces.

With the other extreme, we find the world economy and its "banksters" targeting larger populations. They have expanded at least partially into China and India, thereby becoming even more of an untamed monster that will ultimately destroy itself or the environment. Sixteen of the twenty most polluted cities are now in China, and their huge population is consuming food from other parts of the world, including many endangered species through the black market, at an alarming rate. We must bring nature back into balance rather than consuming it to death, and that goes for everyone. If nature dies, we all die—but like lemmings, we continue to rush headlong over the cliff.

Summary

If there was ever a time to wake up, it is now. If we try, we can reach each of the points I've covered. We can identify who we really are; we can educate ourselves responsibly as a result; we can achieve holistic awareness; and we can change the economic structure to support a new paradigm. I'm not saying any of this will happen. I'm saying that it can happen. None of it will happen by itself, so we must *wake up and act*. Don't be a sheep and wait for others to do it for you. Like Mahatma Gandhi said, "Be the change you want to see in the world." Without doing this, you are not really living.

Chapter One

IDENTITY

Men go abroad to wonder at the height of the mountains, at the huge waves of the sea, at the long course of the rivers, at the vast compass of the ocean, at the circular motion of the stars; and they pass by themselves without wondering.
—Saint Augustine

The destiny of mankind is not decided by material computation. We learn that we are spirits, not animals, and that something is going on in space and time, and beyond space and time, which, whether we like it or not, spells duty.
—Winston Churchill

We are on a journey in this life. The vast majority of us don't know why it started or where it's really going. The path we follow should be comfortable and have a clear purpose, but many seem to have strayed from our true path, or never found it. When things get confusing or when we seek guidance we often turn to religion. It should be clear, however, that I am not a proponent of any one faith, so have no religious agenda of any kind. Most religions of the world state in no uncertain terms that "my religion is better than yours. My God is better than yours. If you don't believe in what I believe, then you're going to hell. And only the chosen ones from my religion will be going to heaven. Everyone else is not going to join us because they're damned." I don't agree with that. We are all God's children no matter what we believe. Since God—the real God—is all loving, then none of us is going to burn in hell for failing to worship Him in the way a man-made religion has dictated. Instilling "the fear of God" into anyone for the purpose of having worshippers defeats God's purpose for us being here to begin with. Despite the separate claims of exclusivity to God, religions do offer one thing that ties everyone together quite nicely—it is acknowledged that we all have a special connection to God. That connection involves the human soul.

That is what is really taking the journey. Despite all of the physical and materialistic things around us that distract us from this higher part of us, including money, cars, sex, television, gourmet food, or whatever our desires can fixate on, despite all that, that inner part of us, the human soul, is the one thing that should be our focus. For the great majority of us, the soul is not any kind of a focus whatsoever and is usually ignored. That is because we cannot see the soul, so people have trouble accepting its reality. Yet those of us who have explored more deeply into the inner realms and have done years of meditation, inner work or introspection of some kind, or have spent time in nature, have formed a connection to the soul. They can understand and feel its presence. However, most of us are caught up in the day to day activity of paying the rent or mortgage, getting and keeping a job, putting food on the table, raising a family, all of the things that are necessary in this physical predicament that we're in. This is survival mode. More and more of us are being forced into this mode for various manipulative reasons by the powers that be, but a lot of these situations still force us to develop ourselves spiritually. These situations are trying on the soul, and a certain amount of progress can be made, but if we are focused on simply surviving during this lifetime and putting money into the system, so to speak, we have little time to productively focus on the more meaningful aspects of life and its purpose. In these situations, the growth of the soul remains stagnant.

We have developed a system that is economically and materialistically based. And when we come into this world we grow into and accept the structure that exists without exploring any alternatives. When we are too young to question things, we just accept them, and the mindset sticks. As you grow up and go through school, up through and including college, and you go out with your friends, you often end up in certain settings whereby anything can happen. You never know who you're going to run into or what can happen on that particular day. A lot of times the most unexpected things can and do happen. Many are high points and become quite memorable. But as we move through adolescence, we are slowly taught to weed out this kind of activity, and start thinking in more structured ways so we can take on the responsibility of doing one specific task in life. We are being "molded" in these years so we can work, pay taxes and be good, consuming citizens. How many people are totally bored with their jobs and look forward only to the weekends or their yearly vacations? It's a clear majority. I am not saying that we need a lack of structure to return to our lives, but we do need more variety, excitement and challenges. That is what life is all about. But our economic system would prefer you to be confined to a certain task and be a couch potato in your spare time—that is, until the TV tells you what to go out and buy. This entire structure is very limiting to the soul, offering little freedom, and at the same time it is something that, in the long term, is destined to fail.

Ask any economist who knows anything about the way the system is set up if there is a way to reverse inflation. Ask them if there is a way to turn things around so that prices will end up dropping, so there will suddenly be an economic system that can start afresh by simply reversing the trends. It's not possible. The only possible way that this particular materialistic economic world system is ever going to end is that it's going to completely crash. Then, at that point, we may have developed enough wisdom to create something far more nourishing to the human soul. But in the meantime, we are slaves to the system. When U.S. currency stopped being backed by gold and silver, oil stepped in and took over the role by proxy. We have been slaves to the oil cartels ever since. When we examine the world economy of oil, and the continually exploding gas prices, and the different wars across the planet that are continually fought over petroleum and similar resources, it makes us believe there could well be another (and better) way of doing things. We have begun to "go green" and are working assiduously toward alternative energy methods; but the transition is painful and legitimate concern exists over the development of a lasting solution. A solid solution will not emerge until we change the way we think first, thereby uprooting and replacing the entire paradigm. This means that the very foundation for an alternative path must be first laid down.

How do we figure out this alternative path? It must start at the root of the problem. We must step back from this worldly dilemma and figure out who "we" are, first. It is essential to understand that it is not the *path* we must examine, which is what we've been doing all along. It is the traveler. Identifying what goes *on* the path, meaning us, needs to be determined before one can know whether or not it is proper for us to be there. We've been approaching things backwards and must now look from the inside out, instead of focusing on outer conditions first. In each individual case, this journey through life is being taken by a soul who is using a body. We are doing this to experience certain challenges and to learn from them.

Most of us do not consider ourselves in that sense. Most believe that we are a physical body that may happen to have a soul. That is the extent of it, since no one can scientifically prove the existence of the soul right now. Although many of us can *feel* our souls, we place more importance on our bodies because they can be *seen*. We might believe in a certain religion or whatever form of belief we've inherited or stumbled upon what seemed to make sense at the time, but their teachings fall short. We more often act like animals rather than spiritual beings because we have very little soul contact with ourselves. We basically consider ourselves to be a human body that may possibly have some kind of a soul. A far better starting point comes with reversing that, and understanding that first and foremost we are a soul that is using a body on a temporary basis in order to learn and achieve certain things.

If we don't know who we really are, then how are we going to figure out what this journey is all about? Let me hypnotize you for a moment. Relax and be open. You are a zebra, okay? A zebra is at home in its natural, wild habitat. You can coax a zebra to run down a superhighway, using a carrot and a stick, but it is not going to be happy when it gets into the city. The zebra *does not care* about the city; it would much rather be free, but has been distracted by its desire to be nourished. For us, it's not about the city, or the outer world, or its distractions. It's a *spiritual* journey, not a physical one. Don't be a zebra, with limited vision. Stop running! Forget the outer desires that limit your vision to short-term results. Looking inward will create the outer change. Zebras are not very bright, so *stop being one!*

We cannot change the entire world structure overnight, but what we can change and what we have the power to change is ourselves. We can do this in a more appropriate way, based on how we view ourselves and on who we really are and what we're doing here. An awakening is needed. By awakening and becoming conscious of our true selves, the biggest thing we must do, as a result, is to *stop acting like zebras*. People who are truly awake don't do this, and that is the main thing I am trying to accomplish with this work. So wake up! You can stop being a zebra now. Turn around and, for the first time, look at who's holding that carrot you've been chasing all this time. You don't need them. They need you.

After we go through this journey and experience this life, the world will be left behind. What we take with us when we leave is suddenly going to be important—more important than being a manipulated "number" and trained consumer in this life.

So what is the meaning of all this? The meaning of life itself? Not just your own life, but all of life itself? That's the one question that has baffled the best philosophers throughout time, not to mention many average people like you and me. It is a complex answer that can be grasped if you understand a few basic ideas.

Sometimes the answer can be simplified in interesting forms like a Zen *koan*, or in the newspaper comics that use a less effective version of its method. One popular comic page motif is where someone has climbed a mountain to ask a secretive, bearded guru at the summit, in a cave, what the meaning of life is. The seeker is often given an answer which is either stupid or completely obvious, to cause a chuckle. That's where the comic ends. With the koan, the answer may seem stupid or nonsensical on the surface, but actually runs deeper and can mean something important to the more astute. A Zen koan may contain great wisdom.

Zen masters of the east often teach their students using koans whenever a situation may call for them. They are often presented as a riddle—like "What is the sound of one hand clapping?" It makes no sense on the surface, but the student is told to think about it and return later with the answer. From a logical standpoint a koan is a senseless or baffling question, statement or anecdote, unanswerable in its presented form, but is really pointing to or expressing an experience of ultimate reality. One of two things will happen when the student returns with his answer. 1) Due to a lack of concentration or energy the student will fail to conclude anything, or 2) The doubt in his mind will become so strong it will virtually take on a life of its own and thereby increase the concentration and energy of the student. The intense focus on the question will then cause an "explosion" of this doubt and, as a result, the student may become enlightened. Another example is the following. What did your face look like before there were your parents? In a strange way the answer to a koan has little to do with thinking. A sudden intuition often appears from out of nowhere, challenging the student to put it into words. But words are really not the goal. Here again we have duality at work—but on a higher level. Because of this duality, it is difficult to reach the answer to a koan—yet it is simple if we can put this duality aside. The point is to transcend it. This is done by changing one's consciousness in a way that allows a glimpse of things from an entirely new perspective. It is this duality, found within all space and time, which causes our confusion.

Duality, which governs our reality, is always striving for balance. Disharmony is constantly occurring, but the forces of balance (whether from mother nature or humankind) always rush in and attempt to balance it out. This entire world is one of duality that continually has to balance itself. That's why we have "the balance of nature." In nature there is night and day, birth and death, prey and aggressor, etc. This duality carries over into human areas, but at a higher perspective involving ethical concerns like good and evil. Because of this, life becomes difficult for us, primarily due to perspectives that disagree and create large areas of gray. Confusion and even warfare often result. Things can become simple, however, if we can put aside the duality through humanity's future strivings for peace, fairness, self-improvement and brotherly love. Such work will allow us to understand a confusing reality that does not seem to have much meaning to it on the surface (like a koan), but it is this duality that causes the confusion. Transcending duality allows a glimpse of Truth. Rather than glimpsing it, we must learn to live it.

Science will tell you that everything in this physical existence is a vibration. These vibrations are found within waves or in particles. In our existence there is either a particle or there is a wave. Quantum physicists have pointed out that it is sometimes hard to distinguish which is which, but our advanced science confirms that it is one or the other. Particles of matter do in fact have wavelengths, which can interfere with each other, while other waves stand on their own as waves. Which is which sometimes depends upon the observer and nothing more, rather than solid science. This fact casts a strange shadow over the hard-line materialists to be sure.

Any physical object consists of a vibrating wave or particle that we pick up with our eyes or with some other sense so that we know it's there. For example, radio waves are broadcast and picked up as sound—interpreted by us in that form, whereas a cement building is composed of particles that are viewed by our eyes and interpreted to be a solid object. But in each case, with either cement particles or radio waves, there are spaces in between them. That, in itself, comprises a built-in duality within each wave or particle because there is space in between them. There is no such thing as just a pure wave without a space in between because when those waves fluctuate, needing that space to do so, only then do we have sound. With particles it's the same scenario; there is actually more space in between the particles than the existing mass itself, but we do not pick that up visually. So the basic structure of everything around us is in a duality-type mode. Nothing is pure in this world, but there is a polarity that continually strives for balance. So from this non-pure, dualistic state, we are able to distinguish up and down, good and bad, night and day. We often experience a natural struggle that results from these opposing forces, which are constantly at play. There's always something that we come up against, built into the system itself, which is a huge challenge for us and, at the same time, part and parcel of what we are here for to begin with. We are here to confront this dualism and are *tested*, while we are here, as to what we do with it.

Instead of spending all of our time caught up in it, there is a need to transcend this duality. It's something that most people will spend an entire lifetime struggling with, without looking outside of the box in an effort to transcend it. We've got people who are always seeing things in black and white, good and bad, saying they're right and the "bad guy" is wrong, and it creates havoc in one's life. There is an important Buddhist concept of having no desires. A lot of meditative practice is geared toward helping one to achieve that desireless state. Desire itself is one of the things that operates in an almost demonic way, pushing people towards continuing to play this dualistic game. On the heels of desire rushes the ego, into our consciousness, to defeat any attempt at a fuller understanding of wholeness. We therefore battle and learn, confronting duality over and over again until we alchemically realize the value of transcendence.

In the meantime, there are levels of waves and particles all around us that we are not cognizant of. We are not able to pick them up—otherwise we would be totally confused. Our senses would be overloaded with the impact of so much extra information, to the point where we would not be able to function. So there is a design or a framework of reality that has been put in place as far as our bodies go, a kind of filter within the brain that allows us to see or experience just enough to function properly. Who or what designed the body and the way it perceives reality is something that we will get into later, but for now let's suffice it to say that these "designs" that we are living in, these bodies, are serving as vehicles for us to come here and operate in a way that allows us to understand the world and operate here in a limited and "safe" way. In knowing that, the question comes up; Did we come here voluntarily to do this? Or, has the designer put us here? It's a very interesting question. Some of the more metaphysically minded will tell you that it was all your choice—you chose your parents, and you came here because of karmic things that needed to be worked out. This life could be of your own choosing (up to the point of karma being involved). Other more conspiratorial minded people will tell you that we have no control whatsoever over our appearance in this world. We are just here to collect energy and be fed off of by hidden forces that we know nothing about—who clearly know about us and manipulate us for their own benefit. The real truth could be a combination of both.

Virtually all who accept the idea of karma also accept, hand in hand, the idea of reincarnation, or being born again into another life. What you reap in one life, you will sow "karmically" in the next. There might still be a degree of choice as to who or when or how you come back, but karma will still determine much. Depending on what was done and who was affected in previous lives, a soul may have limited choices in the process of returning. The only real "choice" involved is determined by the conscious actions that you take in your life because that, in itself, sets up the general situation and context for the next resulting life. There may be those who have cleared their karma to the point where they do not have to return at all, but choose to do so in order to help others still lost in this dense vibration, unable to recognize anything spiritual.

Those critical of the idea of reincarnation will sometimes point out that the population of the earth has reached an amazing size and is advancing exponentially in numbers. If the same souls keep coming back, they ask, then where are all these extra ones coming from? How could this happen when there are actually billions more people today than there were in the past? That can be explained. There are many different forms of life that gradually become conscious to certain degrees and are allowed to become a higher form of consciousness. There are millions of other life forms that have lived so many different times that they're now qualified to become human. This accounts for so many more people being alive at this point in time. It also explains the great mess this world is in because there are so many new souls in it that have not advanced enough, or spent enough human lifetimes, to live in a conscious enough way to take care of the planet or themselves properly and, most importantly, to take care of other people without thinking of just themselves. To advance spiritually requires repeated trips into the physical realm. Despite, and because of, the tremendous shortcomings in this world, including your arrival in complete, blind ignorance, it is *the* place to come in order to do this.

When we enter this world in human form, the reason we do not remember anything from previous lifetimes goes back to a previous point made—there's only so much the human nervous system can take in and be able to digest regarding all the information that's available. Previous lifetimes have information that is not relevant, and it's information that would cause confusion. Lessons that were learned in other lifetimes, things that would no longer need to be worked on, would be all around you, cluttering your focus, and there would not be as clear a path in this lifetime. There would be so many other residual problems surfacing into consciousness that one would not be able to discern the importance of things needing to be done in this lifetime. If you can imagine having about 50 or 60 additional sets of memories of childhood or other similar past scenarios, and trying to sort them all out in your head, you could just imagine how much confusion that would cause. We don't remember other lifetimes because this "blockage" is a very practical, useful feature that is part of nature itself. It protects us and allows us to live in a clear and functional manner that might otherwise not be possible.

So we come here with a blank slate at the very beginning, almost like an artist who has a blank canvas, and we have to create something on it. That can be quite exciting, and I think that's one of the reasons why there are so many people alive. It's because we can actually create here, whereby in the spiritual realm we don't have the physical surroundings and the apparatus and tools in order to do that. What we create is very important because it helps to shape our future. It helps to shape our consciousness and our souls. We cannot advance unless we are able to come here and function here in this physical world, and a big part of that is to be able to create things. Let's assume that each of us is here for a certain reason and that life is not totally and completely meaningless. With this in mind, we have the following features here at our disposal to work with in this realm: 1) The inherent duality of this reality. 2) A physical body. And 3) Our physical surroundings. What we do with all this and what we actually create within these parameters is our test and our purpose.

The dualistic composition of this physical reality provides us with the tools to grow and ultimately, to create a better understanding of who we are. We inhabit physical bodies for a limited period of time, but are really spiritual beings who come from the world of spirit. Duality is less pronounced in the spiritual world. The soul comes here and inhabits the physical body but it cannot directly partake in this foreign, dualistic environment without using the body as its mechanism. It is just an observer here, however, in the sense that it does not actually "do" anything. The most it can do is guide us with unspoken wisdom, through intuition, but beyond this it remains an outside observer. We, meaning our conscious selves, are the "doers" here, not our higher, observing Selves. This is where the idea of a "higher self" and the guidance it can provide comes from. Instead of the term "higher self," however, a more accurate one would be the "true self."

This true self is who we *really* are, but this world is so foreign to us that we (the real "we") can only function from afar, in a more subtle and detached realm. The soul has no duality—it is whole and complete in itself. Since it cannot split itself into a dualistic nature, which is completely impossible, then it must inhabit either a male or female body and *take on* in this way a physical dualistic nature. It may thereby partake in the physical world for the purpose of its growth while, at the same time, its true essence remains hidden. So this is who we are—here to progress and grow spiritually while operating in the denser realm of matter. This world is not our home; we are merely passing through.

It is important to note that animals are not capable of creativity to any great extent. Some exhibit creative traits, but compared to humans, their powers in this area are limited. Creativity is one of the things that is a strong part of the human soul. It is the human soul that is being worked on, developed and strengthened while we're here in this physical world. This entire physical universe including this world of duality is not entirely pure due to its dualistic nature. And yet the one thing that is not part of that, which is capable of being pure, is the soul. The realm of the spirit is not part of the physical universe. So we have come here because it allows us to work within this physical duality. When not here, but in the spirit world, there is nothing physical to work with. You are the sum of your works, but do not have the physical tools on the other side to proceed as quickly—unless you descend and get back to work. Each of us has different things to work on, so we come here to perform certain tasks, relevant to ourselves, in order to build our souls in the proper way and to help ourselves improve—or possibly get back to our unity with God. Many of us fail, accomplish nothing, lose our way or even perform the complete opposite of what we came here for by falling into destructive behaviour. For those with at least some degree of focus, the work here can be rewarding. Success is possible, and our chances improve when one knows the purpose for the trip. It goes quite a bit more deeply than that, which we will cover in the next chapter.

Chapter Two

EDUCATION

Tell me, I'll forget. Show me, I may remember. But involve me, and I'll understand. —Ancient Chinese proverb

Teach men that each generation begins the world afresh, in perfect freedom; that the present is not the prisoner of the past, but that today holds captive all the yesterdays, to judge, to accept, to reject their teachings, as they are shown by its own morning sun. —Ralph Waldo Emerson

We arrive in this life having a clean slate ahead of us, with a new "canvas" to paint on and continue with, through various stages of development. For proper guidance we need to develop an educational system that caters to us as spiritual beings rather than conditioning us to function as workers for the benefit of others. Humanity itself can advance much faster if we can limit the exploitation that occurs for material gain only.

We need to view things more from a spiritual perspective. For example, this journey of life is a walk through maya. In India the mystics call this physical world "maya," which means a complete illusion. When you view the physical world strictly in terms of the spirit or the soul, then everything else is an illusion. Most people see it the other way around: all that is in this physical world is real, and the fact that we might have a soul is a complete illusion. So we have it backwards, or most people do. What we need to do is switch the perspective. Let us consider the soul as the one thing that has true meaning and is the true reality, and start working from that standpoint. Everything that is solid and all around is, in fact, just maya. It is an illusion. And yet, although it's an illusion, it is the necessary tool for us here. This whole physical universe provides us with the tools that we need. Otherwise, with just spirit alone, there's less to work with to create the advancement we're looking for.

Our standard educational systems fail to focus on how and why we come here and operate within this physical world. If we continue to learn within the educational systems that we currently have in place, not much advancement is going to happen—unless the public systems in place start to acknowledge our spiritual make-up, or begin replacing their format with others that approach it from a more spiritual perspective. Something is currently wrong. You cannot teach a duck, no matter how hard you try, that it's a chicken.

Most of the world's educational systems are based on economics rather than spiritual needs. A new perspective is needed to look at life, and its preparation, from outside the standard educational and worldwide economic structure. This perspective should be a spiritual one, based on an accurately discovered spiritual identity. We could then start to logically experiment and see what can be done on a more meaningful level beyond all the poverty, warfare and other resulting things that this Cartesian-Newtonian-materialistic paradigm brings. We've been traveling this path for a few centuries—maybe longer—and it is clearly no longer working.

When we arrive as infants, the body grows accustomed to this gravity before the soul does. Children soon celebrate this fact by running and jumping with delight all over the place. The soul's only remaining freedom expresses itself by projecting outward, from within the limited confines of its new body. Fun is the name of the game, along with occasional trouble. At other times these same children do not seem to be fully with us. They sleep a great deal as young toddlers, being more comfortable in the world of dreams. Coming here is a major transitional thing with the newly acquired apparatus of the mind. As a result, the soul is now relegated to a lesser role and sometimes retreats into itself.

It is difficult to remember where one was before this life began; but the younger one is, the easier it is to deduce or even recall that we were somewhere else. What animates our bodies leaves when the body wears out or is severely damaged, because it is composed of energy. Any scientist can explain the First Law of Thermodynamics in support of this, which is that energy cannot be created or destroyed, it can only be changed from one form into another. In knowing this (or accepting the statement that our essence is an energy form) then the only question that remains is, What form did our energy take before it entered into the body?

Most people equate energy with matter, but energy exists in many different forms without matter being present. There may be a more pure form of energy beyond the type of matter that we are normally aware of in the physical world that is connected to our consciousness. It may also be the specific form we had before coming here, and which we carry with us into the world. It is so foreign to the physical that it goes completely unrecognized and undetected. With this in mind, let it suffice for now to say that we were indeed in a previous world of existence.

There is a modern mystic whom most readers would recognize, but in sharing the following quote wishes to remain anonymous. It reveals a great deal. The information given is meant to clarify our former existence, allowing us to start from the very beginning, in "pre-life." I was allowed to report the memory of events after first recognizing in conversation how important it was. Much was experienced or recalled from the previous world when this person was a young child. It relates to the entry of our souls into this world, and into a physical body, and is quoted as follows:

"Most people would like to believe that the spirit world is inhabited with angels and loving creatures all around. Not so. There are wonderful beings at the higher levels, but when one comes here, a major descent takes place. It leads the traveler down into the depths where safety becomes more of an issue the closer one gets to entering this world. On my way here, into this body, I was pursued. The closest thing these pursuing entities resembled was that of wolves. They were relentless pursuers, right behind me all the way, so if I faltered in any way I would have been caught and possibly devoured in some way. There was no doubt about this—I knew it without question. If caught, my energy or I would have been consumed and I would have not come into a body. This does not mean this happens to everyone, but that it could. The event was real but the exact timing is uncertain. I do not know if this had occurred at the time of my birth or not. There were complications, so I may have left the body only to be chased back—or this could have occurred months previous, at the time of conception or when my soul entered its body.

"If negative entities like this are successful and catch their 'prey,' they might have the power to incarnate, take the place of good souls and inhabit bodies when they do not have the proper energies or qualifications to do so. As in my case I am happy to report that I made it, but that the experience was completely terrifying. Yes, you do not have to have a physical body in order to experience fear. The closest entity during the chase seemed to be panting or 'breathing' very hard, expending all the energy it could in its desperate pursuit and was *extremely* close the whole time. I am grateful to be here. As a small child I would continually re-experience this event at the edges of sleep or waking—although sometimes in the dream state itself. It would always end in my arrival in the physical body. Other times I would experience the arrival into the body without this pursuit.

"This arrival into the body was another event that replayed itself often. Upon entering the body, a certain 'lightness' or freedom of movement begins to fade. Things slow down greatly and an immense 'heaviness' overtakes one's being. The physical operates at an extremely dense level as opposed to spirit, so in making the transition it feels like someone who deep sea dives—who goes from our normal atmosphere down into the depths of the ocean to experience its immense pressure. It's a massive 'heaviness,' which is the best way to describe it.

"Once in the body this heaviness seems most evident around the mouth or in the jaw area and I could not tell you why—but it's your own spirit, or rather the real 'you,' that feels it first. In other words, you are still detached and the first feelings of acclimation to the body show up in the jaw—or at least did so for me. Upon entering the body it is rather repulsive, to be honest. There's a feeling of having to sink to the level of an animal, in a certain sense, but you still do it. For me, joining with the skeletal system itself, rather than the rest of the body, was the biggest turn-off of all—probably because bones are more dense and solid than flesh and organs. I was far more aware of the bones and, yes, it still creeps me out to think about this from that spiritual perspective. The more solid and dense something is the more opposite it is from spirit. The skull repulsed me the most as I 'entered into it' and became wired into the main tool we have in this world—the brain. Although the brain is our best and most useful tool here, it is still a limiting type of 'filter' when considered in a spiritual sense. We become 'confined' and 'imprisoned' in a certain sense within these bodies, but we need these bodies to function here.

"In addition to being repulsed by the skull there was also a certain fascination—much like one who is moving into a new home. Over time we become more acclimated."

This is an interesting account. I tend to believe it, but don't think some of the more frightening aspects are true for everyone.

The old Manichean literature has much to say about this if you are able to find it. Most of their Gnostic writings were burned by early Christians because their dualistic and sometimes more spiritual view of Christianity was considered a threat. Gnostic thought has survived in various forms for over 2000 years. Since you can never kill the spirit, it will continue to resurface and express itself no matter what any earthly power might do.

In assessing the above experience, I would suggest that this person's bright and powerful soul drew the attention of these pursuing entities during his descent into a body because they were lower astral beings. Without much energy, they inhabit a realm between our higher spiritual home and the physical world. This person made it into the world without being caught by hungry parasites drawn to his energy.

If a powerful soul can make it into a material body, its power gets diminished to a certain extent. It was still a choice to come down here—mixing one's soul with matter allows each of us to bring light into the darkness of matter. The material body does create a trap for the soul where one gets ensnared. It is a temporary trap, however—what we do to free ourselves, *and others*, is the challenge. We have far to go, as most people would rather live in the deepest depths of the gross material vibration. They go shopping, watch television, eat junk food and have little concern for others, without any inclination toward compassionate action or spiritual growth. For most people, it's all about their desires, toys or their image.

We do have flashes of our potential, however. We've all had unusual experiences as young children, but when we try to relate them to those who are older we simply haven't mastered the language enough to relate things properly. And then, when we do get old enough to make at least some sense out them, we find that our memories have failed us because our ability to remember such things was not very developed at the time of these occurrences. Some experiences, however, can linger and can still be remembered. The younger one is, the stronger connection there is that remains with the previous world.

From my own perspective, I would often drift off into another form of consciousness when in the early grades. Teachers would claim I was daydreaming, yet it wasn't daydreaming at all—it was an entirely different zone. There is no thinking involved and you're not "dreaming" of anything. There are no images, it's just experiencing a different realm of the mind.

The mind goes down into alpha, beta, theta and all these other different levels. And these lower levels are far more accessible when you're a child because you're still adjusting to this physical reality. Entering into these states will put you into a completely different awareness. You are still aware of your surroundings to a certain point, but are detached and serene at the same time. Later in life many of us try to get these states back through meditation. I, for one, would slip into that state all the time. The active realm of consciousness, the more "natural" and busy realm of consciousness, is not so natural to a younger child. That has to be learned. It has to be acquired. And it happens because we are told or instructed that, "This is how it is. You need to operate on this level." But it makes one wonder... what if there was another level that we could operate on that was different? There is, but we lose touch with it. We are not encouraged to access it in this material world because we would no longer be involved in the frenzied activity of outward theatrics that this mindset requires.

If we could stay practiced in these other states from a young age, then we could better access certain powers of the mind far more readily than we can by simply staying aware in this current state of "normal" consciousness. When we experience all these problems in the world today, it could be because we are operating in a certain realm of consciousness that may not be entirely healthy. Maybe we should seek some balance. This is something that should be encouraged in young children, not discouraged, as is often the case.

For the sake of development, children should be given a mere five minutes of quiet time out of the entire day when in the early grades or at home. They would have to be quiet, and just still themselves. They could go inward, and at least have a chance to keep that part of themselves alive, or stay connected to it. If in school, some parents would complain because children are so hyperactive at that age, but the kids could learn (or be allowed) to stay in touch with a deeper part of themselves if they were given just five minutes a day. Then those "daydreamers" could be told that there is a certain time set aside for this and to wait for it.

Educating people in a more spiritual atmosphere can only make the world a better place. The process should start young and has nothing to do with religion. Certain dogmatic parents would brand such quiet time as meditation and an "evil," and would instruct their children to pray—but this quiet time is not representative of a competing religious idea. It represents the true essence of our being before any labels, religious or otherwise, are attached in this world. It has nothing to do with meditation *or* prayer, which are both *practices*. Meditation requires a certain posture, breathing methods, mantras, mudras, or the focusing on a central visual object or the breath itself. None of this comes into play. This is simply quiet time, an introspection, and nothing more. It has to do with who we already are, not what you or anyone else wants us to become.

This could be the first small step in an inward direction that could prove useful in the development of children and people in general. This could later lead to a meditation time in school for those who are older, but only if they should choose it. There would be objections by some, but keeping this time within a secular framework, offering fair use to all, gives no cause for complaint. Such time could still be used for any purpose whatsoever regardless of faith or belief.

With true spiritual expression nothing is ever forced upon another individual, which is something that could never be said when examining the historical track record of the world's largest religious faiths. Some institutions have already incorporated this simple inward time. It functions along the same lines as prayer in school, but with people using that time in any way they please, without infringing on others. Instead of prayer, which is an outward expression, many would be allowed to go inward.

Going inward is something that is, in large part, taught to be wrong from as soon as we're cognizant of our surroundings. In doing so, it is claimed that one is not paying attention or not being grounded in reality, but there is a lot to be said about this from a spiritual perspective. Although young people may not be able to fully comprehend their spiritual essence on a conscious level, they do in fact know instinctively that there is something deeper going on, within themselves, than just the physical. Because of this, there is much confusion for children who are told not to pay attention to anything inward—that in order to succeed and in order to be aware, then you need to be completely aware of your entire outward surroundings at all times. But there should be allotted certain times for inward development because what we are missing, as we become older, is a genuine inward sense.

This has consequences. For example, as a society and as a race we are sorely lacking in moral values. It is obvious, from a worldly standpoint, that we are lacking a great deal in self-respect and the respect for others. More focus on inward development could, however, contribute more kindness and respect toward others. There have been no studies done as far as I know to support this argument, so I can only say this is a gut feeling, combined with common sense. Many religious-based agendas use the lack of morals outside of their faith as a tool for creating converts, but I am not trying to funnel people into any one particular belief system. I am talking about pure spirit, which can be accessed, experienced and respected from within any religious belief system, or without having any. We can cultivate a direct connection to that deeper spiritual part of us from a very early age and without any religious agendas whatsoever. Having a particular agenda brings separation from others outwardly *and* inwardly, making a pre-determined and exclusively-based agenda contradictory to striving for wholeness. Is there a way where sometime in the future, we would be willing to make a conscious leap away from dogmatic agendas in an effort to reach our true selves? We may be forced to address it at some point down the road but for now, those of us with open minds and a vision of the future, should begin to entertain the question.

Improved Educational Programs

Certain educational programs are in place that could lead the way in this regard. Spiritually based, non-sectarian education has been adopted in a few special places. One of those is the Oak Grove School, fashioned after the spiritual teachings of Jiddu Krishnamurti, located in Ojai, California. It was founded in 1975. This is one school that truly nourishes the youth, especially in the high school program. There are so many positive results for those who have gone through the program, that it should be considered as a model for this kind of spiritually based teaching.

Krishnamurti was a man of great wisdom who wanted to instill a sense of spirit in people above and beyond anything else. He believed that one should not have any dogmatic beliefs because then you are limiting yourself. With strong and set beliefs one is ultimately saying, "This is the way it is," and that is the end of it. This mindset, as a result, closes oneself off from other possibilities when, in fact, the spirit has endless possibilities. The spirit can do amazing things. So when we limit ourselves by saying "this is the way it is," then we grow up indoctrinated—believing in that particular system and that one only. Other effective answers could be available but are rejected out of hand due to incompatibility with the belief system. This is why we have people who stick strictly to their beliefs to such an extreme degree and why we have fundamentalists. They are tied in to their beliefs to such an extent that if you approach them with other possibilities, they shut you down fast. They don't want to hear it, believing that anything other than their own religion is evil or comes from the devil—period! They often shout this at anyone who is deemed a threat.

Open-minded people have often experienced this reaction after having been asked what their beliefs are, by those having the intention to "save" them. A spiritual person is often considered a threat to them, and it becomes clear that there are some fear mechanisms going on in our society. Such people do not want to hear anything outside of their reality tunnel, and are quick to pull you into theirs as fast as they can, if allowed to—whether you like it or not. They do not want to hear of anything inward, or spiritual, because to them you are a heathen with unimportant beliefs. To them, God is not found within, He is "out there," looking down from his throne in heaven, and is judging us all at this very moment. Their job is to convert you. There is no time to hear facts because they have their beliefs. Listening is apparently a skill that only you should possess. This is the kind of mindset we are up against, across the board, no matter what the religion, because this tunnel vision has been ingrained in believers of every faith from a very early age. As a race we still don't "get it," but some are catching on to the futility of this mindset and we are starting to grow tired of it.

There are those who will say, "I believe the way I do because my religion is right. And that's all there is to it." It's the old "My God can beat up your God" syndrome, in that everyone else is lost in the world and are all going to hell unless they see the light. This is despite the fact that there are people throughout the world who live extremely good and just lives. They live wonderful lives, full of kindness, and the fact that they may not have been exposed to the "right" religion relegates them to the depths of hell for an eternity full of torment. There could be a kind-hearted old Buddhist gentleman who has done no harm to even a fly his entire life, who will supposedly go to hell; but in sections of the deep south there's a redneck bible belt "tradition" of people who get rip-roaring drunk, raise hell and crash cars on Saturday night, sometimes beating up people in drunken bar-room fights, stealing anything not nailed down, sleeping around, then going into church on Sunday and singing a few hymns before confessing it all and being forgiven. They go home and say, "Hey, we're absolved from all this. Praise the Lord; thank God for confession— let's go out and do it again next week." And they do. There's a religious mindset going on here that gives people free license to do all kinds of crazy things.

Other religions have the same faults and problems, but that's just one example. As an entire race of humanity, we've got some major obstacles in front of us. There's a lot that needs to be worked on and we are in complete denial, for the most part, because of our religious conditioning. We believe that we've got the answers, through religion, but when viewing things in a deeper way, we simply do not have the proper facts, from a religious standpoint, to formulate the right answers. We have only the answers that we want to hear, the ones that placate us. The fact is, we do not know who we are, where we came from, or why we're here. There's no actual proof of this, but all religions treat these problems as if they indeed hold the answers to them and, from a dogmatic perspective, insist that no followers question it. We can either accept religious hearsay, pawned off as facts, or we can exercise our spirituality through intuitive skills. The only way to develop these intuitive skills is to go within. This is where the answers are.

That is the next big frontier. It may be the last major one we encounter and it is in this position because it scares the be-Jesus out of people. We can go hundreds of thousands of light-years out into space, and what are we going to find? We're going to find more physical matter. We're going to find more physical things. But what will that matter if we don't know who the searcher is? What this means is that the searcher is lost. We don't have to go out thousands of light-years into space to be lost right where we are now. It will not matter where we go, or how far we go, because the answers won't be out there.

Who we are looking for is who is looking. —St. Francis of Assissi

The answers are inside us. That is where they really are. And if we can find ways to search effectively in an inward fashion, which we are starting to do, then the truly meaningful answers will surface. Talk to any of the great physicists in the world today, and they will say that the inner and outer worlds are intersecting, or crossing over. The outer mysteries of matter, meaning the physical world all around us and the hidden levels of reality, are crossing over into spiritual realms the deeper we look into it. We have been working diligently for years and years on all these advanced scientific problems involving physical matter. If we can figure out a way to do just as much work on the inner paths, involving the human soul and consciousness, then we might be able to break through and find the key to everything, the entire key to existence. It may have happened already. Some amazing work in these areas has been going on. The key to physical existence, tied into the spiritual, may have been scientifically found. If so, we are not being told. Religions would topple and our religious mindsets, as a whole, are still not psychologically ready for it.

In another century or two we will look back and say, "Were we ever in the dark ages back then!" This is because we've looked virtually everywhere else there is to look to find all the deeper mysteries and to seek the answers of what's really going on here in this existence, and only now are we starting to look inward. What I'm proposing is for us to offer a start—the glimmering of a spiritual development program within our educational systems, so that our children can explore these realms early on, while they are still sensitive in certain ways. If successful, they may ultimately help to carry on and develop further the general ideas that some of these physicists have started to come up with, and get to the bottom of things. With that accomplished, our identities will be clearly defined within our cultures and our true purpose, on individual levels, can be pursued more easily.

Later on we will be able to apply the powers of the mind in ways that we cannot even imagine right now, but we have to take some initial first steps. If we take them in a way that is very basic, then we will help to set the groundwork. We should think in simple terms in the early stages, and explore more deeply later.

An example of this educational process that I'm envisioning goes back to Krishnamurti. In the early 20th Century, Jiddu Krishnamurti was a young boy walking on the beach with his brother in India when he was noticed by C.W. Leadbeater of the Theosophical Society. It was noticed that he had the most amazing aura that had ever been seen in a young child. The aura is an energy field we all have around the body, but only certain people, sensitive or psychic in certain ways, can see it and interpret it. Leadbeater convinced Krishnamurti's family to take him and his younger brother (since it was best they not be separated) to England so they could be educated. This was to be a highly spiritual education because Krishnamurti, recognized for his powerful presence and spiritual gifts, was groomed to be the next world teacher. He was taught well. In fact, he may have been taught too well. By the time he was a young man, in 1929, he had thousands of followers. Every year at a certain time, they would come and listen to him talk. At one particular meeting, with over a thousand people in the audience, he basically told them, "I am not the world teacher that you've been expecting. I'm not going to be able to save you. You alone will be able to save yourselves but you must learn how to do it." Then he left. He quit. This act pulled the rug out from under all of the people who were looking outside of themselves for answers, rather than looking inward.

Krishnamurti walked away from this organization. Ironically enough, he did become an incredible world teacher. He came, however, long before his time and is not well recognized. He went on to write about one hundred books on spiritual principles, proper education, enlightenment and higher awareness. The Oak Grove School was started in 1975 while he was still alive in order to teach in a more balanced and holistic lifestyle. It promotes no particular religious belief to entrap students with dogmatic limitations. These are teachings of pure connection with the spirit. Of course many worldly and necessary things are taught as well, but its main focus is on the attempt to create a more fully rounded, conscious human being. As a society we are still lacking in educational programs that strive for the most full and complete development—spiritually, mentally, and physically—of students.

Another well-tested, proven program was developed in 1919 by Rudolf Steiner, called Waldorf Education. It is geared primarily for children and the spiritual realities of the developing child. Its stated goal is "to produce individuals who are able, in and of themselves, to impart meaning to their lives." This is one of the fastest growing educational programs in the world, with about 900 schools worldwide in over 32 countries, with about 150 in North America. It has not being given much press, but there is a "Waldorf Movement" growing in the world. Although more spiritual than standardized education, some of the schools are fully accredited and recognized by governmental authorities.

The curriculum covers different religious viewpoints but is not religiously based in itself. This did not stop a lawsuit from being filed in California against two government school districts employing Waldorf methods, claiming that the schools violate the First Amendment protection against the establishment of a state sponsored religion. The court quickly ruled in favor of Waldorf in the 2005 trial. It seems that some fundamentalist Christians are petrified that children are being taught to *think for themselves*. Concerned Christians protested at other Waldorf schools in California, claiming the schools were "rooted in a New Age, cult-like religious sect."

Everyone outside of a dogmatic fundamentalist mindset should be excited about Waldorf education. For example, according to the Wikipedia Internet information on Waldorf, the SAT scores of Waldorf students in the U.S. are usually above the national average, despite the fact that standardized testing is not used as much within its program. In Germany, Waldorf graduates as a group passed their college entrance exams at double and triple the rate of state educated students. According to UNESCO, a Waldorf training college in South Africa was instrumental in the elimination of apartheid, and a Waldorf school in Israel employs both Arab and Jewish faculty for a student body of the same diversity. In 2005, the first Arab-Jewish kindergarten was founded near Haifa in Israel. An international study shows that Waldorf students are more creative than state-educated children. All in all, it has been shown that this type of program can make a positive difference in the world and is the next logical step for us to take in a spiritual direction.

As part of the program, Steiner developed something called *eurythmy*—taught in the schools and described as a new art of movement for the human form. It allows body, mind and spirit to be expressed as a functional unity, sometimes referred to as "visible speech." Steiner was brilliant. He founded the Anthroposophic Society, wrote dozens of books and had a profound understanding of the human spirit. He, like Krishnamurti, was considered by many to be ahead of his time.

> *If called upon to develop a system of education, spiritual science will be able to impart everything that comes under this heading, even down to the instructions about diet appropriate for children. For it is realistic in its approach to life, not vague theory...* —Rudolf Steiner

Mahatma Gandhi proposed an interesting education format for children that consisted of twenty-seven main points, some of which applied only to the children of India, but most can be applied to everyone. They included having coeducation until age eight and as much as possible from nine to sixteen. The special aptitudes of each child should be considered in determining the work they will do, reading should come before writing, nothing should be taught to a child by force, a child should be interested in everything taught to him, the reasons for every process should always be explained when the process is being carried on, and during the last stage of education, from age sixteen to twenty-five, every young person should have an education according to his or her wishes and circumstances. The complete list is available in Gandhi's book called *Vows and Observances*, which also explains his other important concepts of ahimsa, swadeshi, and satyagraha, which should also be included, at some point, in any good spiritual educational program. Gandhi was a spiritual giant who accomplished great things in his lifetime, so his ideas should be of great import to those on a spiritual path.

For anyone with a concern for the future and the education of our children, it is time to meet the challenge of improved educational programs. Much like sports leagues that create two separate conferences or leagues (National and American, Eastern and Western, etc.), an alternative or competing educational system should appear and employ itself—with state sanction, if possible, and acceptance on a broad level. A spiritual or holistic-based school system should be expanded or begun, state sponsored with the backing and support of a group of forward-thinking politicians, with all the basic courses, guidelines, etc., accredited to whatever degree is needed. We should approach the future of our youth more seriously, so that young people can be molded not so much by others, but in a more complete and self-expressive fashion—mentally, spiritually, physically. The public school systems currently attempt to mold children into what society wants them to be, while a more spiritually based system would help to mold children into who they really are. Children will find their paths in life more easily, and it will more often be a true path (more easily identified) rather than a false one (more prone to trial and error). Some people spend their entire lives searching for that true path and not ever finding it due to the various channels they've been funneled into by the system. This is why an additional adult program should be developed along the same lines for those who wish to change their life's path or enrich themselves in certain ways that have been lacking in our society. It's never too late. Once again, such schools would have no connection to any creed or ideology.

I do not personally know anyone connected with Waldorf education or the Oak Grove School in Ojai, but it is clear from the available research that they are good programs and the students have succeeded well. These are proven methods with impressive results. If you look at the people who have graduated from the Oak Grove School, they go on to many of the best colleges in the country. They have also begun a new early childhood learning program, so it is possible that from a very young age children will not lose that connection so easily with the spirit—because I believe we do carry that with us into the world. It also welcomes parent involvement, so parents and their toddlers do not lose the vital connection that they share. The early learning program is more relationship-based, and involves child development experts available to parents, if needed. For later grades the school offers a drama program, computer sciences, horticulture (as far as connecting with other types of life in the world) and much more for curriculum choices. This program is clearly on the right track in a world where there is an extreme shortage of this kind of thing.

Another interesting educational system worth mentioning has been developed by Daisaku Ikeda, who has devoted his life to promoting peace through education. Unlike the Oak Grove School and Waldorf, it is based on a religious framework, being Buddhist, but George David Miller, in his book *Peace, Value and Wisdom: The Educational Philosophy of Daisaku Ikeda*, puts forth in his Conclusion a number of creative applications of Ikeda's philosophy that could possibly be applied without a prerequisite mindset or religious conversion as an aim. Certain spiritual truths cut across all religions and it might be possible to expand parts of Ikeda's brilliant spiritual program into a more secular framework. The motto for his Soka University in Japan is:

Be the Highest Seat of Learning for Humanity
Be the Cradle of a New Culture
Be a Fortress for the Peace of Humankind

Ikeda is president of Soka Gakkai International, which currently has 12 million members worldwide, 1000 cultural centers, 6 peace and cultural institutions, and 13 educational institutions at various grade levels, including universities in Japan and Aliso Viejo, California. Miller reports that the California school goes beyond offering a standard liberal arts education by covering additional areas of study in wisdom, creativity, egalitarianism, value creation, happiness and Socratic dialogue. It's amazing that standardized education has otherwise failed to offer such valuable areas of study.

Our standard educational system has short-circuited the more experiential avenues we could otherwise access and develop from a young age. Without this development or ability to experience on deeper and more meaningful levels, we are left groping for answers. We are told what to believe in many cases, without really *knowing*, and are expected to blindly follow. We often do, because we are, in fact, left blind on deeper levels. The three alternative systems just covered at least offer some direction that we could employ to help rectify the problem. Trying to force such philosophies into the current educational systems in an integrative cross-bred way will not work anywhere near as well as using them directly, so the Waldorf and Krishnamurti-based schools stand a better chance at making a wider impact, over time, through communities willing to test them. In this way, it will be possible for us to allow these relatively newer systems to grow at their own pace and succeed on their own merits.

Self-education and Spiritual Growth

Having worked in the spiritual field for many years, I am constantly meeting others who have said that after their traditional education ended, their real education actually began. Instead of relying upon a teacher, they took it upon themselves to explore more meaningful areas of interest. They felt an extreme desire to quench their thirst with the information that was out there, but they had to search for it. When a person self-educates himself, it shows some real initiative. A lot of that is going on—people seeking out information that is not normally found in the mainstream—more so in spiritual areas than any other area. That is a good sign for humanity, and our overall progress. For those who want to accomplish certain ends, or for those who have interests and want to make the most progress, a spiritually based educational system could also offer some type of correspondence course relating to spiritual subjects using proven texts and effective exercises. General guidance can be found in books, but actual experience and instruction can only be carried out by you. That's when results will start to appear.

Some people have meditated for many years. Using meditation as an example, there are those who have found that it can suddenly pay off with incredible results. In general, one will experience subtle but interesting results over a longer period but there are those who experience amazing results in a short period of time. We are all on different spiritual paths, and these paths that can vary with their results. People seeking answers on their own often do have more success than standardized education. Ramakrishna once said, "All paths lead to the same mountaintop," which is true, but some paths are more direct than others.

We need to be open to different systems of instruction, or education, than what we have today. Based on our spiritual maturity and what we have learned about ourselves over the years, it may be time to expand our approach toward education. A lot of thought needs to go behind this in order to do it properly. It could make a huge difference if done, or could be a regretful mistake if we fail to act.

Most of today's public school systems are light-years behind this progressive mindset, at least concerning spiritual questions. The public school system is there to provide basic, fundamental schooling or an interest in a trade, something that will allow one to operate in the physical world as either a laborer or business person in order to pay the bills, pay their taxes, and live as a "cog in the wheel." The average person works a nine to five job. Many of these people don't like their jobs to begin with. They feel, in a deep-down sense, that something is missing and they can't quite put their finger on it.

Very few people actually enjoy their jobs, although a number of them will tell you that they do. But what are they going to do? Openly admit to you that they're miserable? Deep down, many don't like what they're doing. After a nine to five job they will come home, feed the dog, crack open a beer, and watch prime time TV. And that's their life. *There is so much incredible knowledge out there and people don't even care to explore it.* Yet, if we could be brought up in ways that provide some kind of a spark that develops our spiritual side, then the true self will emerge or come out as we grow older. People will no longer become so stuck, ingrained, ignorant, downtrodden and blind in this physical existence—and will stop reacting in the world with all the ignorance they have collected. Over time, each generation will collect a little more wisdom than those previous, and will act accordingly.

It's amazing how people can be so bored with life when there is so much to discover and explore. Yet people are stuck; they're mired in a deep sense of unhappiness that they have, in addition to life itself, grown afraid to examine. Achieving an answer to this problem has to start at a young age. And it has to be offered by those who have wisdom, true wisdom. There's nothing wrong with knowledge, but that is something different. Those who set up our educational system as we know it today, had a lot of knowledge. And they want people to learn that knowledge. They want that knowledge shared and to be put to practical use. But those who have wisdom can actually create better and wiser people in the long run—people who would act more responsibly and be more kind and respectful toward others. That's the kind of thing we need to nourish for the sake of our children and for the future. We have so far lost that as a lofty aim or goal, and need to reclaim it.

For example, in ancient Greece it was the philosophers who were the leaders and were held in high esteem. Their opinions always mattered and were most often acted upon. And where are the philosophers today? They are teaching in universities, because that is all they are offered. They're not leading society in any clear capacity, and virtually no heads of state are known to ask their advice about anything. Anyone who graduates with a degree in philosophy can become qualified to teach in a university if, by chance, such a rare position is open. In general, that is all one can do with the degree, despite being trained to think clearly and logically at the highest levels.

I never quite finished my master's in philosophy because my aim was not to attain a degree or to teach, but to discover what the greatest thinkers in the world thought in previous times. It was a fascinating study. When that end was met, I left. In my case the knowledge was more important—and functional—than the actual degree. The point is that our society is intellectually bankrupt when those who wish to learn about the world's greatest thinkers have no direct practical application for the knowledge in society, once attained, unless they have a calling to teach. For example, many politicians have backgrounds in law rather than philosophy (although philosophy should be a prerequisite). From a personal standpoint, having this type of knowledge is still recommended for one's own personal growth.

It would be great to have schools that will one day teach philosophical ideas along with spiritual truths to help nourish a society that is missing contact with the more meaningful aspects of the human soul and the human experience. If more people could get in touch with a deeper part of themselves through a new educational approach, it would be a tremendous and positive experiment to see what would unfold (and how fast it would happen). I cannot predict what would happen with such schools but it seems that we have looked everywhere outside of ourselves for answers that have not been found. Now it's time to start exploring on inner levels. There could, in fact, be some tremendous treasures waiting for us there. This refers to each of us, individually, as well as collectively.

After a quarter century of working with and around spiritually based people, I have found that a higher percentage from this group is on a real quest for knowledge than is the general public. Excited people, hungry for knowledge, have visited the metaphysical bookstore I've operated. It is a vastly larger group of self-actualized individuals who come in than those whom I have met in the general public. Most of these people are so *awake* and *alive* and *aware!* It's because they have touched their inner world and all the amazing possibilities it holds. There's a clear zest for life about these people, whereby your average Joe on the street thinks these people are crazy. The average Joes have no idea that this inner world exists.

These "awakened" people tell me stories. I hear them all the time, from so many different people—but none of them know each other. In the mail order division we get orders for spiritual material from all over the world. They often call and say that in their community this kind of material is not available and there's no place to find it locally, but they are all hungry for it. They have found a way to educate themselves and awaken from their slumber; but the average person out there, in comparison, has their life on automatic pilot. They shut down the potential that these other people were yearning for, have found, and are now accessing.

There is a real distinction to be made between both types of people. What is it that separates them? A good analogy is "sleep walking." People in the everyday world are not interested in this kind of material because they have totally shut down. They would much rather stay home and watch reality-based television because their lives are so empty from any kind of excitement, intrigue or discovery that they have to live vicariously through these popular reality shows (that millions of other empty people, just like them, are watching).

Waking Up
A number of the more interesting "awakened" people who are exploring inner worlds, rather than outer ones, come into our store and say, "I don't have a TV. I don't even watch TV," because their lives are so full and complete without it. Is this something the average person could even imagine? I can see it now, all of the couch potatoes when they pass on and check into heaven are going to be forced to admit, "I was living vicariously. I witnessed a thousand lifetimes in this life, but the one life I failed to experience fully was my own."

> *Footprints in the sands of time are not made by sitting down.*
> —Anonymous

1) Turn off the TV.
2) Put your shoes on.
3) Get up and walk.

Let us focus on the self-realized, awakened individuals because that's where we should heading. Colin Wilson, one of the world's best and most accomplished writers, calls this "sleep walking" state of mind "the robot." This occurs when one slips into a situation that requires no thinking. You can get into your car and not even have to think while you drive. You end up at your destination and don't remember what you did while you were driving because you were on automatic pilot. You didn't need to think, so part of you took over and chose to go "unconscious."

The human brain likes to make things easy. It likes to relegate things in a way so that we don't have to think because we're lazy. We are lazy people, in general, and that's one of our downfalls. We've somehow developed this part of the brain that wants to just shut down, relax, and make everything easy. As a result, this "robot" takes over more and more of our affairs so that we miss meaningful experiences. We become numb to the world around us because we don't feel like thinking that day—then the next, and so on, and so on. Our entire existence gets jammed into automatic pilot and will not be moved out of it unless something happens to jolt ourselves awake.

A number of great mystics have tried to wake people up from this stupor. The first that comes to mind is Gurdjieff. Being conscious already, his goal was to wake his students up. He would do the most unforeseen things at unexpected times, much like an alarm clock, and his students or followers would just look at each other in amazement, totally confused, many times, by his outlandish behaviour. But it worked. It was the shock value that he was going for, and it snapped people immediately out of the normal day-to-day drudgery that everyone seems to slip into. He kept people alert, alive and aware of everything around them—and sometimes shocking people is the one thing that will get their attention. Georg Feuerstein wrote an excellent book called *Holy Madness,* for anyone interested in more of this sort of thing.

When engaged in something you truly love, you can also enter into a fully awake and aware state of consciousness. This is the complete opposite of the "robot," which shuts your soul down and turns you into an automaton. When fully awake, you get into a flow and all sense of time seems to vanish. You'll suddenly look up and find out that it's three or four hours later when it only seemed like twenty minutes. As we say, "Time flies when you're having fun."

When not experiencing this state of mind, for example working at a job that you dislike, time can pass slowly and the work becomes drudgery. However, when awake and involved in this fullness of life, this aliveness, look back at what your normal self would be and compare it to how much more awake and alive you are. Be aware of the difference. It will allow you to strive for this state of mind more often, so you will want to grow in a positive direction and accomplish worthwhile things. Life then becomes more exciting and you get to experience things directly rather than vicariously. By getting your true Self involved, life becomes worth living more so than before.

This other self, this robot, tends to take over people's lives to such an incredible degree that it puts you to sleep. You're not even aware that you're asleep—you consider it your normal everyday consciousness. But the real consciousness, the real alive and awake state, often requires a jolt or shock to your system just to wake you up and get you back into it. Then you become open to the more interesting avenues that are available to you. This awareness is the state of mind that should be more natural than the robot. This is the state of mind that is worth living for. This is the state of mind that allows people to grow and allows people to accomplish things that they love and to share the kind of knowledge they have with others. It's far more exciting than this boring robot thing that has put its claws into you to such an extent that you don't even know that you're trapped. You don't even know that you're being carried off and eaten by this thing, whatever it is. However, if you want to be completely free and alive, then pick something you love and set aside some time each day to *do it*, because you never know where that's going to lead. If you don't have something positive that you love to do then find it. Explore and experiment. Your passion defines you. Do not put it off or ignore it in favor of convenient, mindless distractions like hours wasted on television or computer games that trick the mind and rob the soul. An important part of yourself is here to express itself, but will never be able to do so without your cooperation. It's something that many good writers have referenced. For example, the great mythologist, Joseph Campbell, called it "following your bliss."

Unimaginable doors open up to you when you follow your bliss, which I can vouch for from personal experience. You are suddenly aligned with the universe and things happen almost on cue, like it was meant to be. Your life can change at a moment's notice because you are completely aligned with your purpose. Something higher than you "knows" it. Things happen when you really need them to happen—when you have done everything you can from within your bliss and when the rest is up to chance. Then... Wham! You get more than you could possibly ask for. It happens at the right time and place. To others it would seem like coincidence, but to you there is no question that it was meant to be. Some would swear they have a guardian angel; others a higher self; but whatever it is, it all started with you.

If you're stuck in your robot-self, if you're stuck in this automaton mentality, you are never going to grow or go anywhere—not unless it's through pure luck or through someone else's initiative. The robot has no initiative or original thought. Put some real initiative and passion and love into your life so that you can sit down at night and say, once your day is over, that life was worth living that day. All kinds of problems that one might have, whether it be depression, or drinking, no job, little money, or you name it—these things become easier to deal with as you go along, focused on the true passion that drives you. The key is to not lose your focus.

Following your bliss is finding your path. Everyone has their problems, and following your bliss may not get rid of your problems right away. But it will, of course, send you in a more positive direction. In some cases it will eliminate your problems quickly, but it usually takes some time and focus. Changing your life into a direction that *you* want to take as opposed to what society wants from you or what others want is a daunting task. But for those on a true path, who have recognized it, there is absolutely no other choice. When you find it, it's like the choice has already been made. You can create an extremely interesting new lifestyle, if not a completely new and interesting life itself. This is truly the spirit in action. It's the soul at work.

The soul is the deepest part of us and is the thing that inspires people to do things that are passionate. The soul is the one true thing that defines you. It is your fuel. It's your fire. Most people will let their fire burn in small embers to where it's barely discernible. It will only take someone with the knowledge of the pure spark of the soul, your deeper self, to come along and blow a little oxygen into these embers and light something that could turn into a blaze of glory, an incredible blaze of ingenuity, creativity, masterful works of art, whatever it is that your true capacity is. So many people live their lives not knowing what they could have accomplished if they had only tried.

There are stories of those who have gotten older and said, "As a younger man, I wish I would have done this. It was my passion. But instead I chose to do something else. I wanted to be safe, I was afraid to risk, and look at me now. I'm dying as an old and bitter man." There are too many stories like that from both men and women. It's sad.

> *It is quite possible, Octavian, that when you die, you will die without ever having been alive.*
> —Mark Antony, in "Cleopatra"

A different type of education that supports self-expression can change many such cases into ones where those who desire to fly go to the cliff's edge and actually *leap*—and fly—instead of backing off into safety. Discovering you can fly is one of life's greatest and most exhilarating joys. When we are young, while we have this vitality, while we can kindle this flame in us, let's do it. Or be sure that we do it for our children. Let us cast aside this lazy, robotic, automaton-mentality that's got such a grasp on us that we don't even know it's there most of the time. And let's put the fire into our lives. That's what a different educational approach could do. It would bring forth and nurture the personal and expressive flame of ingenuity and the flame of creativity to burn brightly from a very young age, when children still have that sense of wonder. It often burns out a bit later, but it doesn't have to. It's amazing what potential exists for the human family if this power is kept alive throughout life rather than stashed into some back, dark corner of consciousness in exchange for a false sense of comfort and laziness. Humanity is asleep and we need to awaken. The vast majority of us fail to reach our potential.

Is there some kind of a dark force, overshadowing us, that's meant to stifle the human spirit? If this exists then part of our mission in being here is attempting, and even succeeding, to overcome it. That's an accomplishment—especially for the soul because it's on that level that such unseen forces would operate, if there. It is on this level where we actually succeed or fail. Soul work is why we are here, but many people have no idea how to begin any kind of soul work during the *entire time* they are here. They're stuck in this physical muck and mire and spend their entire lives pursuing material things or the almighty dollar as opposed to anything on a spiritual level.

On the opposite extreme are enlightened masters—those few who have reached a state of oneness with God or pure consciousness. Society does not know what to do with these people, so generally ignore them. They function well as teachers for those sensitive enough to gravitate toward their work. It is hard to maintain a truly awakened state for long periods of time, but the best catalyst for getting there is meditation. For more average people, just getting out of the robot is the first step to a new awareness, so one should find something that is loved—whether it's dance, writing, music, any of the arts, crafts, sciences, social work, whatever that passion might be. It does not necessarily have to be anything creative or artistic. Some people are extremely happy providing a needed service, whether it be cleaning, repair work or caring for the elderly. An educational system that supports this personal expressiveness and helps one find it more quickly and accurately could be viewed by more conservative people as being self-centered, but as we grow and evolve more in a spiritual sense, there will be a need for many to step into social programs that help others as opposed to helping themselves. The universe truly does have a way of balancing things and bringing us in line with each other—especially if more of us become in tune with it.

In an enlightened state, when experiencing such bliss, all sense of time gets lost. In the realm of the soul, there is no time. When the soul gets directly engaged with the outer world and is allowed to function within it, then our awareness of time stops. Time is only relative to our physical or outer surroundings. If one is consumed in an inner capacity, then time is not much of a factor—it will pass more quickly because our awareness of it has stopped. Quantum physics will tell you that time is only an illusion, and "soul work" is one way to break through the illusion. You will lose all sense of it, which is a key indicator that you're on the right track. This also means that something is happening on a deep level that you are not fully conscious of. An inner part of you is at work here, meaning the soul. It has so far not been scientifically proven to exist—no doctor has cut open a patient and held up a squirming soul for everyone to see and then applaud about. It is there, however, but not in this physical sense.

The Soul is not Physical

Those scientists who insist that physical properties or mechanisms are the basis for what could be considered a soul miss the entire logical boat. They argue against survival of the soul since the body is a physical organism composed of molecules that disintegrate after death—so nothing could obviously survive. They claim that without a body left to deal with there is no identity left.

Each person, however, is different. Intention, consciousness, inspiration and volition, as well as a number of other human traits, are things that cannot be broken down, reduced or explained by some type of chemical action.

The chemical actions found in the human body, and in all animals for that matter, are quite similar and known, but we are completely unable to account for the immense variations in human personality and character based on these relatively simple molecular actions. Trying to explain these differences by stating that we are a product of the environment also doesn't wash, simply because many of us have innate talents that have never been taught to us, sometimes from an early age that seem to come out of nowhere, including advanced mathematics, music composition, artistic abilities, architecture, the list goes on and on. These abilities do not come "out of nowhere." They are reflections of the soul, shining into this world in a true act of expression—and nothing, absolutely *nothing* from the world of physical science can explain it. And we don't want them to. Any explanation that could be offered from a mechanistic viewpoint only detracts from the truth, has no bearing on it, and we can only hope that someday they will "get it." When enough people do, then a new and much-needed paradigm will begin.

So whenever one is engaged in their passion, or is truly self-expressing, it is the soul within us that is at work. When the soul is busy in this physical realm, then one's purpose in life is being engaged. It means that something on a higher level is happening, and is a reflection of your life's purpose. What one accomplishes in this respect (you could call it being true to oneself) is going to surface later, after you leave here. What did you accomplish in this life?

The soul is something that is not clearly identified in this world. Its existence is hidden or subtle to most of us, but it is here. In fact, it actually *is* us. We are souls that happen to be in a body, temporarily, to do certain things. So if we're tied up in trying to accomplish things that don't include following our bliss, then not much is being accomplished on inner levels. If one has not yet developed a spiritual sense then there are no indicators available for one to spiritually grow or change. Instead, one is merely doing things by rote, or operating out of their robot, which makes people into automatons. The "system" provides jobs for many of the spiritually deficient, while telling them, at the same time, what is supposed to make them happy. This is artificial. No person or system can tell you what will make you happy. That is for you and you alone to decide. The public is told what they need to do as individuals to make *them* happy (those running the economy, the corporate masters, etc.), and you are supposed to be a good citizen and buy into it. Many do, not knowing any alternatives. This is why many people feel dissatisfied on a deep level and do not know why. Going inward with clear intent and actually retrieving something, either immediately or over time, will reveal the steps needed on your path. Others should never dictate your path, no matter what kind of authority they presume themselves to be.

Finding God

Plato, arguably the greatest philosopher who ever lived, had a theory about upper and lower worlds. He believed there is a higher world above this one and we, in this reality, are a mere shadow of it. We are reflecting down here only to a small degree what is the true reality above us. Whatever or whoever we are could be just a small part of a larger consciousness of ourselves—or even of God. That, of course, is only conjecture, something yet to be proved, but it could go far in providing an answer as to why we are here.

There is a Gnostic poem called *The Hymn of the Robe of Glory*, which describes our descent from above, and into this earthly realm. It is an allegorical tale of a person who leaves from another place or a higher world and goes on a journey. Throughout this journey he forgets his origin and what he was supposed to do. We experience this same kind of amnesia in life. For those interested in pursuing their true path, this short tale is highly recommended.

The Gnostics were early Christians. Many Gnostic sects existed during the formation of Christianity and they were generally considered to be the mystics of the time. Their beliefs ran contrary to the more straightforward religious doctrines so their ideas were considered a threat. For example, they were dualists who believed that an all-loving God superseded the more vindictive God of the Old Testament, which they rejected. Most of their works were burned and suppressed and in many cases they themselves, in later years, were burned as heretics. They believed that instead of going into a church and being told what to believe, we can experience God for ourselves.

There are many ways that we can experience God, which explains why there were different Gnostic sects, or approaches to the problem. The Christian church, however, was trying to get organized and too many differing views caused confusion. They needed a simple and easy set of beliefs for people to follow in order to become strong. It became a nuisance for them, having the Gnostics who were saying, in effect, "We don't need the church, God is found within," or "Experiences are more precise and accurate than sermons." The Gnostics offered people separate paths to follow from the church, although some paths worked and others did not. This was a time of exploration and for a time there existed many conflicting choices.

Some Gnostic principals were deeply rooted in psychological truths and there's been an amazing rediscovery of this fact, along with their related Gnostic texts, in more modern times. The word *gnosis* in Greek means "to know," so a Gnostic is "one who knows." For all their knowledge and wisdom, however, the Gnostics were stamped out of existence by the powers that be. It took Christianity 300 years to get organized. Finally, at the Council of Nicea in 325 C.E., it was decided that Jesus was divine and the belief system, as a whole, could now officially follow that claim. Up until then,

Christianity had to work hard at becoming strong. The downfall of the Gnostics was in not being able to organize themselves the way that the church had done. Their strength, which kept them thriving for so long, was in the freedom of belief they offered and the acknowledgement of a more individual spiritual path within a general Christian framework.

Religion is important and plays a needed role in society. However, the church or any organization cannot hand you the truth on a silver platter. Some might believe it and accept it blindly, but you must experience the truth for yourself, and verify it yourself. Only then does it become "real." The Gnostics were encouraging direct spiritual experience. Yet the church was saying, "It is in the Bible, so it is true. You need to accept this one set of beliefs. It is the path to God and based on the authority of the church, this is the way it is."

At that time, government and religion were one and the same, unlike today whereby the state and religion are separate. In hindsight, it is clear there had to be a simplified version of the belief system put in place in order to keep the entire empire in a state of security and under control. You could not have diversity back then because the security of the empire was at stake, and they finally had to get brutal about it. There were too many other competing hoards at the gates of Christianity who were ready and willing to come in and take over with their brand of religion. So things had to get organized. The Gnostics had to get stamped out. It was a political necessity.

Today we are much wiser. We understand now, looking back, how incredibly interesting the Gnostics were and how valid some of their beliefs were as well. We are more intellectually sophisticated today, and more open-minded, so we can better understand their precepts and ideas. This still excludes, of course, the shrinking, fundamentalist mindset that remains blinded to such realities. After centuries of misunderstanding, persecutions, and biased teachings, what we are dealing with in today's world is the label that the Gnostics are "heretics." They were originally stamped out as a heresy. To this day hard-line fundamentalists will say, "Don't explore Gnostic beliefs. It's a heresy." The word has evil connotations.

The word *heresy* does not mean "evil" in any sense; it actually means "choice." And a heretic is simply "one who chooses." Respect for such choices today brings about more freedom because in most western countries our state and religions are now separate, unlike in the past. We can make choices for ourselves as far as our own personal spiritual freedom goes. These choices are now up to us, and should not be dictated by a higher "authority," unless we allow it. It is still difficult, in this day and age, to shake off centuries of conditioning that demands belief without considering the deeper esoteric teachings that were suppressed as heresy in the past. Many people will still accept blindly what they've been told to believe (and what to exclude from their beliefs) because they don't want to think for themselves. Having other people think for them is easier.

This leads us back into this entire "robot" mentality once again. There's a certain comfort zone, which people like to remain in. If people have a set of beliefs, ingrained from childhood or accepted without any real investigation, they don't want these beliefs challenged or shaken up. They want to feel secure in their beliefs because not knowing something is disturbing to them. People are afraid of the unknown. In Christianity, it is said in very simple terms that if you accept Jesus into your heart as your Lord and saviour, then you will be saved. And that's the end of it. Then they can go on with their lives.

It was made very simple on a religious level, but there are other factors involved in a spiritual sense. There is *experience* involved rather than mere acceptance. There is soul work. Most people don't understand the true, deep-level meaning of soul work. They believe there doesn't need to be any soul work because you just accept Jesus and that's the end of it. The acceptance of Jesus, however, should only be the beginning. It is an inward kind of acceptance, but it is *not* actual work. Simply accepting him into your heart isn't going to automatically make you into a saint or into a good person. It takes a lot of work to develop true moral character, good values, and a sense of compassion for other people. Actually living your life like Jesus would live, or attempting to do so, is soul work. There are millions of hypocrites who have accepted Jesus into their hearts in order to become "saved," then do absolutely nothing to really save themselves from that day forward. No attempt whatsoever is made to live their lives as he would. If one lives their entire life without building their character or building on other important spiritual strengths, then one will leave this world basically empty. Virtually nothing will have been accomplished, truly accomplished on your behalf, other than a blind acceptance in hopes of a free ride in return.

So am I siding with heretics here? Would I go so far as to do that? Of course I would—I don't bat an eye in saying that I'm a heretic because I am "one who chooses." I live a spiritual life as opposed to a religious one. I make my choices based on what's inside of me, not what's outside—not what's been manufactured or put together by a group of people centuries ago and passed down through tradition, saying that this is what I have to believe. I'm going to explore things for myself first—thank you very much—and then I'll decide.

There's a distinction to be made between religion and spirituality. Religion is for the masses, while spirituality is for the individual. There is nothing wrong with religion if you want to be part of the masses, but if you want to be an individual and search more deeply, then spirituality will come into play. Religion has been put together by men. It's been organized by people. That's why it's normally referred to as "organized religion." Virtually all organized religion, from inception, has been in constant dispute among its own members and between all other organized religions. There have been more people killed in the history of this earth because of religion than for any other reason.

Then we have spirituality. With true spirituality, if it's recognized within one's self, there can be no dispute whatsoever. True spirituality transcends all religious boundaries. If we can learn to respect one another in a spiritual sense, without bringing man-made religions into it, then it would solve all kinds of problems that we've been experiencing throughout the world. If we ever want to make any progress in the world, then spirituality is the answer as opposed to religions. The sooner we realize that, the better off we're going to be.

I am criticizing all religions—so if you choose to be offended by my criticism of yours, that's fine. Just know that they're all part and parcel of the same thing. None of them have proven, through centuries of trial and error, to be the answer for anything that we've been seeking—unless it happens to be control and manipulation. I am not claiming that religion itself is a complete and total failure. Each religion does succeed where spirituality is employed. But when exclusive dogmatic beliefs surface, as found in them all, this is where spirituality ends and religion begins. On a basic, simple level, individuals can be satisfied with religion. But on the deepest levels of all, in trying to advance ourselves through religion, there will always be the built-in strife and division found within and between them. There's always going to be religious wars and violence and killings because the deepest answers are not being found within a church, synagogue or mosque. The answers are found within.

Religion could certainly be pointing us in the right direction, but it's not going far enough to make any discernable difference, at least on a worldwide scale. Another factor is because each separate religion is completely convinced among themselves that they, and only they, hold the key to heaven or enlightenment. This big "ego trip," common to all major belief systems, is the one thing that will *prevent* you from holding the keys to anything.

Beyond this exclusionary mindset always follows the judging of others. Those who do not follow a particular faith are considered unclean, heathens, heretics, pagans, detested outsiders or, in general, sub-humans who deserve to be punished in often terrible and barbaric ways. And those within the fold who falter are sometimes ostracized, banned, excommunicated or, in the old days, fared little better than outsiders—they were stoned to death outside the village or burned publicly at the stake. We hastily judge others and throw out ethical considerations in every instance, when religious zeal is involved. "Judge not lest ye be judged," is a phrase from the Bible that one should carefully heed before casting stones toward others. Consider what Jesus said when they were about to stone the adulteress to death in John 8:7: "Let the first one without sin cast the first stone."

It's all up to each individual who can put aside their religious zeal. Common sense and one's own conscience should be the guide as opposed to any cruel, outdated religious demand. Spirituality is for the individual. That's where the work is needed, not from within some kind of a "club" that claims to automatically reserve your place in heaven if you become a member and do the "right things." These systems do not work because they involve outward displays; they're just for show and general guidance. We need to accomplish deeper inward work.

Followers in many different religions will go out, in the name of God, and do just about anything in His name. And anything is okay in their eyes, because God is believed to be on their side. That's where most of the wars or jihads or invasions or mass suicides or terrorist acts originate from—because "God told me to do it." Or, "It's okay for me to do it because God says we're the 'chosen ones.'" But killing and warfare in any way, shape or form isn't right in the eyes of an all-loving God because if we're not loving each other, then we're failing. We are absolutely and totally failing when we spend our entire time on earth plotting and planning strategies to take over land, take other people's money, take over other people's possessions, and not even blink an eye in taking their lives to do it.

> *We have just enough religion to make us hate, but not enough to make us love one another.* —Jonathan Swift

And, of course, let's not forget the unceasing efforts to change, often by force, the belief systems of other people. The main spokespeople for the various faiths of the world almost always come from a fundamentalist base, so are of the opinion that if the whole world would just think and believe as they do, everyone would be happy. This is delusional, and a complete impossibility. History bears this out. We are far too different, culturally and otherwise, to ever adhere to one strict set of beliefs; it is not in our nature. And if, by chance, one dogmatic religion was ever advanced upon us through some kind of world change, the sad fact is that we would self-destruct first, before ever accepting it. Whatever survivors that remained would be too shell-shocked to celebrate a religious "victory" of any kind, hollow as it would be.

What we must learn, as a reasonable alternative, is acceptance, compassion and mutual respect. There are many in religious arenas who are preaching tolerance, which is all fine and good, but I will repeat here, in general, what the great sage Vivekenanda said of tolerance. When one exercises tolerance it means that harbored deep within oneself still remains a separation, a dislike and even hatred because one is merely tolerating the other—not accepting them for who they are. What we must do is move it to the next level and truly accept others. Vivekenanda preached *acceptance*, rather than tolerance, and I wish to add compassion and mutual respect to go along with it. With these three facets of relationship in place, we would truly have a chance.

Many of our world leaders sorely lack this kind of insight. Peace advocates have sarcastically suggested that wars be decided by our leaders after giving them clubs and locking the two combatants in a large arena to fight it out. This way only one person dies rather than thousands, and it saves money, too. Instead of taking the violent approach, however, our leaders from every nation should be heavily sedated with valium or some other drug that will inspire tranquility, then lock them all in a room together. Hook them all up to those headphones like they have at the United Nations that allow any language of your choice to come through and force them to listen to songs, all together, that exemplify the rallying cry for peace over and over again like "Peace Train" by Cat Stevens, "Imagine" by John Lennon, and "We are the World," to name a few. Include a large, barbed club for each participant, along with live television coverage, just in case they revert to a normal state of consciousness.

But seriously, what is it going to take to get us to come to our senses and understand that there must be a new way of doing things? Realistically, it might take a couple of centuries to accomplish; but right now, at this very moment, we could make a collective and concerted effort to open our minds and teach our young people how to see things differently than we have. This would start things moving. We come into this world and we are shown that "this is the way it is." And most people blindly accept it, without even thinking. Yet if more people could see what kind of creativity can come out of our young people, and then encourage it, there would be more progress. Education is the key. Instead of having an educational system that structures us so rigidly and pigeonholes us into prefabricated job titles and duties so as to stifle the human spirit, we could develop an otherwise powerful, creative system that would nurture the individual and encourage genuine expression. We have been cramming our young people into "boxes," moving them through a virtual assembly line system in order for them to "proudly serve their corporate masters."

Those who leave high school and college are deemed ready, from societal standards, to go into the world. And yet they often come out more confused than when they started as young children. At least back then you had the security of knowing that someone was there to assist you, if needed. Graduates today are not guaranteed a job in order to feed themselves or get a place to live. Many are forced to move back in with their parents after graduating, asking in bewilderment, "Is that it? Is that all there is that I'm to learn? Is that how they've prepared me? So now what am I supposed to do?" More than 50 percent of college graduates do not get a position in any of the fields they graduate in. Why? It is because they were not *prepared properly*, and this is a process that must start early for it to succeed. It does not mean that one should decide early what they want to be and then prepare for it. It means that a person should develop the means to "know thyself" and be free to explore their true calling without trying to fit into various pre-cast molds. This causes people, as a result, to define themselves more weakly than what their true potential is, limiting themselves due to a lack of proper expression.

In many cases graduates must settle for less than what they were capable of and return to the world as rather unhappy and unfulfilled people for the rest of their lives. There is much to be done to change this general scenario. A friend and brilliant writer, Jack Barranger, was a professor of English and Critical Thinking for many years at the College of the Sequoias in Visalia, California. He had taught elsewhere, took a break for a over a decade, then returned to teaching in Visalia. What he noticed was a degradation in the quality of learning during the relatively short time he was gone. His teaching methods were unique; some would fit well within future educational programs because he truly cared about his students. Using reverse psychology, he would sometimes have them repeat, "Do you want fries with that?" in an effort to save their academic souls. He turned many students around with his personal help, while many stayed in contact with him for years after graduating, which is almost unheard of. Jack, unfortunately, was the exception rather than the rule.

Those who have created their own success rather than depending on what they were "groomed" for by a current educational system often end up with better results than what they were schooled for. Thinking on your feet in the real world can provide a strong jolt of reality, sometimes forcing people to become smarter than the system that was supposed to have prepared them for the world. They realized that they had to depend on their own resources, their own self-determination, their own creativity and ingenuity. And those are the ones who have risen to the occasion and become the most powerful and influential people in the world today. A vast number of entrepreneurs and millionaires have never finished college or had a formal education.

Although school is always recommended, it's not necessarily formal education that makes one successful in this life. Our schooling serves its purpose—grooming people to fit certain molds—but it could play a more integral role in making people successful. Our schooling can, and does, prepare people for normal business careers. But those who have gone on to make a tremendous impact in the world and have proven themselves to be the most powerful and interesting people out there, those are the ones, in a great many cases, who have used alternative means of rising to the top, other than standard education. Many of life's lessons are learned best through living. It is living life, not studying it, that brings tremendous opportunities. Having learned much harder and more realistic lessons, one can maneuver through life more easily without having simply studied it in a classroom. Instead of being told how to succeed, it is better for some to go out and experience different methods directly, until the aim is achieved.

Enlightenment
Besides education and direct experience, what else can wake us up into acting and performing better as human beings on this planet? A few people, including former U.S. president Ronald Reagan, have put forth the idea that if there was some kind of outside threat from another world, then we would all band together and finally act as a cohesive and helpful unit amongst one another. It is a nice idea, quite hopeful, but instead of helping each other to any large degree we would undoubtedly turn all our anger, hostility and violent tendencies toward another completely different race rather than ourselves. We would not change at all—just our focus would.

So what is it that *really* needs to happen, besides a new educational focus, in order to make a major, positive change in this world? It would have to be something powerful enough to truly transform people and society. The best tool to accomplish this successfully would be with a change from *within* people themselves—not from some kind of "outside threat." It would have to result in a new way of seeing things, a different state of consciousness, which is often called *enlightenment*. Only a small percentage of people have experienced this state, which truly does transform individuals and their entire outlook on life. They have moved beyond the simplistic, dualistic nature of things that seems to have been inbred in all of us. In evolutionarily terms, this conscious state is something that many believe we are heading towards. As far as waking ourselves up and breaking free of this robotic state of mind goes, this is the next step. Those who have been awakened view life from a clear perspective. They can see through the veneer of ignorance that acts as a cloak that covers over the rest of humanity. The great seers and mystics of the past have sometimes shared how they became awakened.

When one steps out of this robotic self, it's like a flash. The mind "opens up" and an entirely new awareness comes in. But to stay in that awareness is the most difficult part. Most often, one is not able to maintain this new state when it first begins to show itself. It is hard to maintain because it is so incredibly alive and invigorating and foreign to people, that grasping it in a normal "frame of reference" is not possible. Although quite calm and blissful, it is still foreign and normal mind functions will automatically revert and take hold after a time, throwing one back into the world. Therefore, it is hard to imagine staying in that state and still be able to function normally.

The mad mind does not halt. If it halts, it is enlightenment.
—Chinese Zen Saying

This higher consciousness is not what one would imagine it to be unless it is actually *experienced*. There's a certain calmness that goes with it. When one experiences these brief glimpses of awakening, it's exciting. But when one is truly awakened, when one is a master, then being able to handle the experience is much easier. Living within an enlightened state without coming back to normal consciousness all the time becomes a reality.

A certain calmness overcomes the soul and thereby overcomes the body. This calmness is something that cannot be "thought" in the normal sense. It just happens, and it happens because one is "ready" for it in a deeper sense. It is the soul at work, bringing out an inner "knowing" and allowing the experience to occur. The enlightened person has worked through enough situations to allow the removal of worldly barriers. Experiencing blissful states is not something that is arrived at through rational thought. That is why these masters have such strange and unusual themes to their teachings—especially evident to the common masses that have no interest in approaching such bizarre-sounding precepts.

Great spiritual masters, both ancient and modern, try or have tried to get their students to experience these higher states, but only if they are ready. In most cases these states of mind are experienced through diligence. The student must be devoted to the teachings, which involve a rigorous spiritual regimen. There are those who may have become enlightened through simple, spontaneous events, but in the vast majority of cases, this is something that has to be worked at, oftentimes for a number of years. Then and only then does it come, but it does come for many. When it does it is usually in a flash, often described as an energy, known as *kundalini*, which shoots up through the spine and into the brain. Most of those who reach this point say that a bright light floods into the mind and an entirely new consciousness takes hold.

This consciousness reveals to the recipient what many of our great quantum physicists are talking about today. That being, there is an underlying, all-encompassing "oneness" at work in the entire physical universe, and that all things are connected. You can understand that in an experiential way. It is possible for you to feel and experience the connectiveness around you—all of the connectedness to the world and everything in it and everything in space and everything in time, and an overwhelming sense of belonging and rightness and virtual perfection envelopes the soul because you are intertwined with it all. And for the first time people are able to see that there is an absolute method to this madness. There's a higher purpose and reason for everything, whereby in normal consciousness the average person doesn't see the connectedness at all. You can conceptualize it and understand it in a rational way, but to experience this entire connectedness with the universe is something that is far beyond what you can possibly achieve with the rational mind alone.

For the vast majority of us who have not been enlightened, it is easy to say, "I already knew that. I read about it in my science book growing up as a kid. All things are connected. I can accept that. That's really cute." But until you experiences this, there's no way to appreciate it fully, and there's no way it should be written off in such a hap-hazard fashion. For those who actually experience it, it is an awesome, life-changing event.

> *The raindrop may merge with the sea and lose its identity, but the sea also enters into the raindrop.*
> —Claire Myers Owens

Most people who have gone through this type of awakening end up changing just about everything that they've been doing in their lives. They often become much more creative individuals. They're more conscious of the entire world around them and other people. They're more helpful, more caring, and more compassionate toward other people and all living things.

What is amazing about this mindset is that it could be considered a threat to virtually anyone who operates in a normal day-to-day, dog-eat-dog business framework. Competition is the battle cry, not compassion. When a competitor is down you are taught to kick him—not help him up. There are a number of pioneers who have developed more holistic-based programs, however, where everyone wins. They've shown it is possible to become even *more successful* when operating from a synergistic standpoint. This basic business foundation is coming, and will be employed more and more often as we march into the future.

Businesses are currently structured in a way that demands employees to stay focused in one particular area of expertise, and there is little extra time to expand one's horizons. It is a mad rush, having to live paycheck to paycheck, as most people do, limiting your focus for the "privilege" of paying your bills and your taxes and your rent and your insurance, and the list goes on and on. You are functioning for the benefit of the system, not for the overall benefit of others and, ultimately, yourself. This entire economic system does not allow you—even in a "free enterprise" system—to succeed as one was able to do in the past. Globalization of big business is in command when, in reality, we need globalization of small business to come in and overturn the tables in the temple, as Jesus had done. Thousands of businesses are changing and "going green," while others are beginning to operate from a more spiritual perspective—or both. Instead of pure profit, many analysts now recommend treating others the way you would want to be treated, or to donate a certain percentage of proceeds toward worthy causes. It's infectious, and it works. It is a respectful and spiritual way of doing things, for all to partake in and benefit from.

Many hard-line left-brained business nerds don't get it. They consider such people to be "New Age freaks," and go back to crunching their numbers and plotting corporate takeovers. Yet a new consciousness could be the one thing that, deep down, humanity is striving to achieve. We may not be fully aware of it but those who do achieve this new, enlightened consciousness say that this is really what it's all about, and would never consider turning back or changing anything—even for the sake of greed. This is a huge step for any mere mortal, showing clearly that a personal shift has occurred.

If we can revamp our educational system to be more in line with this kind of thinking, then we could get a head start on a truly positive change. It would allow many more of us, at a younger age, to develop this kind of thinking. It is something that we must pro-actively *choose* to do. It is something that can truly be a conscious direction, chosen and followed by people bold enough to step forward and make a difference. Are you that person? This one moment is all you have right now. Do you let it pass and do nothing? Or do you make a choice for positive change?

Humankind is here on a collective journey. We are all in this together and more and more each day we are discovering the "butterfly effect." What we do affects everyone and everything much more than we ever thought. Revamping our approach toward education can unfold a new conscious map, revealing a more beneficial and collective path that we need to follow in order to better flourish and survive on this planet successfully. At first notice it would seem that we have a tremendously long way to go with this before such a change can be made. However, let us look at the Internet as an example. Look how quickly this particular technology exploded—linking minds around the world with resources and information when just a few decades ago it was completely unheard of. This has revolutionized our thinking and the world's way of doing things—so if we can create and utilize tools such as this, much can be done in short periods of time. It is true that we are more advanced, technologically, than spiritually. So let us use our technology to catch up in the spiritual fields. We can blow up the world dozens of times over and can't get along with the next-door neighbor. We are in our spiritual infancy, but if we can use what we do have, technologically, to help us advance in a spiritual sense, then we should not hesitate to do so.

This entire paradigm has become so dysfunctional, yet at the same time so interdependent, that it will not be easy to break out of. Either the earth itself is going to force us out of this paradigm with a major cataclysmic event, or a focused and concerted effort, primarily through education, must be brought forth by us.

Chapter Three

CATALYSTS FOR CHANGE

Trust only movement. Life happens at the level of events, not of words. Trust movement. —Alfred Adler

Paradigms can shift due to a change in thinking. They can also shift due to slow but major weather changes, or from instant worldwide cataclysmic events that force everything that is lucky enough to survive to start over again. As we try to navigate troubled waters with all kinds of clever, manmade ideas, it is the Earth that has the final say. Native Americans say that the Earth is our mother. There could be more truth to that statement than we realize. There have been cataclysms in the past, and the human race did not survive through them well. As a result, humanity had to be "reborn" again, nurtured by mother earth back to health, and to regain a foothold in the world once more. Legends worldwide, including the tale of Noah and his ark, state that very few people have survived through floods and cataclysmic upheavals during the earth's history. The earth is far more dynamic than we give it credit for, mainly because the cycles it moves through go slowly compared to our lifetimes. In addition, we don't want to recognize how incredibly dynamic these forces are because people don't like to think about impending disasters and things they have no control over.

When we have a massive earthquake or tsunami, those are once in a lifetime events. We will remember it during our brief lifetimes, but during the lifetime of the earth, these events are commonplace. Mountains like Mount Saint Helens can blow up completely, killing everything around for miles, creating huge headlines around the world; but for mother earth herself, it's just another day at the office. It's just earth science. If mother earth could read the headlines, she would just yawn (hopefully not near any human populations). When certain fluctuations occur, the earth's crustal plates can no longer hold and massive earthquakes can result. Evidence also exists for repeated and major shifts in the earth's axis, a "pole shift" as it's sometimes termed, that will cause the earth to wipe out almost every living thing on it. We have been reborn on the earth many times, and the earth is our mother.

Our civilizations have been forced to start over again many times. For an interesting collection of proof, check out the work of Michael Cremo—preferably, *Forbidden Archaeology*. It reveals evidence and actual artifacts proving that advanced forms of technology by mankind have existed in the ancient past. Just one example is a finished ball bearing that could only have been tooled by a machine and was found under a few hundred thousand years of sediments and within an existing piece of coal. Knowing how long it takes for coal to materialize makes this not only amazing, but irrefutable evidence. Similar items buried under layers of coal that can be dated millions of years old have also been found. Where did they come from? Where did the stories and legends of Atlantis come from? Or Lemuria? Where are the remnants of these civilizations? The cataclysms that may have wiped out these civilizations were so dramatic that few physical signs of them exist. We have only verbal stories that have been passed down, or the strange ancient evidence buried deep within the earth, because the trauma was so great when these events occurred.

We have at least two different scenarios going on here. The first involves earth science and nothing more. The earth naturally reacts violently and we are simply along for the ride, taking things as they come and coping as best we can. Ancient upheavals did occur, wiping out entire civilizations as a natural course of events; part of a cycle, and such events are a recognized fact for any intelligent person who should bother to seek out and examine the evidence.

The second scenario is connected to the theories of Atlantis. Instead of strict earth science, some have speculated that those in Atlantis misused their powers and the advanced technology they had developed, and were therefore wiped out. They were not living correctly. If there is any kind of spiritual law at work or maybe even some kind of intelligence overseeing us, whereby if we fail to become enlightened as a race, fail to treat each other properly like the way we would like to be treated, helping each other, showing compassion and not blowing each other up, if we fail to do the right things, then maybe there's a time limit. At certain points in history we may have run out of time and paid the price, courtesy of our overseers.

We were once part of nature and its food chain in the strictest sense, but one day, maybe in the Garden of Eden, we became self-aware. Since then we have been on an upward path, exerting at least some effort away from being nothing more than animals and the "kill or be killed" law of nature and survival. We are making efforts at compassion, and at truly becoming civilized. We are attempting to shed our animal natures and are trying to take on a more spiritual consciousness. We no longer hunt and gather, but have started cities, working together more than mere savages—but still, under all the veneer, we are savages nonetheless. We are trying to break free from it, are learning, with each cycle, how to do it, but have so far run out of time through violent earth changes that have appeared.

Could this time limit really be predetermined by some higher intelligent force, or is it just these natural rhythms of the earth that can be the major cause? One thing to consider is the ancient Sumerian epic entitled *Enuma Elish*, written on clay tablets in cuneiform, the first form of writing ever used by humans. In Sumerian, this means "When Above." It is the story of the ancient gods who, from above, made the decision to flood the earth and drown much of humanity at the time. It includes a creation story as well. In fact, it is the oldest creation story in the world, predating the smaller and less detailed Old Testament version that was sourced from it by at least 1700 years. This is something to think about.

It is not important whether or not we can accept these stories of the gods verbatim, because we only have circumstantial evidence. Regardless of the cause for cataclysms, it is clear that the earth does go through major catastrophic changes from time to time. Should we worry? What for? Just because the ice caps are melting in the most alarming way ever recorded and monstrous chunks have already broken off, affecting the overall balance of that area to some degree, doesn't mean we should panic. Just because the melted water is getting in under the actual ice shelf, especially in Greenland, making it more movable in a violent fashion with every passing day doesn't mean we should run for the hills. This earth has, and always will be, a volatile, dangerous place. It goes with the territory. A giant asteroid could come crashing down to earth just a few streets away from you right after you finish reading this sentence (so I'll stretch it out and make it a long one), vaporizing everything instantly for miles around, creating such an immense black cloud of debris that the sun would be blocked out for months, choking off and killing virtually every other life form in the world that happened to survive the initial impact in an almost exact fashion experience by those ignorant, overweight dinosaurs that were prancing around 65 million years ago, and there's absolutely nothing you can do about it. Nothing.

Early in its history, Earth was struck by a giant asteroid or planetary body far larger than the one presumed to have wiped out the dinosaurs. Ever since then it has been unstable and wobbles on its axis. The volatile tectonic plates constantly move, creating great earthquakes and volcanoes in an effort to stabilize itself. Why is it that we've been put on what seems to be the most volatile and violent solid planet in the known universe? Keeping in mind that all things are connected, it may be because we ourselves are a very volatile and violent race. We fit here just perfectly. We are an unstable people on an unstable planet, trying constantly to create balance in the same way our planet does. An unstable planet offers greater dualistic extremes—making it the perfect breeding ground for life itself, and all its variations, than the average peaceful planet. Nothing is stagnant here. It's the perfect place for duality to operate, and for us to come and learn within such a context. There is much to learn. We spend almost all of our spare time fighting against each other for the slightest differences, whether it be skin color, political ideologies, territory, you name it, the list is long. All we need is a reason to fight and we're there in a heartbeat. And if we don't have a reason to fight somebody else, we'll manufacture one. Sorry to say it, but that is how we are. Based on who we are and how we act, we have a number of things to work out down here.

There may have been a time when a higher intelligence was trying to decide where to send these imperfect souls or spirits. One God may have looked at the other and said, "Send them to earth. Maybe they'll learn something down there. And if they don't learn it, Mother Nature herself will keep them in line. We don't even have to bother." Is it possible that some other higher form of intelligence, whether it be individuals like ourselves or some kind of a spiritual force, could be looking over us? We should not rule out that what may be looking over us is a higher version of ourselves. In stating this I mean our actual selves, connected to us—not some higher or advanced race that happens to look like us. This is something to stop and dwell upon because herein may, in fact, lie undiscovered treasure. Such areas are still a mystery to us, but they are worth exploring.

There are many, many things about ourselves, this world and this universe that are still yet to be discovered, but we normally take on an arrogant self-righteous viewpoint of this and tell ourselves that we already know everything. This is reminiscent of the U.S. Patent Office announcing in 1875 that it was closing down because everything had already been invented. They didn't close. Since that time we've experienced the most incredible explosion of creativity and inventions within modern history—inventing more things in just over one century than through the entire course of previous (recorded) history. Just like in 1875, there is far more out there to tap into. What we did during the 20th Century has only scratched the surface.

The unexplored areas are now found in the inner world as opposed to the outer one. Herein lies a problem. Humankind, in general, is afraid of the unknown. We often label it as "the occult" and many of our religious institutions encourage people not to explore the occult under any circumstances. The word *occult* has been given an evil connotation over the years; however, it simply means "hidden." Just because something is hidden from view does not mean that it is evil. If you don't want to explore the unknown, then you deserve exactly what you get. Nothing. Those bold and adventurous enough to explore new territory almost always get the rewards and recognition. And they are the first to experience the benefits of the discovery. There is often risk involved but to the true pioneer, risk is no deterrent. It is a welcome indicator, as there are no gains without risk.

If you would rather be a couch potato with a serial number stamped on your forehead, then that is your choice. Just go to your nine to five job, pay your bills and your taxes, be a good citizen and, for God's sake, keep that big screen TV fired up. You can be a genuine, unconscious vegetable, or you can be a catalyst for positive change. We all have a choice. When you become much older, however, and are still doing the same damn thing in an old-age home that you did in younger years, do not complain. Just because you could have accomplished almost exactly the same things throughout your life by *being in a coma*, don't complain about it. You made the choice.

If you are in a job or situation that offers some kind of access for you to contribute something worthwhile to the world, in any capacity whatsoever, then do it. Don't spend your life in a box. In order to achieve innovation we are often asked to "think outside of the box." This is because how things are is not really "how things are." They can be changed for the better, but most people don't even try. Have you ever taken a leap of faith and then exclaimed after it was over, "I didn't know I could do that!" There are literally countless things like this waiting for you, but we normally choose to exist in our "boxes" instead. We have cubicles at work and square rooms around them. At home it's the same—we are boxed in square rooms inside a square house, on a city block that is square, and we therefore compartmentalize everything. Is it any wonder? We structure our lives that way. Most people just go along to get along and wish to keep things as they are, predictable and safe, but totally blind to the possibilities.

People need to become more involved and put something back into the world. Many western nations are lucky because they don't experience the immense poverty that is found in other parts of the world. To just kick back, have fun and enjoy things while not putting anything back in is an ultimate sin. We are realizing that we're all connected and there's so many different ways that we can help. You can't single-handedly save the world, but if you donate money to an overseas charity it can help—as long as you know that they're not pocketing most of it like some of them have done. The point is to research these things and make yourself a useful person in this world to whatever degree that you can while you are here.

There are two types of people, those who only consume and those who give (in addition to consuming). Pay close attention to your actions and differentiate between them. Most people are consumers because that is what we are *trained* to be. When you consume you deplete; when you give you provide. Most everyone is depleting resources for their own benefit and that's why we are in trouble.

We have no more right to consume happiness without producing it than to consume wealth without producing it. —George Bernard Shaw

If you're just here to consume, then you're not serving your soul's purpose. You're just "along for the ride." There are many people you have never met who would welcome your help in so many ways. Instead of helping, however, most people prefer to watch prime time TV every night, sleep late on the weekends and involve themselves in trivial entertainments of every kind. For many, giving something back never enters into the equation. It's unheard of because they're too busy being titillated.

When you are engaged in any type of activity ask yourself two questions. First, "Does this have any direct bearing on my life?" If the answer is no, then you're wasting your time. When one is being entertained instead of educated, the answer is usually no. Some forms of entertainment like concerts or sporting events can be inspirational, however, which leads to the second question: "Does this have any *positive* bearing on my life?" For example, gambling can often have a direct bearing on one's life, but in a negative way. Very few people can make a living from gambling, which ruins more people than it helps. Our greed creates an urge to get things for ourselves rather than give.

We've been trained to be consumers and that's what we are. "Just consume" is our hidden, programmed mantra. It is true that those who work hard and make a difference in some way deserve to be entertained from time to time. I don't dispute that. What is bothersome, however, is the huge imbalance of those who care for nothing but themselves—whether it be individuals, companies, and organizations of any kind, including religions or nations.

It is a nice gesture to reach out and help others because this world has so much suffering in it. Any adherent to Buddhism will tell you that one of their major concerns, which is less evident in the West because we don't experience it that much, is suffering and how to alleviate it. There's so much needless suffering in this world, with humans and animals, that each of us should take a stand and do something to help. Thinking this book will encourage others beside you so that you can sit on your fat ass and let them do the work doesn't wash with me. Get up and do something to help, even if it's something small. It's needed. Some may become indignant and ask, "Who the hell is he, telling me to get up off my fat ass and do something?" My response to that is, "Who the hell are you not to? What gives you privilege and makes you better than everyone else?" If each of us, and I mean *each of us*, does something small to help others, then this planet will take off and become a much better place almost overnight.

If you find suffering somewhere in your own community, lend a hand. For some, it is easier and more gratifying to help the local community than to send funds overseas. And if that's the case, go for it. You will be amazed at the honor and gratitude received. It will boost the self-esteem of those who are actually doing something useful with their lives in addition to those who have been helped and would have otherwise thought that no one cared.

So many people are suffering because of one main reason—no one cares. Everyone is wrapped up in their own little worlds. If people reach out of their self-centered worlds it will lessen suffering greatly. It can be lessened but will still remain. What is the initial cause? Why must we have it?

This brings us back to the dual nature of the world. There cannot be good without bad, so suffering is the other side of health, or joy. It is an inescapable part of existence. In this world, goodness is at a disadvantage, so suffering proliferates easily. For example, in order to build something magnificent, like a great building or major edifice, it can take twenty years or more, yet in just a few hours it can all come crashing down in an act of destruction. The 9/11 World Trade Center disaster in New York in 2001 is an example of this. It's far easier to destroy than it is to create.

Evil constantly has an upper hand. It can strike at any time—more quickly than something that takes time, creativity and planning. Bullets from a gun have taken greatness from this work in an instant—with the assassinations of John F. Kennedy, Mahatma Gandhi and Dr. Martin Luther King, Jr., to name a few. There are great writers or composers who have worked on books or music for years only to have a fire take it away; or involve themselves in a deep depression and just burn it all in one night, to regret it later; or to have an accident happen and the wind just blows it away—as portrayed in the film, "The Treasure of the Sierra Madre" (worthwhile for a better understanding of human nature). We need to cherish and value the amazing potential of the human spirit to create such wonders, because in an instant it could all be gone.

Those of us who can tap into our spiritual, creative power, however, are never deterred by threats of loss or destruction. Many millionaires have said, "If you took it all away from me, I could turn around and make it back all over again." So a tremendous power of the human spirit exists within us, regardless of the negative forces that can swoop in and snatch things away from us in an instant. That should never deter us. To confront such things and overcome them is character building. It's spiritual work, "soul work," and it is, at least in part, why we are here.

Chapter Four

DEEPER LEVELS OF REALITY

Every second is of infinite value. —Goethe

The heart of so great a mystery can never be reached by following one road only. —Q. Aurelius Symmachus

We have surrounding us, completely unseen, both good and negative forces. Everything that we can see around us is not the only reality. Other levels of existence intermingle with ours and these levels contain both good and bad influences.

To avoid sounding like a witch doctor, let me approach this scientifically. It is a scientific fact that everything is a vibration. There are just varying degrees of vibration. For example, in the area of sight there are all these different waves around us and we only pick up visually about three percent of them. There are radio waves, microwaves, gamma rays, ultraviolet rays, all of these vibrate at a rate that cannot be seen by the human eye. Yet these things are bouncing all around us 24 hours a day.

We cannot see ninety-seven percent of what's out there, all around us, but it's there. This is good, however, because the brain and eyes together act as a filter. If we were able to see all of this stuff, the brain would become completely overloaded, the nervous system would go haywire and collapse because there would be too much information to try to process all at the same time, in an effort to make sense out of the world. The human design has been carefully planned or thought out by some higher intelligence—or the natural forces of evolution have taken millions of years to develop us in a way that works to the greatest capacity for us to function in the best possible way. With all these energies around us in the physical world, how can we be completely sure that there is not something out there that we cannot see, operating within these unseen frequencies, that has it's own agenda?

Let's move one step closer before taking this leap and examine the more recent research done in the area of ghosts. Evidence now exists that seems to show quite clearly that the human spirit can survive out of the body. Before elaborating, let us make a distinction between the soul and the spirit (these words have been used interchangeably, but it's now time to clarify their terms).

The soul is the innermost part of us. In fact, it is us. It has a connection to God. It is a particle of light. It is what comes here from that other place from which we came. And it is what will return. It carries our life imprint with it when it leaves, and functions while here as a certain form of consciousness. I have taught those who are sensitive enough on how to view their own soul—to actually see it within their field of vision and experience it—and some have succeeded.

The spirit is the result of electrical charges that are generated between the human body and the soul while they are connected. When the body and soul disconnect in a smooth and natural death, these "charges" will dissipate over time. Following death, the spirit will linger for a time—some longer than others. If the human soul is separated from the body quickly in a traumatic death, then the spirit can become trapped here, unable to "fade out" because the death occurred too fast to properly sever the soul from its body. Therefore, the soul connects to the spirit and animates it, having been duped by the trauma to believe the spirit must be the body. The soul and spirit stay connected, not knowing what really happened. The result is what we term a ghost. The soul stays connected to the spirit because that is the only way it maintains its connection to the body. And if it still thinks it has a body, not being "told" otherwise, it will naturally keep its connection to the spirit and therefore not go anywhere. The body keeps us in this world, so if we think we still have one, we will continue to hang around, lost or confused as we might be. In cases of quick and severe trauma, the soul sometimes does not know it has passed.

When the soul stays connected to the disembodied spirit a consciousness is still evident—the same or similar consciousness to the one we had while living. Therefore, the spirit/entity is capable of communicating, having maintained its human consciousness. If, on the other hand, the soul manages to pass over, what sometimes gets left behind is residual "energy," whereby the emotional trauma can still be felt or experienced by local residents or investigators without any kind of intelligence being present. This is called an "imprint," and is an emotional remnant only. This is the result of a highly emotional charge of energy left behind not only from deaths that might occur, but from major events from life itself. An imprint results only from extremely emotional situations.

A stubborn or confused soul may refuse to leave because of unfinished business or a strong human or material attachment. Any consciousness left over is due to the presence of the soul. If the soul can be made to understand that there is no longer a body keeping it here or allowing it to continue its work, it will no longer cling to the ghostly spirit. It will allow the spirit to dissolve, will free itself to the other side and, in the process, free those who have had to put up with its hauntings. Soul animates both body and spirit—without it, neither one can be experienced in an intelligent form.

Our modern "ghost busters" come in and let the soul know that it has passed. They reassure it and provide instructions for it to pass over. These ghost busters have the newest electrical instruments that are very sensitive and can pick up the presence of these spirits. They can detect changes in electrical fields, in temperature, and can pick up visual images on sensitive frequencies and strange unexplained audio. These things are now commonplace in examining potential proof of the reality of ghosts. We all have a spirit; we all have a soul. If one or both should survive the body, why wouldn't we see or at least detect them on occasion? As our technology improves we find ourselves getting far closer to the truth, and at a faster rate than we have ever approached it in the past.

The point here was to show that spirits outside the body are commonly being detected and their existence is becoming more scientifically acceptable each day. It allows us to reiterate that there are positive and negative influences all around us. Some of these negative influences are spirits, as many who have experienced hauntings would tell you. There's good and bad in the spirit world just like there is in the physical.

This universe is far more complex than just the physical surroundings that we can see because, again, we can only see a small percentage of the physical world and everything that's happening around us all the time. So we need to understand that in this world of duality, with positive and negative, much of what we *don't see* is still part of the dualistic system and can have the same positive or negative traits.

There are two interesting researchers in this area that talk about this kind of material and it can become very spooky at times. They are Charles Fort and John Keel. Keel has written a number of books, including *Our Haunted Planet, Disneyland of the Gods,* and *The Mothman Prophecies*. He was influenced by the works of Charles Fort in addition to his own direct experiences. Fort was a man in the early 1900s who was rather eccentric, but very thorough. He collected newspaper articles from around the world about all of the strange and unusual things that occur, documented as fact and considered true. Amazing and bizarre things have happened—only to appear briefly in newspapers. But when they did, Fort was there to scoop them up. He wrote a number of interesting books documenting such strangeness, including fish and frogs that fall from the clear blue sky, modern, state-of-the-art items dug up by archaeologists deep in the earth, and strange, unusual animals that appear and disappear out of nowhere. The list is long—enough so that a complete "science," referred to as "Fortean," was begun in his name and continues the documentation of strange goings-on in the world that have no rational explanation.

John Keel, a more modern version of Charles Fort, had many strange and direct experiences, including tracking down something called the Mothman, a large winged creature with glowing red eyes that appeared for a time in West Virginia. He also had some interesting UFO experiences. On at least one occasion, a strange message was waiting for him at the front desk of a hotel where he stopped for the night, completely at random. I cannot vouch for everything he writes as being verified fact (and I'm sure he couldn't, either), but his material will definitely make you think and is very entertaining to read. Keel documents all kinds of bizarre and unusual things in his books. The conclusion he came to is that we are property. This was first believed by Charles Fort and Keel, after coming to his own conclusions, reconfirmed it for himself and passed it along to us. We are property in the sense that there is some kind of unseen force behind this physical reality that can make us see things that are not necessarily there, or make genuine things happen that go far beyond the norm. There is a huge spectrum of reality that cannot be seen by the human eye. Keel refers to this entire spectrum that contains all waves, including what we are unable to see, as the superspectrum (ninety-seven percent of it is outside of the visible light spectrum).

If we were fully conscious of the superspectrum, we would be able to see, as mentioned before, everything all at once. But it would flood our senses so badly that we would not be able to process it—we would be too overloaded. Keel says that this superspectrum is manipulated behind the scenes by some kind of intelligence, without us knowing. The huge remaining light spectrum, which we cannot see, could also contain or offer access to other dimensions. From a purely scientific point of view, our modern quantum physics has strongly and convincingly put forth the existence of at least ten dimensions. This is according to String Theory, which is accepted by most of the scientific community. We are only in the third dimension, which is as high as we can perceive. What the fourth dimension could possibly contain boggles the mind of many scientists—so what about the six above that one?

What else is going on above and around us within these other dimensions? For example, from our own third-dimensional perspective, when we look at a two-dimensional piece of paper, there's a big difference as to what can be observed. If we were conscious beings in a two-dimensional world as found on a piece of paper, and if someone from a higher dimension were to take a needle and stick it through this piece of paper, the second-dimensional being would only be conscious of the needle as it entered in and exited out of the paper. It would not see it coming. It would not see it going. It would not see the vastness of space around it, nor would it be conscious of any of the things that would be physically in the room or near it. In the second dimension one would only be conscious of whatever is on that piece of paper in only a second-dimensional form. That's it, nothing else.

Now let's take our third-dimensional world and put it within the same scenario, but from fourth, fifth, sixth, seventh, eighth, ninth, and tenth-dimensional perspectives. It's more than plausible that there are things above and around us that can see everything that we are doing and can easily control our environment like we can control that piece of paper in a second-dimensional world. These other dimensions have been with us since the beginning of time, and could be teeming with other life forms—some very intelligent—that we are just not able to perceive. We can often look down on an anthill or into a fishpond and observe things without them ever being conscious of us. So why would we be so vain as to think that we are at the very top of the natural world? It no longer seems like such a stretch to imagine that Keel and Charles Fort could be right.

UFOs could be vehicles used to observe us in this fashion. For more on this, and actual photographic proof of these otherwise invisible objects using infrared filters, one should read the amazing book by Trevor James Constable entitled *The Cosmic Pulse of Life*. Many reports of UFOs have them suddenly blinking out and vanishing right before our eyes, acting like that needle passing through the paper as they either travel between dimensions, or move into a higher or lower light spectrum that we cannot perceive. It is very easy for them; but from our perspective, it seems like an incredible miracle. It's not. There are those in certain scientific circles who know exactly how this works. A great scientist or philosopher once said, "There is nothing out there that is miraculous. It's just science that we have not learned yet."

The second person whose work is important in this regard is that of Jacques Valle. Valle has studied deeply all of these interesting and unexplained phenomena that have occurred throughout the centuries and has come to the conclusion that many reports of fairies, elves, and other strange events in our history, and now UFOs, all come from an alternative reality that has been on this planet from the beginning of time. In fact, he believes we are sharing the planet with this other reality and this other reality does, indeed, have great intelligence and protects itself. It also interacts with us at chosen times, and has been known to do so throughout history. Our encounters with these beings have often been responsible for our mythological tales from the past. Most of these legendary beings appeared in humanoid form as little people, fairies, elves and dwarves. Today we don't see or experience much of them anymore because, according to Valle, our technology has changed. We've become more scientific and more mechanical so now we're experiencing flying saucers, UFOs, and little grey aliens—but it's the same intelligence that's always been there from the beginning of the time. He speculates that they were here before we were, and that they may be a part of nature. The mythological elves and fairies were considered to have a close connection to nature. The little people are here once again, this time in UFOs, but they take on a slightly different form, possibly to reflect what our current consciousness is open to seeing. The entire UFO phenomenon is a mythology in the making, and all of the stories that surround the subject present themselves in exactly that way. What we are seeing could be a reflection of what our society or culture should be expected to see, based on its consciousness.

Because we are exploring outer space, these clever beings may be taking on the form of "aliens" from other planets, to conceal their true origins. They may, in fact, be from this earth and have been here from the beginning of time. They may not have our best interests in mind at all. They're not concerned with our best interests. They are concerned about theirs, so their influences upon us are self-serving and they are intent on staying hidden. This is a good idea since mankind has destroyed or depleted virtually every life form that we could visibly see or put our hands on. When we develop a respect toward all life, then I believe these "others" will show themselves.

It is interesting that we are looking into the far reaches of outer space, light years away, for something that could be right under our noses. Even more fascinating is that there very well could be other races coming from outer space, and they are coming here and inter-dimensionally hiding themselves along with those others that have been here for so long, creating an interesting mix. There is such an incredible, bizarre possibility going on here that is even stranger than many science fiction movies. As it's often said, truth is stranger than fiction.

What does any of this have to do with the expansion of human consciousness? We have limited our view of the world to just the material plane and boxed ourselves in. It's difficult to grow and expand our consciousness when we refuse to accept a much larger view of reality, much less explore it. This is an area that we have only begun to scratch the surface of. We have not searched deeper due to our own ignorance and because the initial discoveries made concerning life on other levels—and they have been made—have been so frightening that at this point we are not ready to proceed. We are not officially told about these discoveries because many people would feel helpless and paranoid, knowing there's a hidden intelligence around us that can manipulate our physical surroundings at will, and there's nothing we can do about it. In considering that we may be victims of manipulation similar to the "pin through the paper" scenario, should we just remain quiet and accept what some scientists are telling us—that the earth is an isolated outpost without visitors of any kind? That life on this world is a "freak of nature" and here we are, alone? That nothing else exists around us and nothing else is visiting us? Far from it. To find these things we simply need to look into the huge remaining light spectrum beyond the visible, vibrating and pulsing with energy all around us—which is easier to accomplish than one might think. Finding ET very soon cannot be ruled out. With the billions of galaxies that are out there, combined with the additional billions of stars, it's only a matter of time before we find other planets that support life. Or they will find us. Many, many star systems are millions of years older than we are and could easily support life that has evolved far beyond us, technologically. Here we are, just coming out of our "industrial revolution," thinking we are at the pinnacle of scientific progress. This egotistical view is either the laughing stock of the universe or other races just look at us with pity.

A few reputable astronomers claim that within the next few decades there is a 98 percent chance of us finding at least one life-supporting planet. By the time one reads this that may already be a reality. We currently know of about 140 to 150 planets, and they are being discovered so fast that it's almost a moot point to even mention the numbers. The point is, they are being discovered quickly, and we are only in the infancy of this kind of exploration. The great thing about it is that it's being done with high technology, without us leaving the planet, which is far more cost effective than the billions spent in the past.

It is this writer's opinion that inner exploration is far more beneficial to us than flying machines and outer exploration, at least at this time. If other races exist that are so much more advanced than we are in a technological sense, as some educated people claim, then let *them* find *us*. We're not going anywhere, unless we blow ourselves up or destroy the entire ecosystem here that supports us. It is more likely that right now, other advanced races have already found us and are here visiting, but they choose not to show themselves. Why? Because we are such a barbaric and backward race, always attacking each other with only the slightest provocation, that we are not trusted on a cosmic scale. That's the bottom line. Humanity is the poster child of the universe for the cosmic "loose cannon," and we are not to be trusted. If we had even the slightest idea of who we are and why we're here, then maybe we'd know how to act. Maybe then could we act accordingly and fit into the cosmic scale of things. But we don't. We still have a long way to go.

Chapter Five

GREED, CONSPIRACIES AND THE MEANING OF LIFE

No man is rich enough to buy back his past. —Oscar Wilde

Fortune does not change men; it unmasks them.
—Suzanne Necker

There are many who wonder about the meaning of life. It's a big question. Most people don't dwell on it much. They're too busy tied up in the day-today activities of just staying alive, working their jobs, raising families, trying to figure out how to put food on the table, and paying their bills. Many people in third-world countries worry about where they can get fresh water for the day, where they can get some shoes that will work, or whether or not they or their family are going to get killed in the newest local insurgent uprising. The average person worldwide does not have time to sit back and philosophize about the higher meanings of life because the problems of basic survival are constantly staring them in the face. Forced into survival mode, their search for a higher purpose and a higher cause is lost.

The people who have time to consider these things are lucky. Those in much higher positions who benefit from all of the struggle and the suffering that's going on are also part of this fortunate group. There are not that many of them; but instead of becoming philosophers in any meaningful or compassionate sense of the word, many who wield real power are too busy enjoying the material comforts and benefits of what this brings than doing anything about improving the state of the world, unless it is from a rationalized approached that serves their own self interests. As the world suffers and many starve, the powers that be often operate from the old mafia adage, "It's nothing personal, just business." World policies based mostly on "business," through the greed of human nature, have killed millions, unmercifully. There are some tremendous ongoing programs in the World Bank and International Monetary Fund that are geared toward helping the poor throughout the world in major ways, with some of them being relatively new. They should be commended, but both of these bodies were formed at about the same time as the United Nations. The world has wrought so many changes since that time, that all three of these institutions need a major overhaul, with better, more conscious people, to remain effective.

Some people in high finance with access to large reserves of cash or gold pay themselves huge salaries or make deals or "trades" under the table. Outrageous unwarranted "bonuses" are commonplace for corporate magnates. For example, in 1991 the Bank of Credit and Commerce International (BCCI) was shut down by bank regulators from a number of countries because their top executives stole as much as $15 billion from its accounts. It laundered major international drug money (at least $90 million alone from Manuel Noriega), and had a hard time surviving unless it engaged in illegal activity—which is what we are discovering about the complete western international banking system itself. Many large western banks are have been or are currently being bought out by the Chinese, who have otherwise steered clear, for the most part, of the west.

BCCI also provided troubled countries like Argentina with loans, backed by a general scheme promoted by the World Bank, International Monetary fund (IMF), and the United States, which eventually blew up in their face because in this case they failed to live up to their end of the bargain and Argentina defaulted. They bought Argentina's debt for $30 million and immediately sold it back to them for $38 million. BCCI had agreed to spend the entire $38 million on assets from Argentina, as an investment and to boost the economy, but only spent $10 million and kept the rest. It seems this failure gave Argentina the right to default, which it did. Greed and corruption operate at the highest levels, and a new framework is needed to work from.

In 1999, when the U.K. mobile operator Vodafone took over its rival Mannesmann, Vodafone's boss Sir Christopher Gent gave himself a ten million British pounds bonus for completing the deal, despite the company losing more than three-quarters of its value over the next three years.

In mid 1994, the Scott Paper Company was worth about $3 billion when ruthless cost-cutter Al Dunlap appeared on the scene. When he sold the company for a profit in 1995, he gave himself a $100 million dollar bonus. In addition to laying off thousands of people at numerous companies, he also, according to *Business Week*, refused to pay for cancer treatments for his niece, failed to support the child from his first marriage, and skipped the funerals of both of his parents.

It is actions such as these that create and support the paradigm that we need to abandon. These people are caught in the materialistic trap, snared like an animal and don't even know it. They are trusted "leaders" from within the field of high finance; but because they remain faceless to the general public due to media silence and less accountable to people rather than profits, they have taken blatant liberties out of pure greed. It has been a continuing pattern, yet we are finally becoming aware of it and have had just about enough.

These are the behind-the-scenes movers and shakers in the world, but the world is overtaking them, their days are clearly numbered, and the power is shifting. Their goal has not been the welfare of the world. The world of banking is equally guilty. Many countries cannot pay back the interest on the loans they must take out to survive. It's a form of "rescue" that is more about profit, power and control. It's about keeping these countries solvent enough so they can still exist—but to the degree that the control of these nation's economies are maintained by others, rather than the countries themselves.

The money manipulators at the world's highest levels would undoubtedly claim that their work alone keeps the world prospering and moving. A number of countries, with Brazil and Argentina being primary examples, would no longer be here had they not been bailed out of complete bankruptcy in the past, only to be burdened with enormous loans to pay back over time. Paying the interest alone is an immense challenge for most countries in this predicament, making them nothing short of slave nations. They are puppets to be manipulated by the purse strings of the hidden worldwide monetary dragnet that has sucked them all in. This system is minimally beneficial to the nations being "helped" because it is the only game in town and must be played by the rules of the money masters, who benefit far more. For example, more than one-third of Brazilians (183 million) live in brick or wooden shacks on less than $2 a day without the resources to improve themselves. Because money has been made the "God" of this world by those who control it, those who control it are in fact *playing God*. And as far as those destitute nations who come crawling to them are concerned, these money masters *are God*. Because they are the only ones who can save them. They don't have just some power—they have *all* the power.

In western nations, virtually everything you do is in their control—what you can buy at the store, what you watch on TV, what medications you can or can't take—their money and therefore their decisions control it all. With each passing day, a long-term pattern is taking shape and a new piece to the unfolding puzzle is added when certain nations and large corporations are forced to dance to the tune that world finance plays. If you don't dance, you don't eat.

Watch how it unfolds in the coming years and recall how the Berlin wall fell in Germany, the Soviet Union collapsed, China opened up massive trade with the West, the European Economic Community was formed, NAFTA and GATT were passed in the U.S., as a number of recent examples. These things came about primarily from world economics and the chosen agendas of the money-kings. In years past, kings reigned in most countries throughout the world. Today they are gone, while hidden kings sit behind the desks of financial institutions and banking conglomerates. They look down and can see that humanity as a whole is barbaric. Instead of trying to heal volatile affairs or stem the tide of this barbarism, it is often encouraged through arms sales and other manipulative means. Our violent tendencies are then exploited—used to their advantage to gain further control.

It is likely true that some organization or group needs to be in charge that can stem the tide of warfare and destruction, but that is *not* being done by these hidden monetary masters. Wars are always raging throughout the world not only because we are inclined towards it by our current natures, but because it makes *money*. Wars also keep populations down and keep people fearful.

We need to expand our consciousness enough to move beyond our barbaric tendencies—to develop compassion for others and educate ourselves in a more spiritual sense, so that we do not have to be ruled by secret masters in a purely materialistic paradigm. If we were led by example it would open the doors for such change, but that is something we cannot count on. It is up to us.

It would be interesting for us to discover and disclose to the world exactly who these money masters really are and how they live because one never sees their names published. Who are they really? What are they doing? They don't want us to know. Figureheads like presidents, prime ministers and heads of state do not have their level of power—or their anonymity. Our visible government figureheads are just the puppets for those who operate the behind-the-scenes monetary machinations of the world. It is a machine, run by hidden masters, and we are all slaves to the machine. The group Pink Floyd had a song called "Welcome to the Machine," for those who would consider its' existence.

> Welcome my son
> Welcome to the machine
> What did you dream?
> It's alright we told you what to dream.

When you wake up and see the machine, then there's a whole new perspective available. You just have to look.

It has been said that major media outlets have been quietly instructed not to print or broadcast the names of certain key people. These powerful people take that privilege because they *own* these media outlets or finance them in some way, and want their privacy. This is censorship to the masses, done so no one will know who most of these powerful people really are or what they are up to. They are not going to allow their own media property to reveal anything about them that could be damaging, based on their personal contacts and powerful affiliations, so the best approach is to not allow mention of their names at all. It is insurance that things will run smoothly.

One of the few world players who has been unable to maintain a low profile is Rupert Murdoch. When The Wall Street Journal ran an embarrassing story about his Chinese-born wife in 2000, Murdoch was not happy. He eventually bought the Journal and its parent company in 2007 for about 5 billion dollars, which effectively silenced such future activity. He owns 175 other newspapers worldwide, the largest printing plant in the world, Twentieth Century Fox Studios, 35 TV stations in the U.S., and as of 2005 owns MySpace, on the Internet, which he bought for $580 million. There were once rumors that his media companies were instructed never to "cover him." If true, this has now been upgraded to positive coverage only. With so much of the media controlled by a few, it has become quite easy to censor anything that could be of concern by the powerful.

> *Everything you read in the newspaper is absolutely true except for the rare story of which you happen to have firsthand knowledge.* —Erwin Knoll

If the large media groups that we rely upon for "the truth" won't tell us the whole story, in many cases, or reveal who is *really* running things, then who can we depend on? If these names were, in fact, made public on a regular basis, it would be found that they were in many cases also members of the Bilderberg Group. This group meets yearly in secret to make decisions about the state of the world, and how they can help run it. Due to their power and secrecy, reading or seeing anything about them in the mainstream media is a rarity. However, the London Times in 1977 did make mention, calling the Bilderbergers, "a clique of the richest, economically and politically most powerful and influential men in the Western world, who meet secretly to plan events that later appear just to happen."

The book *The True Story of the Bilderberg Group* by Daniel Estulin reveals the names of all attendees at the 2007 Bilderberg meeting in Istanbul, Turkey, and includes the names of those involved in the Trilateral Commission as well. The purpose of this work is not to label the people involved in these groups as being "evil." They do the best they can while involved in a paradigm that is fast becoming outdated and inefficient. They will need to make important choices toward achieving a smooth transition into something that may not be entirely of their own design. In other words, they can redeem themselves and those who came before them from this mess due to their positions — but if they fail, the world will fall into ruin faster than most would anticipate. Both groups are quite powerful. Some of their members are politicians but definitely not all because, again, it's all about money. It's all about power. It's about oil. It's about big business. And it's about making a profit through various means of exploitation.

As far as war goes, nothing gets done to stop any wars unless it has something to do with diverting funds into different hands, which will start the process over again with different or more lucrative profiteers. Warfare is just another part of the machine—although a rather important one. It generates income for many of these people, including their ties to the multi-billion-dollar military-industrial complex, and helps keep the banks open and powerful. The truth is, the more you get to know the big players who run the show, the more bloody hands will be seen as they move and funnel money.

Good people are striving to achieve a paradigm that uses money to increase moral behaviour, while this current paradigm is so corrupt that it runs the world, with all its money and power, in a morally bankrupt fashion. Millions are starving, getting killed or being diseased or displaced at the expense of big deals to arms manufacturers who must find ways to use their products. There is far more meaning to life than this—with us being used as tools to achieve their ends.

The Meaning of Life

The most profound question of all could well be, What is the meaning of life? It is often concluded that the question is unanswerable and must remain a mystery. But you can know the meaning of life. It's not so hard to find if you know how to approach it. The question can be interpreted in two ways. The first being, What is the meaning of life, *in general*? This is a big question. Such a huge canvas is not capable of being accurately explained by any separate and comparatively small individual portion of the lifestream. But if one should approach the question as it *should be* approached, then progress can be made toward understanding. The question for each of us should be, What is the meaning of *my life*?

The meaning of life must be approached on this individual basis. Each separate person must determine their own deeper, inner meaning from life, and then act responsibly on it. No one can tell you or show you the meaning of life—it is up to you to *find it*. It is *your* meaning to pursue. Tools to find it can be provided, which I will briefly try to offer.

The next step is to look around. Being self-reflective is the key. Before you can be properly self-reflective, you must examine and understand a much larger context beyond the normal self-serving mode of existence. Here is an assignment. Look at everything that is happening in the world. Take a couple of days to explore this and dwell on your findings. Get a clear and accurate sense as to what's happening on a worldwide scale.

In order to find the meaning of life, one must start by experiencing and observing a plethora of other cultures. Tune in to your cable TV and view as many foreign, overseas news programs that you can for two or three days straight. You may get bored and wish to change the channel to your normal fare, but that should be completely off limits for these three days. Get serious and delve deeply into other cultures *only*. Do not, under any circumstances, revert to old habits or anything other than your focused attempt. Try to become an expert in the short time you have; taking notes will help.

The Dalai Lama must stay abreast of events worldwide and his favorite source of information has always been the BBC World Service Broadcast. BBC news is also a favorite of mine, among a few others, because they cover an amazing amount of interesting and relevant stories that would never, ever be reported on in the same way in U. S., if at all. Use or borrow a short wave radio if you have to—another great addition to television or alternative option if cable TV is not available. These broadcasts might strike some people as boring because of the different way that things are presented, but stick with it. It will be worth it. You will notice differences that, on their own, will be subtle. They might not mean much but when you bring them all together near the end, things will start to shift. You will have "tuned in"—in more ways than one. It will be you, *yourself*, who will be tuned in to what's really going on in the world, rather than the television or radio. A new sensitivity will switch on within you at a certain point, if the process is carried out diligently.

Traveling helps with this process, but if you have not had the chance to see many other countries, then pay close attention as you watch or listen to these programs. There is so much going on in the world beyond what you are normally accustomed to, emotionally and intellectually, that it must be experienced, even vicariously, for you to grow. We can expand our consciousness in positive ways by "experiencing" the views of others half way around the globe.

> *Every man takes the limits of his own field of vision for the limits of the world.* —Arthur Schopenhauer

Our world view is too limited so we must put ourselves into the shoes of others—and walk in them for a few days. Those who are more sensitive, intuitive or psychic will have interesting results with this exercise.

One part of the purpose in life is to make it better for others. Those who are holding the world's power should be ashamed of themselves because they're not doing it. They've sold out to the materialistic illusion that fuels the planet, but if we all act with compassion we can cause this house of cards to come crashing down. Doing small things to help others goes a long way, especially if many others are doing it. It's easy for one to say that everyone else will do it, so why should I even bother? But that's selling out in the same way that those who do nothing at the top are selling out. If you find someone having a rough time, put yourself in their position for a moment and then treat them like you would like to be treated. It's that simple.

The other part to life's purpose involves the soul. It is the soul that defines our life and gives us our purpose. It is us. What defines us is not what is all around us. Nor is it this physical human form. It is the soul, which is something inward, and our purpose involves something inward. So one is never going to comprehend the meaning of life if one is not conscious of the inward. Connecting with your own soul and becoming conscious on an inward level is one of the major keys to becoming aware of your purpose in life. Looking outside of oneself rarely gets people very far, except in the way we have just covered—in heightening your awareness of the human predicament through cross-cultural examination. Looking outward is not very useful unless you are using inner strengths, like developing a compassionate attitude toward others. If you choose to be involved with all of the entertainments, distractions and diversions away from the inner life without being conscious of your spiritual strengths or attempting to use them in any way, then no inner growth will result.

Each of our souls is on a mission here. And people wonder—if life is so important and we've been reincarnated over and over again, why can't we use what we've learned in previous lives to help our situation and help the situations of others? The reason is that if we were to be able to remember our past lives (and I believe that we've had many of them) then we would be too cluttered with extra information to learn anything in this life. We must move on and learn other things, rather than retain old lessons.

It seems that karma may have brought us to the certain position that we hold in the life that we have, and that's where we must act from. We must act from that point forward. We cannot look back. We can only look forward if we are ever going to progress. We do carry an imprint with us, a very deep one, from our previous lives. And that's enough to get us to the point where we can start anew with a clean slate. Then it's time to get to work again.

The meaning or purpose of life is also the same as the meaning and purpose of the soul. Since the soul is to many people just a fabrication or a fairy tale, then the entire purpose of life will remain as a fabrication or a fairy tale, or something not to be pursued. Few people ever live out their purpose in life, because they remain alienated and distanced from their own souls. The stronger the connection to the soul, the more you live your bliss, the more you live your purpose, the more you live a life that is fulfilling. Those who get caught in a materialistic point of mind, or point of being, tend often to be dissatisfied with themselves and with life in general. Materialistic people are never satisfied, because of the entire Buddhist concept of desire and the way it operates on the mind. When the mind achieves a desire it will always, without fail, want more. The function of desire has a stranglehold on consciousness itself. It leads one into believing that having more of one thing or another will bring happiness. Instead, it often brings misery. As they say, be careful what you wish for because you might just get it.

The purpose of the soul is not so much to avoid desire—although that is a good thing to do—but to confront it and work with positive things directly. The Bible says that we will be judged by our works, and our unique ability to *create*, in powerful ways, is a very God-like attribute. The purpose of the soul and the meaning of life itself is to take knowledge and manifest it into material, artistic or meaningful form. I will repeat that because it's important. When you engage in this type of activity, whatever it might be, a number of different levels come into play, including mind, body and spirit. All facets of your being are used to manifest representations of your meaning or purpose in life. The purpose of the soul and the meaning of life is to take knowledge and manifest it into material, artistic or meaningful form.

Stop and think about this for a moment, as it deserves some serious thought and introspection.

We must take our knowledge and bring it out into the material world. But as a prerequisite to this, I recommend that you examine the material world first to see where your knowledge may be applied for the greater good. This is not being taught in our schools today on the deepest and most soulful level. It is being taught in certain places on a limited basis. This kind of teaching is only now beginning to emerge. What we are talking about is wisdom teaching that can make an impact and get people interested enough to respond in meaningful ways. There are ways to approach life so that you feel comfortable doing what is right as opposed to looking out for your own self-interests for personal gain alone, or acting out of greed. Our world leaders and corporate giants should know exactly what we're talking about here.

Conspiracy Theories

They may have some concern for the general spiritual well-being of the people of the earth, but for the most part those behind the scenes who really pull the strings are more concerned about keeping people in line, keeping them under control, and not having too many revolutions, uprisings or wars that could disrupt the economic balance that they are trying to control so thoroughly today.

There's an interesting line of research that one can perform, as suggested by the leading conspiratologists of the day, and that is to examine all of the major companies in the world and see who owns them. Once you discover what group or company owns them, look further and see who owns that company. And you keep going up the scale as far as you can possibly go, and you will find that there are only a small number of people at parent "umbrella" companies who control and own everything. And now what you need to look at is what organizations are these companies connected to? We are talking about the Council on Foreign Relations (CFR), The Trilateral Commission, The Bilderberg Group, the Brookings Institution, the Club of Rome, the European Central Bank, the Federal Reserve Bank, the World Bank, the International Monetary Fund (IMF), The Committee of 300, NATO, The Royal Institute of International Affairs, The Tavistock Institute for Human Relations, The World Trade Organization (WTO), and, yes, even the United Nations. It will take some intense digging, but you can find out. What are the agendas of these organizations? What are their missions? What are their stated and unstated goals? In general, the agendas involved have nothing to do with spiritual growth, and have nothing to do with the enrichment, prosperity, or the enlightenment of the masses. The masses are always the victims, not the benefactors. The entire system is designed to keep us in ignorance, and to keep us from knowing who they are and what they're really up to. The best way to do this is to keep the masses busy. We have less and less free time these days and that is no coincidence. If the masses are kept busy, no one will be able to do anything about changing the current paradigm. However, the complete failure of this paradigm, despite its control over us, is forcing everyone to take an urgent and concerned look at it. It doesn't work—but is so cumbersome that it will not collapse unless we force it to.

This current paradigm is restrictive and freedom is the one thing that's being lost more and more every day in this world. One needs to look and see exactly who our freedoms are being lost to, and what our freedoms are being lost for and ask, at what expense *to ourselves* is this happening?

This leads us into is the idea of the "New World Order," as it is sometimes called. There's been a popular analogy made to this hidden encroachment regarding the masses. If you place a frog in a pot of water, put it on a burner and then slowly raise the heat, the frog will not know that it's being totally *cooked* until it's too late. And that's our situation. This control and our loss of freedoms are being slowly, ever so slowly, brought over on us so that we do not even see it happening. And the few who are starting to see it happen will never rouse the others in time to accomplish anything—it's just going to be too late. Everyone considers those who see it coming as crazy and nothing will ever be done on a scale that could allow us to change this course that we are on—at least that is "their" plan. The water is not yet boiling, but it's starting to get uncomfortable. In these situations, however, the power of the human spirit should never be underestimated.

Let us look at this situation from the other side of the coin. This New World Order is a loosely interconnected worldwide group of people who have developed a power base so strong that they control most of the economies of the world and thereby everything else that goes along with it. This is not a fantasy or a subject only for conspiracy buffs. One only needs to read *The Web of Debt*, by respected Los Angeles-based attorney Ellen Hodgson Brown, for a complete understanding. It took more than six years for her to write and it has become the seminal work on this subject, containing valuable, documented information, some of which is not otherwise easily obtainable. The International Monetary Fund, Bilderberg Group, Trilateral Commission and the international banks, among others, all play a role in this web. If someone from this NWO group were to approach you and ask, "Well, do you have a better system? What else can possibly be done or better engineered to control this, because it is extremely complex? Populations are growing exponentially. It's virtually out of control. There's got to be a way to handle it so that it does not get chaotic. With so many people in the world battling over so many different interests and conflicts, it's best to get as much control over them as possible. And it's best done economically. Otherwise, there could be chaos, there could be worldwide nuclear attacks, there could be all kinds of insidious things that could go wrong if somehow the economies were not controlled in a certain way."

This is a good argument when examined from a materialistic/economic point of view. The sticking point is that materialism will never be the answer to humanity's problems. We need cooperation instead of competition, and a focus on compassion instead of profits. Above all, we must be nurturing instead of parasitic. Instead of breaking down the Berlin Wall we must break down the walls of banking, at the highest levels, and liquidate the limited form of consciousness that spawned it.

Growing Pains

We have moved almost completely out of the Cartesian-Newtonian-Marxist paradigm and its supporting materialistic philosophies. We now have quantum physics, Heisenberg's Uncertainty Principal, and the discovery of solid matter actually "melting" into waves, depending on how it is perceived. The new physics has created a vision of reality that reopens the doors to ancient wisdom, but with the added benefit of scientific "proofs." This means that we are, in fact, starting over with a new paradigm, ever so slowly—but it requires a different form of consciousness. We cannot immediately change it, but must first begin with a new and more rational point of view that might *evolve us* into a different form of consciousness. There is no doubt that we need, and are actually developing, a new form of consciousness to replace the old. Jump-start yourself and get involved.

There's a saying that goes, "The only way out is in." If one is looking outward all the time, then the inward path is never viewed. It's behind you. It's not even in your field of vision. If your consciousness is a bag, and you operate from within that bag, then you can only look outward. So it's time to turn the bag completely inside out. Turn the bag inside out and *there you are*. You are suddenly viewing your inner world, your *Self*, rather than some big outer materialistic drama. What a shock. The answer is staring you right in the face. And it's been there all along.

We need to start educating our children in more meaningful, spiritual ways. The current vessels of education are hollow, empty shells, and as a result create hollow empty shells for people. More depth in education will result in a new and deeper consciousness. This new consciousness is not going to happen by itself. We have to care enough to point ourselves in the right directions.

This is like having a child's room that is messy. It will never be cleaned unless we tell them to do it; unless we give them direction. When the educational system begins to change and clean up its act then, in turn, the actual children will get direction. It's the same with our minds; our consciousness. It's cluttered with all the material distractions around us. One might argue that this is all we have in this physical world—material things—but that is a soulless view. Material things are nothing more than temporary tools for us to use and grow with, nothing more. They should not be mistaken for "reality" or for what is lasting and meaningful because, as they say, "you can't take it with you." What we should be focusing on and exploring is what we really *can* take with us.

Let us say, for the sake of argument, that a spiritually based educational system is adopted and strengthened throughout the world in various countries. Let's look at the pros and cons of this new mindset. What kind of resulting path would we be on? We would have to explore, as one of the pros, the entire subject of enlightenment, whereby the cons would fall under the possible breakdown, over time, of the religious institutions worldwide. This is because a more accurate view of divinity results from the clarity and deeper understanding of enlightenment. Religious shake-ups and the problems that go with them comprise the biggest hurdle involving the coming new paradigm. Yet this threat to religions may still not happen at all if we approach it in the right way. A new view of God does not necessarily have to result in the complete destruction of any religious system—as long as the system can be flexible in its understanding of Deity. A difference in religion should not matter because, once again, religions are man-made; and spirituality, or actually the soul itself, is not. If we recognize ourselves for who we are and acknowledge our proper connection to Deity, shared among all, then there should be no religious differences between us. My God will no longer have to beat up your God because we all share Him equally. Or rather, He shares us equally.

All religions were put together and formulated by man, although each religion will separately insist that theirs was ordained by God. Research into all of the major world religions will tell you that, although each of their founders claimed to have had inspiration or contact in some way with the divine, they themselves, and not God, were the primary instruments in putting these religions together. Not once, and I repeat, *not once*, has God ever come down and personally said to anyone—despite what they might claim—that this is the religion that all the world shall follow, because if God had meant that to happen, he would have created one religion and one book for everyone. He would not have told separate religious leaders different things and pitted us all against each other. We are all God's children. When we learn mutual respect maybe then will He bring us all together. In the meantime, there are no "chosen ones" who are supposed to rise up with their one brand of religion and control all the others. The idea is preposterous, but believed to be "God's will" by fundamentalists of all stripes.

God has no religion. —Mahatma Gandhi

Again, if a loving God were to have directly bequeathed a religion to us, he would have made sure to include all of us within it. God loves all his children the same, and would not be exclusionary in this matter. An all-loving God would not have us fighting amongst each other over which "God" is stronger. Like spoiled brats we insist, "My God can beat up your God." Which God is stronger? If there is only one God and that one God were to come down and make himself available, it would not be to a chosen, select few. He would also not punish those who happened to choose the wrong religion (whether it be a conscious choice, or due to a cultural difference, or having been exposed to the "wrong" set of facts) by sending them to hell to burn for eternity, or just exclude them from the wondrous, happy place, sometimes called heaven, that everyone else gets to go to.

If we decide to wake up and approach our existence from a respectful, spiritual standpoint, then it's not going to matter what religion one believes. Each religion, however, may feel threatened by whatever slow advances we will begin to make in our educational systems and its accompanying spiritual viewpoint, but with time, as people grow spiritually, the threat, and the ignorance, will diminish. This will take time, as wisdom comes slower than knowledge.

Unfortunately, the last ones to come on board this common sense bandwagon will be the fundamentalists from every religious group. These are the people who currently pose the greatest threat to a spiritually based life, mainly because they are still operating out of the "My God can beat up your God" mindset and "Every religion for itself." None of them will be satisfied unless their particular brand of religion can dominate and control all others. Yet, Christianity has admittedly learned one lesson that some of the other ones still haven't, which is that they are not going to take over the entire world. They know they cannot impose their religious dogma over the entire populous of the world—it's not going to happen—so they have become more respectful than in the past.

Out of the office of the Pope in the year 2000, there was acknowledgment and actual respect paid toward other religions as opposed to the standard party line of subtly, or even openly, downgrading or attacking them. It's a sign that we are evolving in a spiritual sense. Christianity has come a long way from the times when we threw people to the lions in Rome and, in later centuries, were burning people at the stake for contrary views. That does not happen any more, and it is because we are spiritually evolving. We're going somewhere. We're learning something—and we have not been able to learn it overnight. This all is taking time, and the process is continuing.

But what direction is it that we are heading in? It is definitely in a spiritual direction, and the views expressed here are an attempt to help steer us into that direction a bit faster. It seems clear to this writer where we are going, but it's in a collective sense and collectively, we are moving slowly. It's a learning process, done by souls in this physical world, so, in a certain sense, it is an alchemical process as well. We have been working through all the things that we need to work through, transforming ourselves and advancing. Realizations have been met, and yet they have not been met completely. We still have work to do. In this modern, technological age, when there are so many material things that can distract us, it's good to point us back to the spiritual, because that is our source. With our amazing technology and wonderful gadgets come all of the distractions that keep us from the entire basis of our spiritual foundation. We must find ways to ground ourselves to this foundation, which is our source and our true connection to God. Therein lies our true humanity here in the world and, at the same time, our ultimate salvation outside of it.

Humanity is having a hard time staying focused and learning the important spiritual elements of who we are because attention spans are so short. Everything has been geared towards a quick sale, with a quick jingle. Before the days of radio and especially television, attention spans were much longer and for a few centuries the main avenue of communication was through publishing and books. Without the endless flow of short, snappy distractions that we are bombarded with today, people were able to sit and research books that were written very thoroughly. Without a doubt, many of the best books ever written were created before the days of television and radio. Back in the early 1900's about the only major marketing tool they had was the Sears catalog, but now *everybody* wants to sell you something. We are now being barraged from every direction and every angle with all kinds of cute and mindless presentations that blatantly insult our intelligence.

> *Your vision will become clear only when you look into your heart. Who looks outside, dreams. Who looks inside, awakens.* —Carl Jung

Each of us is being used like a rag doll, being pulled at from all angles by marketers, banks, agencies, the government and major corporations. If you feel that your self expression and life's path is being robbed, you have very good reason to feel that way. We need to wake up to the reality of who and what we really are and get our *focus* back. By doing so, we will have the power to choose our own paths in life. If we fail in our endeavor to reach this realization then we will continue to be manipulated and others will make our choices.

Chapter Six

MIND CAGES

Yet we sit there, eyes glued to the set, watching this explication of the obvious in hateful fascination and even find ourselves compelled to stay tuned to whatever follows.... Consciously, we despise ourselves, yet we are fascinated... as any savage before his totem. —Richard Schickel

Fish see worm and not the hook. —Chinese Proverb

Kill Your Television
    Do you recall the first television commercials that you saw as a young child? I do. The first time I began to pay attention to television I thought, "These people are stupid. What are they doing putting music into TV shows or dancing around to it like idiots in a commercial? What's the point of that? If they want to tell you something, they should just tell you." Even at age five I could figure out that using music to try to sell people something was just a stupid gimmick. It's a marketing trick. Just have someone sit down and tell you the honest value of a product and why you should buy it. What do you need to bring in a damn orchestra for? Or a brass band and circus animals? When you talk to people do you carry around music to play for them whenever you ask somebody a question or try to convince them of something? It makes no difference to me whether or not it's done in person or on television—so therefore it is an outright insult to my intelligence. And then the completely stupid things that people do in commercials to try to get you to buy something. They'll go to any extreme. It goes way beyond what reality would be like in real life, and I make the same distinction with people's actions as I do with the playing of music. People on television commercials do the stupidest things, and we're expected to believe that there's enough basis in reality for their stupid behaviour to warrant us buying whatever they're trying to peddle.

Let me put this as plainly as possible. Television is by far the biggest detriment to our spiritual development than any other thing on this entire planet. There's a bumper sticker that says "kill your television." There's also the Nike slogan that says "just do it." Put the two together, act on it with religious zeal, and you're halfway to enlightenment already.

As far as the human soul goes, television is almost always pure poison. We are here to grow and learn and experience things, whereby television only offers a vicarious form of life. Absolutely nothing is accomplished by watching most of what's on television. Like the saying goes, "Life is for living." And if you're not going to *live your life*, then what are you doing here, vicariously living through somebody else's? You came here to live your life, not snack on popcorn and watch it go by. Wake up! These reality TV shows are the most outrageous theft that mankind has ever perpetrated on each other or ever concocted in the past.

When I had set out on my spiritual path in a very determined fashion, I was also working in the television business. There was a huge internal clash. As I became more spiritually aware, I also became more and more physically ill from working in the television business. I used to sit at the big lit-up boards and put various television networks on the air in Los Angeles. It was called master control, because you control everything on the airwaves for that particular network. In this job you are forced to watch all of this "bubblegum for the brain" repeatedly every night, and also deal with hands-on, direct responsibility for providing it to millions of people. This, obviously, was not my calling. At the same time, I was meeting many interesting people in the areas of spiritual exploration in Los Angeles, which was a mecca for this at the time.

My eyes were gradually opened to the amazing potential that we have as spiritual beings. Yet, I also realized that few people knew about the reality of who they are. I now write and publish in this area in order to contribute something meaningful to people, rather than mindless entertainments that pollute not only the airwaves, but our minds.

Are we being spiritually advanced by watching other people engage themselves in competition by eating horse testicles and live cockroaches? Is the popularity of such things the defining element for humanity today? Or can we actually define ourselves in other more meaningful ways? God help us if this is the only way we can bring meaning into our lives.

Another television comedy phenomenon was a self-proclaimed "show about nothing" a few years back called *Seinfeld*. They bragged about its lack of content by spoofing its own mindless creation in the show. Here we've got three or four dysfunctional dimwits who are so self-absorbed that they're unable to perform anything meaningful at all within each episode. They offer us virtually nothing of substance except a display of their own neurotic tendencies and vain stupidity. The only thing they're smart enough to do is get themselves into enough trouble to prove how vain and self-centered they really are. And every moron in America loved it. They just ate it up, while the creator of the show, Jerry Seinfeld, became a millionaire and retired.

In coming here to live life, it's not our purpose to spend it by sitting in front of a box watching imaginary stories. Before too many people have caught on to this and awakened to the fact that this is what they're doing, wasting their lives, the networks have broadsided us with reality shows. "Let's show them some real stuff." So millions who are dissatisfied with their own lives now choose, and in some cases need, to live vicariously through others on these reality shows, which makes it all the more sad.

If you took all the hours that an average person watches television and were able to replace that time and use it in more constructive ways, and were able to apply that to each television watcher, not only in the United States but throughout the world, a complete transformation would occur from this alone. I propose a day—just one day a year—where the entire world shuts off their TVs and does some kind of positive service instead. What a day that would be! Amazing things would happen. Just think how much good could result from that, rather than wasted time. Just think if people would apply themselves with that time to help others, or to teach others, or to do things that had real, true meaning to it. And yet, we sit like morons and couch potatoes watching mindless BS for hours upon hours at a time. And where does it get us? Where does it lead us as a human race? Into any positive areas?

There's a small amount of television programming that is dedicated toward positive ends. But in the long run, when you look at television in general, everyone should kill their TVs immediately—or at least break the addiction and be more discerning. If you're not going to throw your TV off the top of a building and destroy it or give it up or anything like that, which is actually a very hard thing to do, then at least be aware of what you're doing to your mind and be more discerning. Try to limit the time you spend watching because most of it drags you into a fantasy world. It's all a big illusion, and it is already enough of a problem for us to fight the serious illusions that life itself throws at us.

What we're really here for is to operate within the realms of life itself, not within some fantasy box. The real illusion we should be facing is life itself and we're here to try to figure *that* out, instead of heaping more illusions on top of it. Let us address life's challenges. We need to make some sense out of life and add meaningful things to it that can impact one another directly. Television, movies, computer games and all of that stuff, when overly relied upon, are an incredible diversion.

When you're watching television it actually transforms your brainwaves into a hypnotic state and causes you to function in ways that are similar to that of a zombie. Professional marketers intentionally design the musical beats of commercials to coincide with suggestive and submissive brainwave patterns, so you'll be more open to buy their crap. As a result of this carefully researched mind control, you will respond to their commercials like a zombie. Or you'll buy into whatever latest gimmick is that they're throwing at you, whether you need it or not. There are many useless things out there that television can convince you that you need.

Turn on QVC or Home Shopping Network and look at all of the clever gadgets and amazing new "must have" junk that they throw at you. Once in a while you might find something useful on there, but it's mostly a showcase of inventions that perform functions you could otherwise do *with your own two hands* and an IQ just above the range of an idiot. The commercialism in this world and on television is way out of control.

Every organization wishing to make an impact on society uses television as its main tool. Political speeches, rallies and events are televised; religion has its televangelists, and virtually every business with financial clout targets their preferred demographics with it. Why? Because they can reach more people and, more importantly, know how easily television can program and manipulate the masses. All people respond to advertising on some level, whether they know it or not. A great number of us depend on television to make our decisions for us, rather than having to think for ourselves.

> *Powerful churches, political parties, and vested financial interests... have a strong desire to program the rest of us into the particular "Real" universes that they find profitable, and to keep us from becoming self-programmers. They want to "take responsibility" for us, and they do not want us to take responsibility for ourselves.* —Robert Anton Wilson

We need a spiritual infusion put back into our society so that we can start living in more meaningful ways. In the meantime, millions of people will sit in front of these boxes in a zombie-like state because television does in fact change human brainwave patterns. It changes our brains like mush to the point where it's addicting. Believe it or not, there is a powerful addiction to this certain brainwave state. It is just as powerful, if not more powerful, than any known narcotic. There are television addicts in massive numbers. It is more powerful than any known drug addiction and does just as much damage—not to the body in this case, but to the mind and human psyche.

Later on down the road when we've matured enough as a species and can look back and see what television had actually done to us, we would find that on a spiritual level it had stunted our growth far more than anything else had ever done. We will have made some incredible advances in the future, but we'll suddenly look back and say, "You know what? We were fools. If we hadn't had television, we would have reached this point much faster."

Television has people in its stranglehold to such an extent that virtually no one sees it. Most people view it as normal entertainment and spend every day zombied out in front of this thing. I hereby propose a worldwide day to abandon it, in the spirit of service to others or the personal growth of oneself. Let this day be the longest one, with the most sun, so that people may be encouraged to spend the most time possible out in nature, under the glimmering light of what gives us life, rather than sitting in front of an artificial source that, in a certain sense, sucks the life right out of us. It is encouraged, on a personal level, to commit more than one day a year to avoid television, but then I might be asking too much. Try to take just one day a week (since most people watch every day) and don't watch—do something else. Do something else with your mind that's far more proactive, interesting, stimulating or creative. Offer a service or do something artistic. For just one day a week create something rather than consume it. There's so much out there that people can grow and have other forms of fun and entertainment with, or challenge themselves in certain ways rather than vegetate by watching TV.

Reading is great, but many have been diverted from it. Fewer and fewer people do it. The lack of reading is a major cause of the dumbing down of society. Studies show that children who read more than viewing television are more intelligent and responsive than those who do the opposite. And for adults, the vast majority of good information—meaningful information—is still found only in books. Some is on the Internet, often lacking depth or much detail, however. The best information is definitely not on television, and it's rarely found on videos or dvds. By far, the most important and meaningful information is still found in books and is often not going to be found elsewhere. Those who love books or work with them know this for an established fact. People are missing a huge amount of important information in exchange for sitting in front of a television set and infecting their minds with comparatively useless information or outright garbage.

Television actually runs many people's lives. There are those who exist for the sole purpose of television. It rules and dictates what they do on any given day. There are many people who cannot and will not do anything unless they know what is on television first, as opposed to what's going on in their real lives. It's really sad when you put your main priority in life on a box that shows pictures in your living room as opposed to living a genuine, vibrant, and meaningful life. All of the amazing potential for millions of people, including your own potential, may be sacrificed—completely given up for almost an entire lifetime, wasted on stories and pictures that have no direct bearing on your existence and what you're really here for. Wake up!

So how does one awaken as an alternative to the bombardment of materialism all around us and the hypnotic waves of the television? How does one escape this trap, this mentality of always wanting more and more and more of this materialistic existence and all of the things in it and never being satisfied, truly satisfied? How does one escape this and actually move into a level of bliss and happiness and contentment, or at least know that one is on the path to achieving such things? It is entirely possible to do that, but first, one must step outside the box.

This box is composed of the materialistic things all around us that we are constantly yearning for, or trying to achieve. Yet, if you can find that quiet place deep within and knows how to access it, then all of the material things that are constantly being craved for suddenly do not matter so much.

Paths to Spiritual Freedom

How does one go about finding this new way of being? It is usually done by exploring one of many different *spiritual disciplines* that religions often warn against. Searching for your individual Self instead of being part of the "flock" is a severe threat to any organized religion. They do not want you falling away from them and diminishing their herd, or flock. They see you as a sheep, so followers are part of the "flock." When someone fails to reach their unique inner potential by being branded as part of a herd, it is a spiritual death of sorts. So I tend to view any religious "flock" as cattle being led to a spiritual slaughter, rather than experiencing any kind of salvation. I call it the "herd." Do you want to avoid the "herd"? Step out. Be an individual! Because the truth can only be found within your own being. There is no organization out there, outside of yourself, which has your truth. Only you have your truth. And if you're not willing to look for it within yourself, then you will never be able to find it.

With that said, meditation has always been the method of choice for most people, with centuries of proven results. It works well for many who attempt to contact a deeper part of themselves. There are a number of different meditation schools and techniques to experiment with to find out which one is comfortable for you.

The first thing we should do, however, is to define meditation. What exactly is it? If prayer is "talking to God" then meditation is "listening to God." It is a way to relax the mind so fully that an elevated state of consciousness can be accessed, and the listening can begin. Sometimes this listening can evolve into a powerful "communion." This state of consciousness really can be accessed, on deeper and deeper levels. Over time, an enlightened state of consciousness is possible. It is there, waiting for us. It comes as such a blissful and unusual event that many who experience it think that it is something they have achieved. Some teachers point out that this higher state of consciousness, meaning enlightenment itself, cannot be "achieved" because we already have it. It's just a matter of accessing it and knowing how to access it. There are those who claim that being an enlightened master is something that only a chosen few are able to achieve. Yet, again, one does not achieve it. We all have it. In the future, it will be commonplace. We just have to start taking the proper paths to becoming aware of this potential.

Meditation requires an inward focus, sometimes with the eyes closed, sometimes opened. With the eyes closed, one will often focus on the breath and simply be aware of each one going in, then going out, without having any thought involved. It is just an observance of the breath and the existence that we have been blessed with because of the breath. Other people are more comfortable with focusing on some object or small outward, visual point while the eyes are open. Although the eyes are open and one is gazing outward, the fact that the focus is set so strongly and unwaveringly on just one point does succeed in shutting out everything else and causes one, although looking outward, to actually be looking inward. Gazing at one strict outward point, if done correctly, does not avail to us any of the other distractions surrounding us in the physical world. So a pinpoint, or the center of a mandala, or a dot on the floor can all narrow our focus inward.

Using mandalas is a great way to meditate. A mandala is a rather complex, artful picture, usually circular or square, and made for this very purpose. It always has a center or focal point. All of the symbology that surrounds this center has significant meanings in a very spiritual way. Although one may not be aware of it, during meditation a lot of these symbols go deep into the psyche and can produce some very positive results. Our modern idea of audio subliminals is a cheaper rendition of the same idea, but uses sound instead of images. With mandalas, we are looking at powerful, meaningful universal symbology that has great significance on spiritual levels. Although most are from the east and may therefore seem culturally exclusive, one should remember that symbols speak in all languages. Symbology has a universal language of its own. Those in the eastern world who have created mandalas over the centuries have a great deal of wisdom in putting them together. I, for one, have used mandalas, preferring those from the Shingon School, because I'm a visual person. Others may find that closing the eyes will produce better results. It's a personal preference that each should be willing to explore for themselves. When one finds they are comfortable with a method, they should stick with it at length, which is important.

What is often found when you reach these deeper meditative states is that when the mind ends up relaxing to such a great degree, the body then follows. People most often meditate in a sitting position and sometimes in the lotus position, with up-turned heels. Although that may look uncomfortable, those who are able to reach such relaxed states can sit like this for hours upon end. When one is experiencing blissful states, it is often easy to have the physical body, as well as the mind, withdraw from the outside world.

Those who have never meditated before, but want to start off on a very powerful spiritual adventure, should consider taking a meditation class or at least purchasing one of the basic, how-to books on the subject. Often people will experience great relaxation, but for many years will not experience any advanced blissful states. The key is to be steady and constant in the practice. After a morning session, a certain clarity of mind follows many people around for the rest of the day. It's always good to pick a certain time to meditate and stick to that on a daily basis so that it becomes part of your natural schedule. It then becomes easier to reap the benefits.

There are short-term benefits to meditation, but positive results are also accumulative, meaning they increase over time. One will experience, over time, an overall more relaxed state of mind—and physical changes often do occur, like the lowering of blood pressure, increased awareness, and an overall more spiritual view of things. Make no mistake about it—being in touch with a higher part of your self brings forth a clear, moral purpose and a caring attitude towards others, more than those who do not meditate. Serial killers are usually not meditators. People like Mahatma Gandhi are. There's a clear existing pattern between the types of people who engage themselves in reaching higher states of consciousness and those who do not. Those who do not are often devoid of higher moral standards and spiritual awareness and, as a result, act accordingly.

One of the most important long-term benefits of meditation is that you may have an encounter with the divine. The divine presence that you may have an encounter with and may be *directly experienced* is actually a part of you. What could be more incredible than to experience a part of yourself that is in touch with the divine presence of the universe? This is by far the most amazing part of your self that would have previously gone unknown and unexperienced. This divine presence has been, throughout history, described as a spark of light within us. This spark of the divine, which is actually us after we leave here, holds that godly connection. It is "trapped" within this physical body of ours during life and we are not conscious of it in the normal sense. Some would call it the soul. It is not able to reveal its higher purpose to us because when we are brought into such a low material vibration, we lose touch with this divine nature. The body serves as a vehicle for the soul, but in coming here the soul loses its "normal" abilities in the denseness of matter. The physical world is so dense that pure spirit cannot function well or survive long without a body.

Meditation can help us experience higher consciousness, allow a connection to our soulful identity and in some cases bring our memory back to us as to what and who we really are. At the same time, meditation is not like taking a magic pill and you immediately become enlightened and one with the divine. It doesn't work that way. It takes years of devoted and concentrated practice, dedicating yourself to higher states of consciousness and bettering yourself in a spiritual way in order to reap important benefits.

What can make it easier, however, is the hemi-sync meditation technology and other similar forms of audio. The wonders of technology have created a kind of audiotape that we can listen to (with headphones) that syncs up the brain waves and puts us in a meditative state much faster than sitting in a cave and chanting for many years, like in the old days. After years of research, the first to come out with this patented technology was the Monroe Institute in Virginia. The two audio tracks sync up both sides of the brain into one unified wave pattern. When the right and left hemispheres of the brain are completely in sync, they cancel each other out and the brain, or its normal thinking processes, can no longer get in the way of higher consciousness. As a result, we can reach these higher states and experience them more easily. It just takes a pair of headphones, the proper audio program, and a quiet room.

According to most people, during their normal day-to-day activities the brain is always chattering. There's always this "voice" going on in our heads. Meditation is a powerful tool to still the mind, to take the constant current of thought and make it like a pool of water on a warm, summer day, where there's no breeze whatsoever. The water is just completely like glass. When the mind can be like that, then it can accurately reflect back to you *who and what you really are* as opposed to all of the ripples and turbulence that the mind can create in its normal state of consciousness.

The mind, in its normal state of consciousness, has often been compared to a chattering monkey that won't be quiet. Those who meditate regularly, however, can function in the normal day-to-day world in a way that allows them to control the mind more easily. And although one is not in a meditative state during normal consciousness, it becomes easier to still the mind when needed, to become more clear and focused and to make decisions that contain more wisdom in them, as opposed to a non-meditator who may react spontaneously, which might be regretted later on. When one can quiet the mind and reach up into the higher self, even for brief moments during the day, then decisions can come down to you that have more wisdom. It's only obvious.

In a literal sense, when one can push a chattering monkey aside and listen instead to the wisdom of a sage or grandparent who's had more knowledge and experience in the ways of true being, one will always choose the latter. When one becomes aware of this choice it is an important realization, but does little good unless steps are taken to access these higher states and to listen. Many try, but soon revert back to a chattering monkey that's off in a million different directions all the time and is easily distracted. That is how most people live their lives, running off of pure emotion and their short-sighted, impatient chattering monkey with incessant desires. In general, these monkeys are the kinds of people that one must deal with on a day-to-day basis. It would be nice to encounter those with true wisdom throughout each day, rather than those whose minds are essentially racing and operating in a more confused state.

We have been in kindergarten for far too long and need to be looking toward at least the second and third grades. Only when we begin the think more clearly and logically while in touch with our true selves will we ever improve our own lives, the lives of others, and the planet in general. We need more people in the world who are of sound mind, and who can operate in ways of wisdom as opposed to acting out of impulse and immediate desire—especially in positions of power and authority. The entire world is highly impulsive right now and driven by surface desires, as opposed to a higher form of thought that is seldom accessed and often not even acknowledged as being there in the first place. This world is living in darkness. We have a long way to go and we need to get started.

Hurdles and barriers

I recommend that people read books about those who have become enlightened. A great one to start with is *Kundalini: Evolutionary Energy in Man*, by Gopi Krishna, as well Dr. Lee Sannella's interesting study of multiple cases called *The Kundalini Experience*. Of course the actual experience is recommended as a priority, but these books will also provide you with a good understanding of human potential and the future of consciousness.

One of the common factors for those who have had incredible awakening experiences is that they were, in most cases, meditators. It's the description of these higher states of consciousness that one should pay attention to. When it happens, there is absolutely no mistaking it. In the future, as time goes on, there will be an infusion and eventually an explosion of the kinds of people who have experienced these states of consciousness. For now, however, such people are considered freaks of nature. Yet this more awakened form of consciousness will be far more common in the future. Many people in the so-called New Age Movement are the only ones paying attention to this rare but important phenomena and society, in general, does not recognize people who think this way.

Mainstream television and media pay little attention to higher forms of consciousness because they're trying to get you to buy something. Material pursuits are what it's all about as opposed to those pursuits that are spiritual. So those who pursue higher states of consciousness are often considered to be well out of the mainstream and a bit quirky or strange. There is an interesting saying that one should remember in this regard: "You laugh at me because I'm different, but I laugh at you because you're all the same." Who wants to live a cookie-cutter life and be like everyone else? Apparently, most of those in our culture do.

When the neighbor gets a brand new SUV (sports utility vehicle—which most people in suburbia really don't need), people can't stand it. They've got to get a brand new SUV. The neighbor gets a surround sound in-home television theater, and then you have to go out and get one too, just so they don't one-up you and cause everyone in the neighborhood to think they are so much better than you are. They go out and get a dog; you've got to go out and get a better dog. It's sad, but that's how the vast majority of people in this culture think. Eventually there has to be a transformation from this way of thinking before we can move out of this material focus, which is dragging everybody down.

The only people to whom it's helping are those at the very top of large corporations, whose presidents have five homes in exclusive vacation spots all around the world, spend money like it's water, and are laughing all the way to the bank while you and everyone else in this culture instantly respond to your television marketing brainwashing programs, like Pavlov's dog, after having been brought up and trained to buy everything that they tell you to buy, and insist that you need. What *I'm* telling you is you don't need the vast majority of this stuff. It's the basics that are needed to get by in life, as well as close family ties and good, trustworthy friends. It's often been found that those who cut back to the basics, not the bare necessities, just the basics (there's a difference there), then a deeper appreciation develops for those other people or family members whom you're sharing those basics with. And the focus doesn't stay on getting more and more things. It's focused on what is shared together, what we have as a family. People value each other much more when not having to engage themselves in a race to see how much more they can get, or how much money they can spend.

> *Most men pursue pleasure with such breathless haste that they hurry past it.* —Soren Kierkgaard

Without a sense of family or bonding, can we separately become happy by buying all of this stuff? No. But together you can become truly happy as a family by sharing basic items of need and sharing the values and the cohesiveness of what a family really is. It can't be bought.

Happiness is an elusive thing, but once the right atmosphere for contentment is created, it becomes more possible to achieve it. We are only human and can falter in spite of this, but all in all we can become better people with more values and less material "junk."

When materialism takes the place of the cohesiveness that a real family should have together, then that family will often break down. That is one of the problems we have in our culture today, and yet few people see it. It's already too late for many who are hypnotically responding to the cultural mantra that's been fed to us from birth.

> "Buy me. You need me. Get me now before it's too late. Spend and consume. Spend and consume. Just listen and we'll tell you what to buy. Obey us without question. Don't offer your

ideals to the State. Just take and consume and spend. That is all you want. That is all we want. Money is your God. You worship by spending. Your soul is a myth. Just be a consumer."

The bottom line is that this is just one big giant economic machine that is in the process of chewing you up. And when it's done, it's going to spit you out and leave you there after you've served your purpose—a purpose defined by them, not you.

But you do have a choice as to what purpose you really want to serve in this world. It's about time people started waking up and seeing that there is such a choice. Otherwise, you're just meat for the machine, another warm body that will consume X amount of items to keep the machine running during your lifetime. And then, like many older people who have reached the end of their days and look back on their lives, they often wonder, "What the hell happened? What did I do with my life? If I were to do it all over again, by God, I would have done this and I would have done that, but now it's too late." The wisdom often comes too late to do anything about it. So it's time for us to tap into the higher source that is within us that can provide such wisdom, so that a direction in our lives can be taken that has far more meaning than just the materialistic purpose that we are set up to serve, quite slavishly, from a very young age. We spend our lives serving it, by acting on selfish motivations, placed there on our egotistical, self-serving "plates" by those who control the materialistic markets.

Do yourself a favor. Take some quiet time and go deep within yourself. Explore what you really want to accomplish in this life. Understand that those who have actually succeeded in accomplishing their goals will tell you that anything is possible. If you can conceive it, you can accomplish it. Incredibly great things have been accomplished by people who have gotten away from all of the barriers and stringent societal demands and boundaries that have been put upon us. Those in touch with the spirit have performed some of the most incredible accomplishments that we have ever seen in this world. They've led a spiritual life in many key ways, were extremely focused and driven by passion—so get in touch with that part of yourself. Once you have a clear focus as to what you'd like to accomplish, then that's the first step.

When going deep inside yourself, either through meditation or introspection, a form of intuitive guidance often appears from a higher "place." When that happens, you no longer question your actions. Your actions simply unfold in a way that seems perfectly natural. Once it is determined what path it is that you're on and what you're here for, there can be no questioning—there's absolutely no questioning as to any decisions you make. You just "know." This remains the case as long as your higher goal is kept in focus. When we get sidetracked into other things that really don't matter, that are tangents off to the side, and we start to take these side tangents, then it becomes a distraction and even a deterrent to what we're here for. But the great men and women of this world who have accomplished the most monumental tasks have always kept their focus on their goal and their purpose in life. As a result, anything they did was strictly in line with that purpose. Suddenly, someone who may have been wishy-washy, uncertain of themselves, having a self-esteem problem, not a strong personality, meek, mild, easily intimidated, or having any other character flaw that could serve as an obstacle—all of this goes out the window when that focus is achieved.

On the surface it may seem that people like Mahatma Gandhi were easily intimidated, but they were grossly underestimated. There was a totally unwavering purpose in the lives of such people as Gandhi, Dr. Martin Luther King, Jr., the Buddha, Mohammed, Jesus, and the founders of various other religions. These people changed the entire world around them during their lifetimes with nothing but the power of the spirit. They did not have great armies. They did not have large sums of money, which is what we're always groveling for these days. They had none of that. They may have acquired some level of power at a later date, but what got them there—what they all started with—was nothing but an idea and a passion for the truth.

I often refer to this as a "triumph of the human spirit"—the title of one of my previous books covering those who changed history in this manner. I am not claiming that all readers of this book can suddenly become movers and shakers to completely overturn the existing paradigm and change the world itself, but the possibility does exist to do that. Aligning one's self with the spirit and generating a path that is true to one's self brings forth an incredible sense of security, power, and comfort. This all happens on the inner levels first, but then self-confidence shines through and is seen by others. One is no longer uncertain or confused about so many things from the past. When we successfully get on our spiritual path, the possibility does surface that we can change the world in positive ways. And it sure beats not trying. It sure beats sitting at home becoming a vegetative couch potato watching prime-time television, munching on suicidal snacks and screaming at the neighbors once in a while. If you want to do that with your life, that's fine—but just remember—it's an empty, petty existence and you now have a positive alternative. Make the choice. And make a commitment to the choice.

When we suddenly have entire communities (not just individuals) that are getting in touch with a more noble purpose, then society will start to experience some changes. Maybe the types of schools we've previously discussed will continue to spread and crop up here and there. Maybe we will start experiencing less violence in our streets and a more sympathetic, caring and compassionate culture in general. It does seem, however, that the driving force of our economies have us heading in the completely opposite direction from this, while, at the same time, a growing number of us are indeed *waking up*.

Religious and cultural differences have been so diverse, and so much anger and dualistic thinking has been stirred up because of it, that our culture seems to be facing in the wrong direction for positive change.

The sad part about this is that as long as greed, profits and money remain the focus rather than the well being of the planet, its people and, yes, even its animals (which are being horribly slaughtered and abused), will continue to suffer. We may be forced to experience even more devastating repercussions around the world with certain forms of violence. Only then may the masses truly start to wake up. If you live by the sword, you die by the sword. With such terrible, violent negative possibilities looming on the horizon, the one good thing about it is that its severity could actually wake us up.

Chapter Seven

PRIMITIVE POLITICS

In the case of political, and even of religious, leaders it is often very doubtful whether they have done more good or harm. —Albert Einstein

If the only tool you have is a hammer, you tend to treat everything as if it were a nail. —Abraham Maslow

Mankind is capable of the most detestable and horrific acts against one another. What we have still not figured out is something that we should have figured out a long time ago. And that is, that no matter what we fight about, there are no winners. Nobody wins. It may seem there are winners on the surface, but deep down, on many levels, there are no winners at all, just losers. When the world finally comes to that realization, then and only then will things begin to change. Without this realization, all we're really doing is fighting fire with fire. Violence begets violence. It's just one continuous cycle and it's extremely hard to escape. In this day and age, and in the realities of this world, it is often required that we respond with violence for our own self-preservation.

As much as we would all like to become peaceniks in the spirit of the 1960's and just shut out the realities of the world, thinking that love is the answer, it will never happen through political means or through foreign policy. No government anywhere will ever establish a state of peace through legislation. Tranquility of your heart and mind will never be produced through laws or pronouncements. It must come from you. Everyone is waiting for world peace to appear through governments. It will not happen. Governments are war machines. They create weapons to protect their citizens or in preparation for the event of a war—which invites the violence. Entertaining the thought gives it the energy.

For example, let us equate war with darkness and peace with light. We are constantly battling our governments to end their warfare and we have continued, through the years and at present, to engage in anti-war rallies and demonstrations in an effort to stop it. This is like the crazy man who gets up in the middle of the night in a dark house. He grabs a bucket, opens the window, and spends the whole night trying to bail the darkness out of his house. Turning the light on never occurs to him.

Instead of working for peace and putting our energy toward attaining it, we try to rid our reality of something that will always be inherently there. Our focus has been misdirected. That is exactly why all of the 1960's anti-war demonstrations created more turmoil than peace. For the opposite reasons this is why the peaceful methods of Mahatma Gandhi and Dr. Martin Luther King, Jr. succeeded, despite their violent deaths. *Their focus was directed correctly and that is what made them so powerful and successful.*

The lesson here is that peace is not simply the absence of war. Stopping violence does not automatically achieve peace. Peace has an essence and power unto itself that needs to be focused on, worked at, and cultivated directly for what it is. And governments do not do it. Governments spend their time and energy *fighting for world peace,* which is absurd. They do not have branches that are devoted toward establishing peace in peaceful ways—they instead have armies, navies and agencies like the Department of Defense that engage in the complete opposite. In troubled areas of the globe they often employ a "peace-keeping force," which is a contradiction in terms. You cannot force peace to occur. Peace is not profitable for the powerful military/industrial complex that is the life-blood of war-based economies, so little incentive exists for establishing peace in the first place.

> *A nation that continues year after year to spend more money on military defense than on programs of social uplift is approaching spiritual doom.* —Dr. Martin Luther King, Jr.

Our leaders need to step up and change their thinking before the world sinks even deeper into this sinkhole of violent behaviour. But we cannot depend on them. They will never change before we do. That is a fact. What is more relevant to you?—some leader out there trying to legislate peace in some way, or you, right where you are now, actually creating it?

There is no more excuse for you to expect others to do it first. You are not an insignificant number off in a corner somewhere with little power. You are a microcosm of the entire creation itself, and can reflect a positive and powerful direction for the world by your actions. This is your reality and from your perspective it is the *only* reality—so live it in the way that represents your highest values. You should not care what others are doing unless it is positive in nature—like turning on a light in the darkness. Powerful world leaders are crazy—they're trying to bail out the darkness with buckets while you, and others like you, can shine a spotlight on their foolishness and make a bigger difference, collectively, than they ever could. Their positions of power are nothing but illusion, and this can *only* be proved out by our actions—yours and mine. Stop fighting against negative things, like we do most of the time, and instead be a beacon of light. Focusing on the negative feeds the negative and draws attention to it. Put your attention on the positive. Don't whine and complain about a problem or an injustice, hoping for a result—step up and do something to stop it from harming yourself or others. The world needs this desperately, in many areas. Much of the western world is more concerned with entertainments and material pursuits while huge, legitimate concerns pile up all around us. The alarm bells are ringing and guess what. It's time to wake up because your inaction is voluntary suicide. We need to act, as individuals, even in the smallest ways.

> *Insanity in individuals is something rare—but in groups, parties, nations, and epochs, it is the rule.* —Nietzsche

If we were to suspend military spending for just one day there would be enough money to feed the world for a year. This is a staggering truth, which would prevent the starvation deaths of more than 40 million people during this year and the needless suffering of millions of others who barely manage to survive. This glaring fact is something that we, as humanity, should be totally and completely ashamed of. Until we do something to correct this, we will remain a race of uncaring, selfish brutes, devoid of any higher spiritual sense and clearly qualify, by Nietzsche's standards, as being completely insane. *Except as individuals.* It's true that overpopulation and limited resources are a problem, but turning our backs and allowing people to starve to death is not the answer.

> *Every gun that is made, every warship launched, every rocket signifies, in the final sense, a theft from those who hunger and are not fed, from those who are cold and are not clothed.*
> —Former Five-Star General and U.S. President, Dwight D. Eisenhower.

Some will argue that it is human nature for us to fight and to foster all the conflict and misery in the world. We are aggressive, territorial animals, they will say, wrapped up in human skins. Human nature may be responsible, but our *true nature* is still hidden. And it is our true nature that is starting to emerge. When it completely comes out, the light switch will be turned on and the darkness will be of little consequence. The potential of darkness will always be there, but when we choose to operate in the light, and are focused entirely on its advantage, then darkness will not be allowed to take effect to the degree that we currently experience.

Is politics going to save us? No political system, from the right or left, has ever solved humanity's woes. Developing a worldwide system of socialism, under the guise of "globalism," is not the answer any more than it would be for any other political system.

Most liberal Democrats lean toward ideas of advanced consciousness and are on the right track, but they do not have the proper system to change things. It must be carefully built and fostered through the four-point plan outlined in the *Introduction* of this book, or through some other more ingenious but similar philosophy. Republican conservatives have the right idea as far as less government and free enterprise is concerned, but when conservative politics get stronger, freedoms get sacrificed. Right from the get-go, conservative-minded policy makers are reluctant to change anything—unless it makes money. The current system will never change with the mindset of profits as the primary motivation, or continuous legislation with new laws, taxes or controls. We must grow up as a species and rule ourselves through conscience and wisdom, providing needs through compassionate service whenever these needs arise.

Again, the proper system to carry out such positive change, without having all the baggage and problems we have now, is not in place. What is happening in the political spectrum, not only in America, but all over the world, is a kind of balancing act. The constant struggle for balance means only one thing: that the entire system is *unstable*. Two different factions of liberals and conservatives always fight against each other when election time comes around. Some countries have additional independent parties that can actually operate on an equal footing with the two main opposing choices; but for the most part, there are only these two factions that compete. This fits perfectly into the dualism of this world, whereby the opposing view to yours is automatically processed as "evil" by the mind. We have to have a bad guy or an enemy to "blame" in support of our particular cause. If people are kept busy fighting against each other, then the *real truths* are often never revealed.

Just because you beat an enemy doesn't necessarily mean that your answers are right, and the more passionately you can get people to fight each other, the more of a distraction it becomes. This is much like three people coming into a store to shoplift. Two of them create a distraction by pretending to fight, bringing all the attention to them, while the real motive behind the facade—the theft—is never seen. People will talk for days—maybe even years—about the big fight (or big election), never knowing what the real motive was that day, which was successfully carried out. The one time we did catch a glimpse behind the curtain was in the 2000 U.S. presidential elections (an embarrassment to the "puppeteers"), which *clearly* involved enough vote tampering through a new computerized system to sway the election and actually change the outcome. It's a proven fact, swept under the rug. This view has been painted by some as a shallow Democratic "sour grapes" claim, but the more deeply one looks into it, the more veracity it has.

Looking back through the history of politics, we can clearly see, if viewed from a higher perspective, that being a liberal or a conservative is not the answer. Yes, each side does provide temporary answers. Too much liberalism brings chaos and too much conservatism brings dictatorship. There are never long reigns of a particular party in any country unless a complete dictatorship is in effect and no elections are allowed. Why? Because when the system goes too far in one direction, it has to be balanced out by getting the other party in power. Policies must always be reversed at certain points in time— and that's the only way that politics is able to survive. It therefore makes no sense to be a staunch supporter of any political philosophy. Intelligent voters should gauge the direction the system is lacking, as far as its health, or balance, is concerned and vote that way. Those who fanatically support just one political party are not only annoying, they've been blinded by party politics and political dogmas without considering the bigger picture. It's an elastic system that operates within a fixed framework, only allowed to go so far before it must be pulled back and balanced. A certain equilibrium must be maintained. As a result, entire political structures are manipulated in much the same way money and interest rates are controlled by the Federal Reserve in the U.S. and the IMF, throughout the world, respectively.

When the manipulation of money worldwide is coupled with pre-determined leadership, they function together like an orchestra playing. Politicians and governments play the instruments (make policy) while the banks and their cartels are conducting. If it starts to play out of tune, you adjust some of the strings—in this case, the purse strings. An "elastic" Federal Reserve is normally kept in tune through this method. Although the method has worked in the past, the orchestra can no longer play the tunes accurately, if at all. By faking it, the system has managed to continue, due to the poor attention span of the audience. Lately, however, the audience has had no choice but to pay attention. The system is becoming outdated.

Parts of the system, like the failing environment and exponential population growth, previously not considered as having much effect, are growing unmanageable, creeping in and causing disruption, and getting people's attention. In our fast changing world, the song is too old to make everyone dance effectively. It's not working anymore. The masses have begun to listen to the tune more closely and don't like it. They understand that a far better tune is needed—and *can be played*—than the one that we have repeatedly heard over these many years. Much of this current path, again, has to do with consumerism. In order to keep the money flowing at an increasingly "sustainable" rate, the same outdated tune must be danced to in a frenzied, speeded-up tempo.

The problem is, as the system grows, it's getting harder for it to work and stay manageable. The population is exploding and we have more problems in the world—more suffering, more starvation, less clean water, more wars, less of a protective ozone layer, and more terrorism. So how do we change the system before it's too late? The people at the International Monetary Fund and the World Bank have become experts at plugging all the financial holes throughout the world and are keeping this system patched together because they have enough control to do it. They have it down to a science—but a science that needs increasingly elaborate levels of patchwork to maintain. The Bilderberg Group, the CFR, and the Trilateral Commission are among the organizations that play a role in this international maintenance. Some of the members of these groups are politicians, but many are not. The political figures are nothing more than political *figureheads*. They are there for the public to see and are objects for people to focus on as far as policy goes, but the real policy is carried out behind the scenes, by others, whose names seldom, if ever, appear in any of the newspapers or media. They and their decisions are not publicized. They're quietly sitting behind the curtain pulling the strings while we have to dance to the tune that they orchestrate. The political seats of power that we are taught to respect are not as powerful as they once were because our politicians have sold out to these more powerful organizations and lobbyists with their agendas.

> *My choice early in life was either to be a piano player in a whorehouse or a politician. And to tell the truth, there's hardly any difference. I, for one, believe the piano player job to be much more honorable than current politicians.* —Former U.S. President Harry Truman

In order to change this, it would seem we would need the cooperation of the powerful organizations that control and influence politics. But maybe not. Time could make the difference. If we carry forward an educational system that would bring the importance of the spirit into people's lives from an early age, then maybe, in later years, a spiritual view could become a bigger part of world affairs and this dualistic, violent, egocentric and materialistic paradigm might begin its immanent demise a bit sooner.

When people have attained a certain degree of spiritual maturity, then adhering to any type of polarized political system will not be quite as necessary. When consciousness is elevated and we are more spiritually aware, then the path of heart is followed as opposed to the path of any sort of political ideology. We are still many years away from having this kind of awareness being dominant in our society or in our culture, but it is more than possible at a later time. It is definitely something that can be realized, but it will not happen by itself. It is something that we should strive for and set the foundations for. We need to plan it for the planet.

We are definitely evolving in a spiritual way, but our knowledge in scientific and technological areas has sky-rocketed ahead of it. We have not grown wise enough to handle our technology responsibly. In fact, it was Albert Einstein who said, "Technological progress is like an axe in the hands of a pathological criminal." So mankind is like a child and immature, but in charge of dangerous weapons. We have the ability to destroy the world and everything on it in a matter of hours if we wanted to. Yet if we knew what it really all meant, would we contemplate doing such a thing? People understand *how* the world works, but they don't know why. Our scientists have broken down everything into the smallest particles and examined them in a scientific way, so we can see how things are put together. But again, people don't understand *why* everything is put together the way it is. If we looked at the bigger holistic picture instead of breaking reality down, tearing it all apart to see how it works, it would be an equally valuable perspective—if not more so. The world needs to form a successful holistic view of things, almost from a godly perspective, in order to see why it works and to actually keep it working. And until such time that we do this, there will be no understanding and no sanity in this world to keep it all functioning together. Things will remain in relative chaos.

> *Our scientific power has outrun our spiritual power. We have guided missiles and misguided men.* —Dr. Martin Luther King, Jr.

At the moment we are totally blind, living in darkness as to the higher purpose and reason for the existence of this planet and ourselves. We must come to understand that we originate from a higher source and in a certain sense remain connected to it—but without this knowledge we remain floundering ineffectively in the dark. Our power is this higher source and our connection to it. This realization could bring us far beyond the threatening attitudes that we pose toward one another and the planet itself. Once we make this realization we still have to act on it—by connecting to our power and then learning how to use it. That is a major goal of this work.

In summary, we've seen where politics falls short, and we've seen how science and technology is failing us.

Chapter Eight

HOLISTIC WORLD VIEW

Every truth passes through three stages before it is recognized. In the first, it is ridiculed, in the second it is opposed, in the third it is regarded as self-evident. —Arthur Schopenhauer

We live in succession, in division, in parts, in particles. Meantime within man is the soul of the whole; the wise silence; the universal beauty, to which every part and particle is equally related; the eternal One. — Ralph Waldo Emerson

We are beginning to view the world holistically in an ecological sense, which is extremely important. Our actions in this direction are crucial and will determine the very life of the planet and ourselves. Religion will also be covered in this chapter because it has been the one major dividing force in the world throughout our history, preventing many forms of holistic thought. Viewing *ourselves* holistically is equally important to our view of the earth.

It is important to know that we are all part of God. This statement is often expressed in ways that mean very little, or as a figure of speech, but a true understanding of it can elevate your consciousness. If you ask any quantum physicist who knows anything about the origins of matter and the physical makeup of the material world, then you will see that such people have come to the realization that spirit and matter have crossed paths in such a way that it's hard to differentiate between the two of them within the deeper levels of reality. This has thrown the scientific world into an awkward state of confusion because we know so little about the spirit. When one looks at the spirit, one must eventually be confronted with the idea of God. And that is, in fact, what some interesting scientific research is starting to explore. Some authors are highly trained scientists and have now turned their attention toward God. When we look at atheism in light of this new research, it becomes a much weaker field of thought. Many atheists have based their arguments and premises on science, but the more advanced forms of science have started to overturn the purely mechanistic ideas of the basic functions of the world. The best atheists can do nowadays is to gravitate towards theories like Stuart Kauffman's—who views the creative force in nature as God. As of this writing it is yet to be determined completely in a scientific way, but we are starting to discover that we are, in fact, all part of God. This idea has also been a core belief of many spiritual schools of thought for many centuries.

What often comes from the New Age metaphysical community is the statement that we are all connected. In general, few of the metaphysical gurus who make this claim back up the statement very well. They keep us thinking within a materialistic framework. They present this idea to us—that everything is connected—and then don't go any farther beyond that. We are just supposed to accept it.

If, however, one looks on a very deep spiritual and even scientific level, it will be seen that everything really is connected in discernable ways. If God created this reality, and we are all part of God, it naturally follows that everything is connected. It would have to be connected to and through us. It would also naturally follow that the statement, "You create your own reality" would also be true—despite our being so totally sick and tired of hearing it from the same empty-headed New Age gurus who fail to explain why. Your reality does not turn out exactly how you are trying to create it because we constantly run into other co-creators whose paths intermingle and effect ours. Therefore, our ultimate "perfect plans" don't come to exact fruition. We usually get a lesser rendition of what we want based on the other collective activity going on all around us. We are acting upon the stage that we created, but the story line is more complex than just one single actor's vision. How it all plays out together and what we can learn from it is why we're here.

You create your own reality. Certain metaphysical gurus, however, will repeat this statement over and over again, giving us the more simplistic concept of the idea, which everyone loves to believe. That is, that we have total and complete control over all of the elements around us, including ourselves, so that we create every single facet of our lives and all of the events that are occurring around us—which is total nonsense. We have limited control over what other people are going to do around us. That is part of our reality. We do not have complete control in creating it, like writing a novel, as it unfolds during every single minute. That's not our job. Yet some New Age gurus have people believing this total fantasy.

One must be careful when exploring the whole New Age metaphysical movement. There are people out there who will completely mislead you and spew out happy ideas that one would like to believe, but offer no basis for them. It would make life so much easier, but it is simply not the case. Sadly, there are many seekers who will stretch their minds to accept a fantasy, something bordering on the absurd, because they *want to believe it* so badly. Some teachers, knowing this, design metaphysical programs around what people want to hear, rather than what they need to hear.

It is better to be inclined toward ancient truths and philosophies, as the ancients were no fools. In many cases, they were far wiser than we are today. The idea that we are all part of God goes back a very long way. It is a powerful statement because it is based on deep spiritual truth. All of humanity has a deep, ingrown drive to find that oneness with God and, if successful, to express it. That's where our separate religions have come from. While engaging in this search for God and our place in the universe, however, we are like children stumbling around in the early morning shadows of darkness, waiting for the twilight to grow brighter so we might better understand our surroundings. We have so much more to learn. We have collectively reached the same psychological stage as a four-year-old child who won't take no for an answer. They will throw temper tantrums and attack their siblings over any item desired or the idea that they are right, and that's it—period! Anyone who has ever experienced a three to four-year-old child knows how incredibly hard it is to control them. That's the situation we have right now with humanity. Why? Because we have been given free will. Give a four-year-old free reign and they will run all over you. Like children, we can refuse to accept the consequences of our actions or we can choose to confront them and learn from our mistakes. It is time to start accepting the consequences of our actions and to confront our mistakes instead of leaving them for our REAL children and future generations. God, or whatever higher power there is, is not going to come down and discipline us. As we spiritually evolve and grow, we are developing self-discipline. A separate "God," apart from who we are, will not do it for us. We are on our own to learn certain things—for example, a holistic view of the world is coming into focus and with it will come wisdom. If we have begun to learn anything, it is about time we prove it and start acting responsibly.

If we are all part of God, then in a certain sense God is already here—through us. He therefore cannot completely separate himself from all of the millions of souls upon this earth in order to exert His *personal will* upon us or try to direct us. Although we have a connection to Him within us, God does not control us. Instead of this dictatorial idea of control, we have free will. Yes, God is watching. He is even here *experiencing* this material creation, through us. From our point of view, witnessing the rest of humanity, God's involvement may seem to be in scattered form, through millions of different souls—but from His point of view, He is experiencing the whole picture coherently, and processing everything at once. We can be inspired to do things on behalf of God, but because He is a spiritual being, He cannot "reach" down and work directly in the physical world. That is our job.

Everyone prays to God for a miracle. We are the miracle. Religions express various miracles that God, or those representing Him, have done. Religions, however, offer metaphorical events in this regard, in an effort to convey spiritual truths. Knowing this should not lessen the importance of any religion, or demean any who follow their faith. Religions have always offered these valuable stories, but we are growing out of religions with faith in such miraculous events, and into the direct spiritual experience that these stories entail. This can still be done within the religious context, but the dogmatic frameworks they offer remain woefully outdated. The more strictly one follows a belief system, the more rules it demands one follow. A direct experience of God has been thrown by the wayside as a result. The enforcement of rules by intermediaries has derailed us from the paths laid down by the founders of our religions. For those who care to look, virtually none of our major religions follow the original teachings of the founders.

The concept of God is important and had to be developed. Religions filled that role—but one of the main lessons we need to learn is that none of the religions are completely right. None of the religions are completely true, but to a certain degree they all are true because we as humanity are the learning instrument, using religion as a tool. We don't realize that we are the focus of this learning (not the religion)—the truth we seek resides *and operates* within us—there is no God up there sitting on a throne in the sky, looking down and judging us.

To the contrary, many who have come back from near-death experiences state that they reviewed their own life and then *judged themselves*, because a higher part of them—and you—has tremendous wisdom. Only after one has left this physical plane does it become clear that this is the case. A higher part of us oversees us in this lower material world. And when we leave, it is, in fact, that higher part and extremely wise part of us that does the judging. You do not come before a man with a long beard sitting on a throne who does it for you. That's absurd. This is something that is your journey, your experience, and your learning. We are here for a reason and we know what we've come here for, but when we enter this material world the vibration is so incredibly low as compared to spirit that we forget where we've come from and what we're really here for, in virtually every case.

Some people intuitively know their calling and do noble things in this world. Most others are totally and completely lost. They must find their way on a blind and difficult path, as their spiritual growth comes slowly. We are all going somewhere and this is all being done for a reason, despite the world's difficulties. We will learn how to overcome our challenges, but only when we as individuals are ready.

Spiritual Truths

It is a known scientific fact that everything is a vibration. In the larger view of things, the dense material world sits low on the vibrational scale. Everything in the universe operates on a certain vibration. Because of the different rates of vibration, we have the different structures that we see all around us. It may sound odd, but light is the basic component for all in this physical vibration. Even if something appears solid, light is the basic component for its vibration. In scientific terms, matter itself is known to be light that is trapped in a gravitational field. There are major implications regarding the truth behind this existence if all in this material world is simply light, but in differing forms, vibrating at various degrees.

An interesting fact is that many of the ancient religions of the world, the ones that seem closest to the truth, have always said that God is light. Nearly every religion in the world still claims it today, with it being passed down in one form or another, including Christianity.

> This is the message we have heard from him and proclaim to you, that God is light and in him is no darkness at all.
> (1 John 1:5)

So if God is light, then God is everywhere around us—in all of the stones, plants, rivers, buildings—in *everything* that you see. We have God within us. People and living beings have more of this light within them than inanimate objects because we hold an awareness; we have the potential for wisdom; we are able to do things that are God-like to a certain degree. Because we are searching for God more actively than all of these other vibrating things, then we, in fact, do have more of God within us. We are much closer to God than we might think. In religion, when people find God it is said that they "see the light." Enlightened masters—those who truly connect to God and have their consciousness totally transformed—always report becoming "one with the light." That is why they call it en*light*enment. Yet we continue the centuries-old dogmatic trend of fighting each other, and killing each other, over the idea that God is to be recognized within our own primitive tribal belief systems, rather than within our own Selves.

We are all God's children. We are all part of God, but at the same time, we're acting like fools during our search for Him. He's right in front of us, or rather within us, and virtually nobody sees it. It's time to wake up, to see the holistic reality, and then transform our actions and ourselves.

We have created different forms of religion in an effort to grow closer to God and learn more about Him. To a certain extent this has worked, but it takes faith in the particular belief system. God has not come down and made one—*not one*—personal physical appearance in front of any of the *billions* of congregations or religious meetings that have ever taken place in the history of the planet. Jesus never claimed to be God incarnate, although the Catholic Church claims it today, after it having been decided that he was by the Council of Nicea in 325 CE. The closest Jesus came to claiming this was in two different quotes—the first being when he said, "I and my Father are one." (John 10:13) He never said, "I and the Father are one *and the same entity*," which would have been different. Jesus clarified this same figure of speech in a second quote, in response to his disciple Philip, who said, "Lord, show us the Father, and it sufficith us," Jesus said:

> Have I been so long time with you, and yet hast thou not known me, Philip? He that hath seen me hath seen the Father; and how sayest thou, then, "Shew us the Father?" Believest thou not that I am in the Father, and the Father in me? the words that I speak unto you I speak not of myself; but the Father that dwelleth in me, he doeth the works. Believe me that I am in the Father, and the Father in me. (John 14:9-11)

Based on the information in this chapter, we can all claim this. The difference is that Jesus was awake enough to know it, while most of us are not. As a result of our spiritual ignorance, people continue to have faith and look outside of themselves for God. Yet Jesus said, "The kingdom of God is within you." (Luke 17:21) Isn't it time we start looking there?

Because of human frailties like greed, prejudice and the lust for power, we have created trouble in our search for God. Religion has a deep and dark history of controlling others rather than enlightening them. That is why we have had, over the centuries, various groups that have broken off from the mainstream religions. Every major religion has dozens if not hundreds of various splinter groups, sects, denominations or cults that crop up, based loosely upon the original. They are searching. Their existence demonstrates that our search for God involves a conditioned reaction to look outside ourselves, by continually trying to depend on a group or outside "authority" to follow. If one doesn't work, we must try another. Maybe Joe over here has the answer since I can't find it with Fred. It is a continuing pattern. These groups are formed because not one of the major religions, despite their popularity and long-standing existence, has risen to the top and proven themselves to be (or unequivocally become known as) the true path to God. Ironically, the groups that *have* made the most progress in the direct achievement of union with God have been persecuted, stamped out, and experienced tremendous violence against them by the dominant religions in power at the time. When it comes to religion, in almost every single case, power and control become more important than the enlightenment of the individual.

The Gnostic Path

In early Christian times there were those who were called Gnostics. *Gnosis* is a Greek word that means "to know," therefore a Gnostic is "one who knows." This knowledge refers to spiritual knowledge from direct experience as opposed to religious belief, so Gnostics were considered to be the mystics of early Christianity. Many of them were experiencing God for themselves instead of being told by the church what to believe. The Gnostics have continued to resurface over the centuries in new and different forms, but have continued to be persecuted each time they appear. This is one reason why their ideas have failed to take hold. Another is because it is more of an individual-based movement, lacking cohesive strength through a rigid system of belief. Everyone, as an individual, has to discover and experience God for themselves. What works successfully for you might not work as powerfully for me. If you want to experience God rather than just be a "believer," it takes work—on a deep and personal level. Many do not explore that deeply, or know how to, because the surface teachings of religion are used and lack the required depth.

The teachings of mainstream religion are often ineffective on deeper spiritual levels because they have been simplified. The generic form of any belief system brings more common people into the fold, and makes the religion stronger because of added numbers. It is often said that religion is for the masses while spirituality is for the individual. The Gnostics of earlier times were the seekers of deeper knowledge, and that is why they keep returning and will never be eradicated. This search is part of us. There is a resurgence of interest today in the Gnostics because we have become more sophisticated and intelligent. We are also becoming more awake and alive, and are growing in this direction. Dogmatic belief systems are rigid and stagnant while spirituality is totally alive within us and allows us to grow.

Historically speaking, the Gnostics have always been warned off as "heretics." Despite the conditioned negative reaction and the urging we've received to avoid such people at all costs, the word *heretic* actually means "one who chooses." That's all. When one chooses not to take the standard path of the traditional religions, there's tremendous freedom in that. But just like the word *occult*, which simply means "hidden," the word *heretic* has been given a negative spin by society so that people believe it to be something terrible. We've been conditioned to accept a different meaning for the word than what it truly means.

As a species, our search for God is relentless and seems to be one of our most powerful urges. God is not so easily found through the various belief systems that we have erected. The more elusive God becomes, the more new denominations we create (this is true in Buddhism, Hinduism, Christianity, and in all the major religions worldwide). Or it may be the other way around. The more new denominations we create, the more elusive God chooses to become because *we just don't get it*. God is not to be found in man-made religions or their offshoots!

It is an individual inner search that will produce a result, and this is what the Gnostic strives for. All of the denominations that break off from the main foundations are striving for this as well—in order to find something—to find a connection to God that the religion has failed to do. When new denominations survive it is because the teachings remain simple enough to attract enough adherents. Those who search even more deeply, the direct experiencers, have had some organizational success but they're never allowed to flourish long enough for the movement to grow and succeed. The power of an individual person always gets sacrificed for the sake of the organization and its survival. Power comes in numbers, but it's really up to the individual. Historically speaking, individuals have been weak when it comes to standing up against a long-standing dogmatic structure, *unless the time is right for change*. We have reached that time once again. It is individual "heretics" who have created and inspired all new religions, which then became organized later. How can people retain individual spiritual freedom, experience God directly through means of their own choosing, and prevent religions from attacking them as "heretics?" This is an important hurdle that we are facing today.

Ancient and Modern Shamanism

How can this dilemma be approached? Where have we seen success at finding God? When we look at attempts to find union with God, there are some interesting ones. Way back, far before Gnosticism, there was shamanism. Primitive tribes always had a shaman, one who was able to leave the body and go into other worlds. Some of these tribes are still in existence today. The shaman goes into these other worlds by using substances like mushrooms, ayahuasca or peyote, something that will change his consciousness into a higher vibrational state where he can leave the body and gain additional information that is not readily available to us at this lower vibration we inhabit. The spirit has access to higher vibrations and the shaman knows how to get there through trance or the use of natural entheogens. They sometimes go into a trance through chanting or drumming and then enter into these higher worlds. A holistic view is encountered and many answers are given. For example, if someone is sick they go into this other reality, diagnose the patient, come back, have a cure, prescribe something, and the person will often miraculously recover. However, to them it is not so "miraculous"—to the shaman it is just another day at the office.

In our modern, western world of medicine the shamanic approach is considered to be nothing but superstition in action or the cures are attributed to the power of suggestion. But to these shaman and to these people in primitive tribes, it is trusted medicine that has been tested through trial and error for centuries, with these techniques being passed down, generation to generation. To them, it is not hocus-pocus at all, but a powerful and viable tradition, still used today in many tribes throughout the world.

Many outside of primitive tribes have tried to trigger higher states of consciousness with the help of plants, pills, chemicals or natural entheogens. Back in the 1960's when LSD first exploded onto the scene, it was the result of young people who knew that opening their minds in a blissful new form of expression was better than the accepted form of mainstream expression, which was supporting war, violence and death. The Vietnam War made little sense to them, along with the senseless murders of our most loved and moral leaders like president John F. Kennedy, his brother Robert, and Dr. Martin Luther King, Jr. The use of LSD during this time could be considered a misuse because it was used more for recreation, a form of escape, or sometimes even protest, rather than for spiritual growth. But these people wanted to celebrate life just as much as those who would wish to improve it. Attempting to experience other forms of reality or consciousness will always be a deep spiritual part of us—one that seeks to reach beyond this flawed existence into something more meaningful.

This is not to condone the use of illicit or even legal substances to reach higher states of consciousness, but merely to illustrate that we have an innate desire to reach them. Since our culture does not educate our youth in any spiritual sense, many know of no other way to attempt a higher journey but to take a "shortcut,' through the ingestion of an outside substance. The people from this whole flower power generation could not move to Siberia and learn to become a shaman, but they knew that what their own culture was expressing and experiencing was something that they wanted no part of. The one thing they did have was the freedom to express themselves the way they wanted to, which was in direct opposition to what was going on at the time.

Freedom does have a lot to do with the spirit, but the paths we sometimes take in expressing it may not always be the right ways to go. We are still learning. We are still trying different ways to reach the level of consciousness that gives union with God. Religion only goes so far, demanding faith and belief rather than offering personal experience. For young people just beginning their search, mind-altering substances will sometimes play a role in the attempt at that experience.

The youth of today is experimenting with all of these new "designer drugs." It's the same search. The direction is right, but the substances are often poisonously wrong and dangerous. The methods being used are not the most effective. We are grasping at whatever is available to grab while being too spiritually immature to understand that these short-term, mind altering trips are not a proper path. With the answer already within us, ingesting something in an effort to explore in this direction, especially when we are not fully prepared, is foolish. It is still an answer for some young people because it offers a way to stand up against the current system, inside an acceptable subculture of rebellious outsiders. Although it may not be the perfect answer, it is an answer at the time. Nevertheless, any kind of hallucinogenic or consciousness-expanding substance is a temporary shortcut and can damage the human brain with extended, and sometimes even short-term, use. Only an indigenous shaman, with natural substances and a lifetime of both preparation and training, constitutes an exception to this statement. Otherwise, such usage is nothing more than a crutch.

There are other interesting ways to explore the inner realms. After LSD was outlawed, Stanislav Grof developed a system, after experimenting for years, demonstrating that one can reach these states of consciousness without any drugs whatsoever. His workshops, taught by himself or others trained in the work, are incredibly powerful and involve listening to primitive drumming, music or chanting while simultaneously engaged in a form of breathing called holotropic breathwork. It's quite powerful and will move you into those states where awesome things can happen on deeper levels. For many, a higher awareness comes down from elsewhere and enters into this third-dimensional expression of ourselves. Grof has written a number of books, highly recommended, but at the same time, no written words can replace what the experience has to offer.

Such a powerful experience may not be for everyone. Some people can reach a stage of oneness and bliss with God just by going into a church and praying. People can find answers suitable for them by being a fundamentalist Christian. But when one believes that this is the only answer for *everyone* and starts to force these ideas upon others, then it becomes a problem. Just because you believe it, doesn't make it right. It makes it right for *you*, and you only. When a religion represents itself in this way and becomes too dogmatic and forceful, then it becomes dangerous. We should all be free to express our connection to God in any way we choose. In order to allow this, we must develop our compassion and our ability for mutual respect more fully and move beyond the tremendous violence and intolerance that is based on our beliefs. We are living in the dark ages as far as spirituality is concerned. We are blind to our own natures because we are spiritual beings and don't see it. We will leave here as entirely spiritual beings—but only upon entering into spirit will most of us finally recognize it.

Identity Crisis

We will leave behind these physical bodies that will be burned into ashes, or as corpses that will rot, get recycled within the earth, and eventually left in the dust, while another part of us moves on. Yet we ignore the more lasting part of ourselves and focus on our material existence, which will be nothing but dust or ash in the future. The ideas and policies that control this material world will remain here and mean nothing to us in the next world. The material world continues to allow people to kill each other and disrespect each other, so while we are here we should be resolved to not remain in the dark or to assist with the continued cycle.

There are those at the very top of some religions who are completely convinced that it is their job to make sure that their religion takes over this world. They are not light bringers; they are nothing more than a reflection of the darkness in which we dwell. No single religion will ever take over this world. The human spirit is far too strong to allow any such thing to ever occur. The only possible way this could happen is for someone to wipe out the entire world with nuclear or biological weapons and have a small religious cult underneath the ground somewhere protecting itself. The earth would be so poisoned by then that they would, by the time they emerged, never be able to survive anyway. Yet some people are totally convinced that without weapons, but with the force of their minds alone, they can convert the world to their form of religion. The egotistical belief that by using their compelling ideas and personal magnetism, all people would, no doubt, see the same "truth" that they see, is a fantasy. They think that as long as they can deliver this "truth" to others, it will one day result in a world conversion—but this is easily one of the biggest fairy-tales and delusions that has ever come upon the face of this earth—proven as false over and over again for centuries.

We are finally moving in a different direction than that. We're moving into a world of diversity that is becoming far more respectful than that. It's taking time to develop and it's not happening overnight, but we are definitely moving in that direction.

We are all part of God and we have that light of God within us, no matter what one's religion might be. In a previous book, *Triumph of the Human Spirit*, I explain this light—how we can access it, what it looks like, and how important it really is. It is an extremely bright light, much more luminous than anything earthly, yet it is clearly part of us. It can be contacted and experienced, and is known to be the soul.

There was some faulty research done by a doctor named Duncan MacDougall in the early 1900s purporting to show that when someone dies a person's body loses about 21 grams of weight at the time of death. This was not properly verified and in all probability, has turned out to be false. Anything with weight has mass, which would thereby make these 21 grams a physical object, subject to the laws of gravity. The human soul consists of light, so does not have any weight. Oftentimes when people have died in the hospital they suddenly find themselves looking down at their body on the operating table, having floated upward, weightless. They don't drop to the floor and scurry around like a bug. From above they witness the doctors or nurses doing things, which they later accurately describe. We are so entrenched in this physical reality that we somehow believe that we should be able to *measure* everything. A soul cannot be weighed. If the soul had any physicality whatsoever it would be material, not spiritual, and would have undoubtedly been discovered by now. It would be a shame to leave the body upon death, only to be stepped on and *killed again* by some clod carrying your bedpan around. The good news is that souls do not have weight, cannot be stepped on and continue to live on after the body expires.

We are not our bodies, we just use them for a time. Without our bodies we migrate out of this world as luminous particles of light. For now, however, we are trapped here, inside a low material density and within time itself. This light—or our souls—is actually part of God, and this migration of the soul at death is a journey back to the place from whence we came, freeing us from the heavy spell of forgetful "sleep" we endure, along with the bondage of time. God was and is a complete, powerful, and all-inclusive spiritual force. At death we are free to connect back to this source once again, if we have progressed enough to do so, while bringing with us whatever lessons we have learned in life.

The Creation

God originally existed before there were any material forms, so aside from God there was an empty void instead of the material universe. God was a complete wholeness with nothing else around except a void of nothingness. There was no universe, galaxies, stars or planets. God was a powerful mass of untested consciousness and wanted to know it's potential. There was a completely stagnant ball of energy with all of this incredible potential, and nothing had "happened" yet. In order for the God force to know its own potential, it must separate out. Material things are consciously born and thrust into the void, providing endless means of discovery and expression for God. Vast galaxies fill the void, along with stars and planets, with just some of these planets lucky enough to support life through a natural balance of living creatures. It is the living creatures that bring forth much of the needed growth and expression.

> *It (God) was not created in the past, nor is it to be annihilated in the future; it is eternal, permanent, absolute; and from all eternity it sufficiently embraces in its essence all possible merits.* —The Mahayana

We may be the result of what *seems* to have been a random process, but it is all by design. Our world is amazingly important—and what we do with it reflects things on a cosmic scale. From the perspective of the universe and its size we are tiny, but the universe is actually a *hologram* so we reflect the entire cosmos in what we are and what we do, right here and now. What we do consciously and collectively here on this earth is *hugely* significant.

Consciousness

Before the original separation, however, God was just pure being. In the Bible God says, "I am that I am." Whoever or whatever says that is trying to denote the fact that there is nothing but pure being involved. When we get in touch with that part of God within us, it becomes a powerful statement for us as well. When you know without question what you are doing here in this life and cannot do anything else—because you are being true to yourself—then "I am that I am" defines you.

Because the universe is a hologram, we are reflective fragments of its full design and power. Therefore it is possible for God, as an unfragmented and pure being, to maintain this essence in a dualistic universe. It is done through all consciousness, collectively, and includes us. Our powers don't equal God's because we are much smaller fragments, but we are all connected and share the same God-like qualities. Separately we cannot see it, or fathom it—only God can perceive our unified "mind" from the collective level. Individually, we are stuck in a dualistic mode of thought. The collective level operates in a more expansive mode that cannot be accessed directly by individuals unless, for a brief moment, we experience "enlightenment." Enlightenment occurs outside of our normal time-space continuum, so it is hard to maintain the experience. As we continue to evolve, however, the experience of enlightenment will become more common and comfortable for us, and the blessings of God's wisdom will rain down more often into our lives. We can look forward to this in the coming years.

Can the true God actually come here in the image of a man, as portrayed in the Bible, and say, "I am that I am"? Or was this merely a lesson—something to give us the understanding that each of us have enough Godly potential within us to make this statement ourselves? The point is that we are an important part of God. We are not separate from God at all, nor are we separate from each other.

> *We once thought we lived on God's footstool; it may be a throne.* —Clarence Day

All of us, collectively, the human beings on this earth, share in the total and pure consciousness of God. In that respect, we, in fact, are God. Those entrenched in religious dogma will consider this statement blasphemy, but an interesting and credible scientific theory has emerged that recognizes *consciousness* as the main component of the universe rather than matter. The first to propose this theory from a quantum scientific standpoint, rather than a purely mystical one, was Amit Goswami, Ph.D., in his 1993 book *The Self-Aware Universe*. Modern New Age thought claims that everything is connected. If this is the case, what is it that serves as the connecting principle? It could be consciousness. Quabalist and Biblical scholar Carlo Suares once said that the universe is spirit that is becoming self-aware by projecting from itself a cloud of consciousness upon which it can self-reflect.

In the old Hermetic books, which are more mystical than scientific, Hermes states that God holds everything within Himself as *thought*—and the entire cosmos itself is a thing composed of consciousness. These ideas are not new and revolutionary. They compose some of the oldest and wisest mystical teachings the world has ever known—the only thing new about them is that they are being rediscovered, sometimes with advanced scientific backing.

Since we are all conscious beings, we share in this connection to God. We remain unaware of this "God-consciousness" because the vast majority of us are not ready for it and it is therefore operating at an unconscious level. Our search for true meaning is right in front of us, but because the consciousness of God has been scattered out into creation and shared, we fail to comprehend it individually (except in rare cases). God is not only observing though us, but experiencing what becomes of a perfect wholeness when it becomes fragmented. This consciousness is exploring all of the options of what it truly can be and what God's potential is. That is, in fact, who and what we really are. Remaining as a stagnant ball of perfect, unfulfilled energy was not God's purpose. People wonder, why are we here, who are we, where are we really going. The answer is that we, in fact, are God. Collectively. From an individual perspective we are blind to this fact, but from a collective sense—which an individual's consciousness cannot normally reach—the answers are clear. When we *collectively* realize our true identity we will immediately begin to act accordingly. This realization is a major component in the development of a holistic world view. Our collective link to God can create a better world through large-scale unity with everyone involved.

Mankind is not perfect and we make mistakes all the time. When the consciousness of God enters into an imperfect being like you and I and into a dense world of imperfection, It is forced into the background as an observer. The dualistic nature of matter takes precedence and *splits* the human mind into opposing concepts like good and evil, right and wrong, and in using the left and right hemispheres of the brain, etc. The unitive mind of God, which we are all individually connected to, does not act in a direct or conscious way upon our lives but can still influence us through intuition, if we know how to listen. Great things often happen when we tap into the "higher Self." Those who experience enlightenment lose the mind's dualistic view and experience a blissful "Oneness"—which is what God-consciousness is. Humankind is evolving toward this higher awareness.

During our lives the experiences of each of us go into the mind of God and are all equally valuable. Each of us is on a "mission" in this world and when we pass on, we will return to the source with the fruits of our work. If our lives were good, the knowledge we bring back will be helpful.

> We shall not cease from exploration
> And the end of all our exploring
> Will be to arrive where we started
> And know the place for the first time.
> —T. S. Eliot

Could a universal consciousness play a lesser role in our conception of God and our identities? I don't believe so. Scientists continue trying to prove otherwise, in an effort to show that consciousness and all other facets of reality originate from a creative process in nature rather than the reverse. In support of this thesis we have the work of Stuart Kauffman, addressed in his 2008 work, *Reinventing the Sacred*. He considers God to be the creative impulse throughout the universe, with consciousness being a mere offshoot of it—recognizing consciousness as "a real feature of the universe." Kauffman states that, "God, a fully natural God, is the very creativity in the universe." In stating this, he means that God is much like nature, replicating and growing, without possessing consciousness as its primary, driving force.

It is my opinion that before you can have creativity, you must have consciousness. That is the case with humankind and it is probably the case with the universe and with God. If God has no consciousness, then what is its definition? Kauffman states that God is "our chosen name for the ceaseless creativity in the natural universe, biosphere and human cultures." His theory is one of emergence and self-organization that parallels my theory of God as consciousness, but for his to actually work, in my opinion, it would require the involvement of a conscious intelligence as a prerequisite for this ceaseless creativity. He believes that reality as we know it arose without a Creator God, while I believe that we, along with all things conscious, are in fact, the creators. We are growing back into full consciousness after a "big bang" major fragmentation, separate souls now, on an awesome journey of self-discovery. The soulful part of Kauffman's research is not present; it is purely scientific. He sees consciousness as being part of evolution instead of evolution as being part of consciousness. My views would no doubt seem mistaken by those in support of Kauffman's work, but we do share in the opinion that a physical God as an independent, judgmental personage is something that is long outdated and should be left in the past. All ideas that move us in this direction are needed so that we can openly explore them and progress.

Spiritual Evolution

When we learn new spiritual lessons and are aware of them, we become self-reflective. This self-reflective state touches the higher self, or "Godmind" within us. This brings us closer to God—often better than with religion.

All of the separate religions in the world are engaging themselves in pure folly by trying to locate God through an exclusive path—one that reflects their version of God based on a specific culture or strict set of beliefs. The only path to God, however, is one that will bring us together on a collective level, beyond the religions that separate us. Maybe, when we get wise enough, we will reach a certain critical mass that will trigger us to completely disband religions—at least in the dogmatic way that we express them today. Once that critical mass is reached, then everything will become completely clear and we will come together as caring and compassionate humans. But until such time that this happens, we are destined to fight amongst ourselves in a barbaric, tribal world that is completely stuck in a materialistic and territorial mode of thought—complete barbarism.

The answer we've been seeking is not "out there." *We* are the answer. The illusion of duality is our only obstacle to finding it. When we experience the wholeness of ourselves, we experience the wholeness of God. Everything truly is connected to us and to each other. We are not separate fragments of "us and them," to be fought against or dominated. We are all One. But to have space, and material things, there needs to be "up" when there is "down" and "bad" when there is "good." There cannot be one without the other. The dualistic illusion we live under was created by God with the birth of the material universe. It is a necessary evil because without it nothing would happen. Everything needs an opposite to create the context of "events." Even our brains have a left and right hemisphere.

The key for God Himself to return from this dualistic reality is for us, his consciousness, to *collectively* reach the realization of oneness and our identity with God. God cannot magically pull his consciousness back together after it has been fragmented in such a way. The consciousness itself must do the work, and move past the illusion. For example, we must understand that when we hurt others we only hurt ourselves. Any seemingly independent and greedy action has its eventual consequence, which will surface and impact its originator with the same negative energy that spawned it.

> *Violence and injury enclose in their net all that do such things, and generally return upon him who began.*
> —Lucretius

In the same way, when one does something to help the lives of others, the eventual results that surface will enrich the originator's life in a similar positive fashion. Many businesses are now incorporating extra services or plans of action dedicated toward worthwhile charities or helpful research. People in turn respond to these businesses as a result of their concern and willingness to support their causes.

At the end of this great lesson of unity lies a more enlightened society, along with each individual contributor. When we examine the mindset of a truly enlightened person, it is clear that they hold a more compassionate view towards others. The realization of enlightenment involves an inner search, however. We hold the answers that we seek within us. When we spend time going inward on a spiritual quest and searching deeply within ourselves, oftentimes, enlightenment does occur. Such people do exist, but when we spend our time praying to a God who is supposedly up in the sky, out there somewhere, and spend our time going to a church, which is made of bricks and mortar as opposed to the spiritual substance of the soul, then there are virtually no known instances of anyone becoming enlightened using such a path. The best way is the inner way, which can be successful. The world's greatest spiritual teachers never achieved their incredible wisdom by sitting in a pew or in any kind of environment that is dependent on a teacher who has them seeking answers outside of themselves.

Great teachers have been known to trigger a deeper understanding from their students, but this is always done through personalized methods not found in a standard religious framework. Enlightenment is not for the masses. Therefore, it is not taught to the masses.

Recognizing and experiencing the actual part of God within yourself often brings enlightenment. It is a union of sorts—some would term it a "reunion." The outer world, however, is in a fragmented state. When you split something apart that is whole and complete (in this case the original God-consciousness), the result is a set of opposites. That's why this whole world is based on opposites. You've got an opposite for everything—night and day, up and down, good and evil. So people ask, "Why does God allow evil in the world?" It is not so much "allowed," but a natural part of the whole equation. Anything that is whole, when smashed into almost endless separate bits, has an endless array of opposites. It's a natural occurrence, with a negative for each existing positive. All reasons why this is playing out this way is unclear, but it is clear that we are playing a major role in God's own self-realization.

We may ask, "If God is all powerful, why does he need his own self-realization?" If we go back to the complete void and nothingness that existed, which is rather hard to imagine, it seems that it would be an extremely boring existence to just "be." There would be nothing there. It would be a fullness with no action or existence, without knowing what existence would be like or could be.

I think that an all-powerful God would *want to use* that power. That is what is being played out right here and now. Once that power has been made manifest through us, in every conceivable possibility and experience, I think that there would be some kind of tremendous benefit involved at the end. It seems that the most important facet of all this has something to do with consciousness. It's hard to imagine exactly what that facet of consciousness or its payoff would be, because we live in such complete darkness in that regard right now; but there are indicators that seem to show that that direction, and the conscious choices we make, is leading us to something. What we do with our consciousness, in a collective sense, is the most important aspect of what is being played out in the world today.

Although this seems to be presented in abstract terms, the idea that we are all part of God is becoming provable with each passing day. The only thing we cannot prove with no uncertain terms is exactly what God is, because God is so far beyond what our small minds can conceptualize. But what our greatest minds have determined, to the best of their abilities in scientific terms, is that God is a powerful, all-encompassing force in the universe that does indeed connect everything, is found within all matter and is related very strongly to the entire material world.

Also, light plays a very big part in this connection to God. In fact, it is the Gnostics who said way back during the time of Christ that we are all sparks of the divine. The Gnostic conception of the universe is something that is worth being closely studied. It is the general belief of Gnostics that some part of God broke away, but at a higher level than where we are today. They believe that there was some fragmentary, lesser and therefore inferior force of God that created this physical world—in essence, choosing to create a world that is not under the strict domain of God. They believed that with God in charge and still in His complete power, there would be no division of opposites. There would strictly be wholeness and complete harmony, which in its original form they called the "Pleroma." Instead, we have a world that was created by something that had broken away from God. All of the evils and sufferings that we have are not something that God would have wanted us to experience, according to the Gnostics. An all-loving God would not want his children to suffer.

There are a number of Gnostic holy books that lay out the story of how this may have happened. *Pistis Sophia*, a Gnostic gospel, talks about how the material world was manifested. The best version of that work was translated by G.R.S. Mead. We also have the *Nag Hammadi Library*, which was discovered in Egypt in 1947, about the same time as the Dead Sea Scrolls. The Gnostic texts offer a fuller and more interesting version of creation, and of religion and humanity itself.

Traditional Christianity considers these books to be blasphemous, and warns people to stay away from such things. These warnings were added into the Bible to keep the faithful away from competing ideas, which any good religion would do, and to keep Christianity in power. Yet, as we become more knowledgeable and more spiritually aware, it is time to look at these older documents. The Bible itself does have its flaws, including endless contradictions, and many of us have outgrown it. All religions—not just Christianity—need to put their biases aside and start looking at the world in more spiritual ways. Most Gnostic teachings do not purport to reflect historical events, but contain deeper messages not found on the surface of traditional Christian dogma.

Carl Jung, the father of Jungian psychology, termed himself a Gnostic and said they were, in fact, the world's first depth psychologists. At the time of Christ they knew a great deal about the human mind, how it worked, and therefore how to relate spiritual truths through parables. This was not only during the time of Christ, but continued in the centuries that followed. Gnostic thought has appeared in and influenced the *Book of John*, and many of the original teachings of Jesus could be termed Gnostic. This includes the *Gospel of Thomas*, the largest known collection of his sayings, discovered as part of the Nag Hammadi Gnostic texts. Much of these works focus primarily on inner teachings and deep spiritual truths.

Suffice it to say that the true connection to God that we are all seeking comes only with a devoted and intense inner work, as opposed to outer worship. The inner work must be done in an individual way and is generally not taught to the masses because the masses, in general, are followers. It is not normally a follower who takes it upon himself to do this deep inner work. That's not what followers do. Followers, in general, are standard church goers and are happy with it. It gives them comfort, it works for them and it's all they need. But as we grow and progress, when we continue to spiritually evolve, there are growing numbers of us who feel something is not quite right. Something is missing.

Many with strong religious convictions, however, are convinced that there is nothing wrong with their belief systems. We can contrast these people with the many others who are "waking up" and concluding that something is not right with these very same belief systems. Those who cling the strongest to their beliefs are most often the ones who become so incredibly angry, outspoken and even hostile towards anything that goes against their strict religious dogma. Threatened and insecure people often react in this way. The fact is that far more people today are falling away, in large numbers, from their traditional religions than at any other time in recorded history. There's a reason for that. It's an idea whose time has come and we are beginning to spiritually awaken. This provokes fundamentalists into deeper and feverish study of their own beliefs, activism involving the aggressive recruitment of others into the fold, disrespectful attacks on other lifestyles or forms of belief while, at the same time, dismissing out of hand any information presented to the contrary. One example of this, which was unheard of until recently, is the picketing and demonstrations by fundamentalist Christian groups at gay people's funerals—people they have never met. While loved ones grieve, picketers hold up insulting signs and chant nasty, anti-gay rhetoric, including how the deceased has been damned into hell for eternity, at a time when solemn and respectful attempts are being made to put someone to rest.

Any person or religious group that must demean others to make themselves look good exhibits by their actions not only tremendous insecurity, but mental instability. These actions are also the result of desperation and anger against a culture that is becoming more tolerant. Although feeling threatened, they should understand that there is a transition taking place. It has nothing to do with religion. It has everything to do with spirituality. This so-called New Age "religion of the devil" is not organized as a religion at all, but a spiritual movement of self-discovery. It should not be interpreted as a serious frontal attack against religion. It's just a natural opening of the spirit that transcends mere beliefs.

True spirituality never "attacks" anything. It is respectful. Nevertheless, many have been taught to believe that spiritual experience as opposed to religious belief is of the devil. That is the easy way out, a convenient excuse to postpone their own spiritual growth. It allows them to dismiss the entire question and still cling to their beliefs with the comfort that they desire. Having a belief system requires very little inner work. It makes it easy for us to turn our energies toward clinging to our beliefs rather than working with ourselves on a deeper level.

Religion requires more of an outward expression than an intense inner search. Followers are encouraged to act and believe like the rest of the group in order to keep the religion strong. This makes the religion more important than the spiritual growth of the individual. Spirituality, however, puts the individual first. It allows us to step outside the fold and any strict dogmatic rules that might hinder a full exploration and experience of the divine.

There are as many ways to God as there are souls of men. —Sufi saying

Each separate religion claims to be the one and only path to God. Religion functions as more of a social mechanism where you go in groups either to church or to the mosque or wherever they worship, and engage in ritual, song and/or prayer with the other followers. Little is done on an individual level, but that is where most of the effort is required for us to advance on a spiritual level. If we are more ingrained and indoctrinated in this group situation, then a feeling of togetherness develops. It then becomes too frightening to stray from the flock and go on an inner exploration of our own. People don't like that. It moves them away from a comfort zone and it becomes too scary for most. We have just now reached the point where we have evolved spiritually enough for people to become more open to this inner quest, so we are starting to see positive change in our society and in the world.

This trend will continue. If you look around and attempt to recognize it, it becomes clear that this flower is already starting to bloom. The transformation, the movement, is beginning to occur on multiple levels, and the most interesting feature of it is that there's no organized "program" set up for it in an acceptable, mainstream sense.

The Power of Giving

Positive spiritual change often occurs in a spontaneous fashion and comes from the heart. When it is seen to work, others continue the trend. That is what we are beginning to experience today, and that is the way it's always been throughout history. The best catalysts for positive change have always been spiritual giants. Yet *everyone* is on an individual journey, as far as making a difference with our own true Self is concerned, and many who succeed are finding ways to spread a positive spiritual outlook to others. It is in the act of giving, without expecting anything in return, that is the most effective method. We consider God to be like this and therefore this conduct is very God-like and inspiring.

Today, people have begun to catch on. An amazing amount of compassionate giving to needy people is occurring around the world. We can expect this to grow. Whenever there is a major disaster, famous musicians come forth and raise more money through benefit concerts than all governments and relief organizations combined. Hollywood movie stars often get involved in social issues and donate generously. Professionally they work at pretending to be other people and this can be hard on actors attempting to define themselves, especially when the public worships them for it. Some try to make up for this identity deficiency by involving themselves in worthy causes in an effort to define themselves properly, which we must respect and admire. They have more marriages than average people because their identities always change in their work, allowing them to grow and mature faster on a spiritual level than most people. They are not immoral people, as some would claim. They can and do learn lessons from living the experiences of others, quite often in meaningful ways. The ones who fail to grow and learn these lessons fall by the wayside, victims, usually, of drug and alcohol abuse. Few of these troubled actors or musicians are ever found working for worthy causes, and that is no surprise. One cannot take care of others without first caring about themselves. Our worship of movie stars and sports stars of any status is terribly misplaced, but the best of them are using their fame and influence to become examples for positive change.

The book and film "Pay it Forward" was about a young boy who, for a class project, mapped out how one good deed could be passed on to others and grow, exponentially, to make millions of people happy. It caught on and people began to do just that—pay it forward. It is still happening today, years after the concept originated.

Oprah Winfrey had a reality TV show called "The Big Give." Instead of trying desperately to win something for themselves, as we often see, contestants competed much like guardian angels to see how much they could give, in various ways, to help the truly needy. This is the complete antithesis of the trash we normally see on television. This show is only a small part of what Oprah has done, and is doing, on television and in the world, on a spiritual level. She is an angel who truly "gets it," and is one of the very few at this time who is using television for spiritual growth to a mass audience. She is an historical figure, with her work in Africa and elsewhere, helping children and building schools, and she deserves the attention of every compassionate and thinking person.

The only other reality show on this same level is called "Extreme Makeover: Home Edition." They find people who have given everything of themselves to a good cause, without expecting anything back. They are desperate for a home that is not breaking down, but have no money to pay for it. Sometimes they or their children are disabled, or they have lost a spouse, or provide a community service that people are grateful for but might otherwise be discontinued due to a misfortune they have endured. Great kindness sometimes gets even greater kindness in return, as this show builds these families an amazing new home, customized for their specific needs, and arranges for a payoff of the entire mortgage at a time when all hope seemed lost.

Bestselling spiritual author Dr. Wayne Dyer recently shared some research on serotonin, the chemical in the brain that fights depression and keeps us happy. When we receive a gift or some kindness from someone, the serotonin levels in the brain of the receiver rises. These levels were also shown to rise in equal amounts for those who did the giving. Even more amazing is that those who were simply present and witnessed the giving experienced the exact same level of serotonin increase. So just by being in the energy field of this event we become happier, without giving or receiving anything except bearing witness to the kindness and experiencing it vicariously. We truly are all connected. This research proves that God-like acts such as this are part of what connects us together. It is inspiring—not to see the dismal state of the world, but to see how powerful spiritual actions are not only spreading, but beginning to *change it*.

Direct action by individuals and corporations is taking the place of churches and religious organizations, worldwide, which have always functioned historically as the "stewards of kindness" in the past. All that is changing. There is no more monopoly on the giving of kindness, either directly from the heart, or in exchange for devotion. Both forms of giving are still practiced by churches worldwide, and we are completely grateful. Any church should be happy to see unconditional giving spread throughout the world, especially at a time when it is so desperately needed, and no church or combination of churches could ever fill the needs that now exist.

Religion is a good starting point for this positive change for many people. It is a long-standing tradition to show kindness through your faith. Most of the churches have set a positive example, continue to do so, and religion is pointing us in the right direction.

Spiritual Lessons in a Material World

Apart from giving and being of service to others, many don't know how to look in deeper ways for a powerful, inner revelation. This is also starting to happen, despite the main hurdle of getting beyond the fear of looking. There is hope. There's a glimmer of light for us all in the future, and religion is an important, beginning beacon, pointing the way for us there. When we become more directly tuned in to the energies of God and the energies within ourselves and experience how they connect us together, then we will gradually move away from the more conceptual religious institutions. We will one day know instinctively that there is other work to do that involves the spirit directly, rather than with any man-made intermediary religion. We may not see it now, but it is our destiny.

The spirit we will learn to better connect with has always been there with us. It is you, from a personal standpoint, and always has been you. Once this body is used up it will be cast away and the spirit will continue in another world. In that other world, religion has little to do with spirit except to have done some general preparation for us while we were here in the physical. If the preparation work is not complete, as is usually the case, then we come back for more learning. Breaking news: Heaven is not an exclusive, private place for those of your religion. Egos are left outside the doors of the spiritual world. You cannot bring them in. In the physical world, religions involve a battle of the egos. Therefore, religions don't go in, either. Just the spirit—your pure spirit, without any ego-based labels. What we learn in a spiritual sense, however, goes with us because it transcends the ego we leave behind. Your brand of religion may get you to heaven's gates, but you will also see those from other faiths entering with you, because all good souls are seen as equals in the eyes of God.

We are on a spiritual journey in this life. Most people don't even know it, but we are evolving in this way. We are all part of God and we all, each of us, have a role to play. On this deeper, more all-encompassing spiritual level that we are operating on and that few people see, we may actually be God, collectively, and are discovering certain things while here that will bring the dense material world back into the kingdom. Our *consciousness*, and what we do with it, is the key.

> It is not God who will save us—it is we who will save God, by battling, by creating, and by transmuting matter into spirit. —Nikos Kazantzakis, *The Saviors of God*

There's an old saying that has come down through the mystical, Hermetic traditions that says, "As above, so below." The material world is only a shadow image of what is above and is not the true reality. The great philosopher Plato discussed this, saying that this world and everything in it is just a mere shadow, or inferior copy, of what is in a higher world.

This inferior material world may get back into the kingdom of God if we can realize our involvement here and succeed in our work. So far, however, we have struggled in the dark. What is it that prevents our success? In the Gnostic tradition it is believed that a demiurge or a false god is the one that actually created this material existence because it is inferior to God's wholeness and perfection. There are so many flaws in this material world, along with its suffering and cruelty, that the Gnostics wondered if an all-loving and powerful God would create such misery in the world. The answer, at least to the Gnostics, is that He did not. They believed in higher spiritual levels containing angels and other beings. In these higher realms, there were other entities, godlike entities, and one of them broke away from God and began to play God for himself. This material world was created in this broken, inferior way because the entity involved was nowhere near as powerful as the real God—unable to recreate a perfect system out of a shattered wholeness.

In contrast to my theory (which I hold to) of this reality being a personal quest or experiment by God Himself, involving consciousness, the Gnostics believed that our consciousness, as separate sparks of the divine, became trapped here when this blind "god" broke away. They claim we are trying to deliver our own godly sparks back home, where we belong, by becoming more conscious and working our way back. Alternatively, we could be "fallen ones" who, instead of being trapped by the main rebel, made a conscious choice with him to break away from God, thinking we could do it better among ourselves. We are now paying the price. If that is the case, we must earn our way back, through various lifetimes and karmic cleansings, trapped in a cycle that is difficult to escape.

Either of these two theories are plausible, more so than standard explanations, and I am much in line with them except for the idea of a lower, imperfect God as Creator. This I believed for many years and my Gnostic friends and students may be disappointed in this change of thought. If the material world has more of a basis in consciousness than previously thought—discovered by quantum physics—then its creation is aligned with the Godly forces of consciousness that we all share in. My research into consciousness and my separate intuitive insights have led me into the acceptance of us having a more direct and personal connection to God, via consciousness. If we accept our collective consciousness as coming from or even *being* God, and this same overseeing consciousness is responsible for material creation, as accepted through some theories in advanced science, then an intermediary, rebel or ignorant God is removed from the picture. In other words, some segments of modern science have eclipsed the purely Gnostic view of a creator God and I am open to accepting that.

> *Mind no longer appears as an accidental intruder into the realm of matter; we are beginning to suspect that we ought rather to hail it as the creator and governor of the realm of matter...* —Sir James Jeans

It is not possible to create a perfect world at such a dense and low vibration. This world is terribly imperfect and to Gnostics it does not reflect the work of a perfect and/or compassionate creator. However, in order to carry out the work of consciousness, then matter, and its resulting opposites, cruelties, and imperfections *had to be created*. Imperfection is the testing ground for both free will and experience. Without flaws and dangers there would be no free will, choices, experiential events, discoveries or spiritual advancement. Nothing could be explored or experienced in a world without contrasting opposites—and that is the whole point. One cannot actually know beauty or perfection without *experiencing* its opposite. Take a moment, close your eyes, and experience some deep breaths. Be grateful for life, with both the good and the bad, the love and the pain, and use them to their fullest.

Matter and spirit work in completely opposite ways in the world. Because we are so focused on the material, there is a huge chasm, or separation, between us and God. It was by design. Matter is of a far lower vibration than spirit. When we come here and enter into this low vibration, we lose direct touch with the spirit, but we do not lose touch with it completely. It is always there. Most of us, throughout our entire lives, remain completely unconscious of the spirit and our true potential. But we all have a direct connection to God. It's there. This physical vibration is so low that we do not relate to this higher connection or identify with it very easily. Most people think we have lost this connection to God and must speak out through prayer and look outside of ourselves to get it back, but it is something that is *totally with us* at all times, staring us right in the face. We are just too blind to see it.

In today's world we live in the spiritual dark ages. Only later will it dawn on us who, in fact, we really are, where we really come from and why we are actually here. None of this we seem to know, at least to any degree that will cause our lives to be filled with unquestioned purpose. Those few who are able to get on this path are "following their bliss," as termed by the great mythologist Joseph Campbell. For those who are following their bliss and know that they're on the path that was meant for them, everything resonates with them, rather than aggravates, and falls into place perfectly. The spirit is calm. There is no worry or anxiety. Their energy field does not allow disruption. They are completely comfortable in their own skins, but these people are few and far between.

Most people don't have this and feel that something is not quite right. They are always yearning for something, never knowing quite what it is. This is where desires come in and completely take over. Temporary answers appear, but they are short-lived. Because we do not consciously know what it is we are supposed to be looking for, we immediately think that each desire that comes up *must* be what we need, because we desire it. As a result, people remain focused on the various worldly distractions out there that lead away from a true spiritual existence.

> *To pretend to satisfy one's desires by possessions is like putting out a fire with straw.* —Chinese Proverb

Everyone wants a bigger car or they want a better house or they want a big screen TV. They want a whole myriad of things—a better computer, video games, the best designer clothes, you name it. The list is growing exponentially. And what we might eventually learn from this is that the desires will never be quenched. If you are on this never-ending treadmill of desire, then once you achieve one thing that you want, you will always want more. And it will never stop. That's part of the mechanism of the trap, this whole material existence. We *want* more things because we are unconsciously trying to get everything back together again, to make things whole again, or complete. Those on higher spiritual paths recognize that they must complete *themselves* first, so set out on an alternative inner journey.

It's a huge trap being here in this material world, but at the same time it's an opportunity to work at spiritual development. When you work in a spiritual sense here in the material world, then you are fulfilling your destiny. In such cases you would be following your bliss, and there is purpose in that. That is the true answer. You can only achieve true happiness by following your heart, by following your bliss. Anything short of this means that you are cheating yourself and denying yourself of your own destiny. William Jennings Bryan once said, "Destiny is not a matter of chance, it is a matter of choice; it is not a thing to be waited for, it is a thing to be achieved." Go out and *achieve* your destiny; waiting for it postpones it forever.

There is much violence, misery and greed in this world. People in power are pushing their own limited, shortsighted agendas from within a failing paradigm. They believe if they can change others to follow their materialistic world view, more control and profits will result and people will fall in line with the agenda. But when everyone is trying to manipulate everyone else, nobody is really happy. There are not enough physical resources available when control of them all is the key issue among competing countries and corporations. The key to happiness has nothing to do with manipulating people and resources. How much suffering, cruelty and lack of compassion do we need to heap upon one another in order to demonstrate that the way we live is with absolute insanity? When physical existence is played out in a non-spiritual fashion, nobody wins. Once we fully realize this, once we finally *get it*, only then will we act.

This paradigm must shift before everyone can start winning and experiencing a planet that offers mutual respect and gratifying relationships between all peoples of the world. And this paradigm will never shift until people's thinking shifts. Our thinking must shift into a more spiritual form. It's not going to happen overnight—it's going to take some planning and in-depth thinking about how to shift this, in part, with an educational process. It has to start somewhere, and education is a major key.

Who on the world scene has the power to do something about this? Who is going to step forward? This is a call for action—but so far it's been ordinary people who have had the vision and determination to answer it. Lasting change works best from the bottom up, so a growing influence will continue. When you go up against an entire paradigm where all of the people who are operating it have a vested interest in every single facet of the materialistic mindset, and its greed and prison-like control on both them and us (since they're in a prison of their own making), then it is difficult to make any progress. Things will happen slowly until it is decided at higher levels, among world players, movers and shakers who have the money and the influence, to actually do something. Those who act will be the visionaries; the first to see the inevitable shift and to devise a stake in it. Only then, when someone steps forward in this regard, will others join in who can shift things more quickly, as we've seen in the past. The slow part, from a grass roots level, is already having an effect.

The first major players who act will probably be considered crazy by their peers. They may even lose their lives if they have enough power to install measures that could effect some of their cohorts throughout the world in a negative economic fashion. Yet, these people are smart enough to know how to put things in motion in a deliberate and careful enough fashion so that negative repercussions will not occur swiftly. After all, those at the top of the world scene have become so powerful over international economic systems, having done it over a slow and gradual acquisitional campaign, that it is now clear that other goals could follow a similar pattern, if needed. A little research into our current world economic structure will show that relatively few people own the vast majority of the largest corporations in the world.

If you want to call that the New World Order, then so be it. The sad part of this is that the agenda of such a system has nothing to do with spirituality, and that is what is urgently needed at this point in time. It may seem that such a paradigm shift is impossible to achieve or is far from occurring for the moment. Yet shifts of this nature can happen quickly—like the fall of the Soviet Union or the Berlin Wall coming down, which were both big steps toward freedom that happened quite fast. Powerful economic systems always end up crashing, eventually. There is a built-in shelf life that lasts only so long, unable to bear its own weight when inflation reaches an unsustainable cap, and we are nearing the expiration date of today's version. Only secrecy and behind-the-scenes manipulations keep many facets of the economic system strung together today. More self-sustaining, cooperative systems whereby everyone is more concerned with each other rather than themselves, stand a far better chance at surviving over the long-term.

This is not a sales pitch for socialism or communism. Based on spiritual values, who knows exactly what kind of system would develop or evolve? That is for us to discover as we go; but we can learn from those who brought forth spiritual success in the past. Mahatma Gandhi developed and promoted a concept called *swadeshi*. This is a self-acting law requiring a person to identify himself with the entire creation. This means being conscious enough to recognize a connection to all things; to see things holistically. According to Gandhi, the first duty of one with this mindset is to dedicate himself to his immediate neighbors. If prominent members in each community would focus in such a way, it would spread. A tremendous cohesion would result, along with local wealth, brotherly love, teamwork and a strong sense of community. This would create the fabric for a new economic paradigm, right within your hometown—one that could replace the current paradigm that is destroying innocent lives and the environment on a world scale. With such a system in place we would no longer feel helpless and would no longer *be* helpless. Each of us would command more power. We would be proactive, with more direct control of our economic success. An amazing synergy would result and we would be far less dependent on unseen forces.

A great example of this is the new explosion of CSA farming, which stands for Community Supported Agriculture. It has spawned an entire movement sweeping the country and although it might not have been inspired by Gandhi's *swadeshi*, it could very well have been. This is when individuals, families or restaurants prepay a local farm in early spring for a certain weekly percentage of its yield. Depending on the size of the farm, hundreds if not thousands take part, insuring the freshest of food with the knowledge of exactly where it comes from. I know of a local restaurant that gets fresh produce in this way every single morning for their customers. Since most of these farms are organic, people have the knowledge that there are no pesticides, chemicals, or preservative coatings in or on their food. This setup also saves on costs to industry and the environment by eliminating the fuel and transportation to markets, and gives the local economy a big boost, especially in the face of so many farms going under. Between the years 2003 to early 2008 CSAs in the U.S. almost doubled—going from 1000 to 1800 farms. If short on investment money, some CSAs offer work shares, so if you help out on the farm they will pay you with an equivalent percentage of food. If there is no CSA farm near you, go to your local Farmer's Market and seek out the organic food. Either way, *you save money* by cutting out the middleman and purchasing directly from local farmers, who need your support.

This is a good alternative to supermarket foods from out of the country laced with pesticides or poisons, or that have wax coatings or unhealthy preservatives meant to keep it from rotting before it reaches your table. Wax coatings keep the pesticides and herbicides from washing away, locking them in so you eat them, while organic foods contain higher levels of key nutrients. Another thing to keep in mind is that this local approach could be directed toward other goods and services—not just food. A strong local approach is a good response to globalist multi-national power, which makes us more dependent upon a system that is unhealthy, unfair and exploitational. Aside from education, food choices are a good avenue for change, because we all need food and can therefore have a collective impact if we choose to act, and eat, wisely. This puts control of your own personal health and the control of the local economy back into the hands of the people.

Water, the Key to Life
The one thing we should concern ourselves with most is water. Water is our lifeblood, without it we are dead, and hidden powers and organizations are taking steps to control as much of the future water supply as possible. Whoever controls our water, especially when in short supply, controls our lives.

What is the future of this most precious resource? Saudi Arabia, with its huge oil profits, has built a number of desalinization plants—converting salt water into fresh water—but the costs are enormous. As this is being written a similar plant is being built in Southern California and it seems that, despite the costs, this may be our only viable answer to current massive contamination and future water shortages. The filtering process in most cities fails to eliminate endocrine disrupting chemicals, which people ingest, pass through their bodies, and end up in the water at the sewage treatment plants. These chemicals include pesticides, pharmaceuticals, hormones, steroids, antibiotics and industrial compounds. We drug our water, flush it and then drink it again—adding more contaminants with each cycle. In isolated amounts, it may not be worth mentioning; but continually ingesting these things over time shows evidence (through initial animal testing) of causing genetic problems, birth defects, and sterility. Tests in major U.S. and Canadian cities show this contamination to be a widespread problem, proving that we have completely trashed most of our cities' water supplies. What about more rural areas? In the year 2000, the U.S. Geological Survey tested 139 streams in 30 states and found that 80 per cent of them showed measurable levels of contamination, including birth control pills, sunscreen, estrogen replacement drugs, insect poisons, and hundreds of other drugs and chemicals. Bottled water is not immune—in fact, many people are beginning to forego it in favor of investing in major, super-charged filtering systems for their taps. One word of advice. Get the best.

The coming desalinization plants could be an answer to this problem—if we can afford them. The question is, who ultimately will foot the bill and who, in turn, will we be beholden to for the most important thing we need for our lives? Also, will only those who can afford the higher costs of water, based on the desalinization process and construction costs, be able to get it? As the world gets more controlled by fewer people, just remember the saying that power corrupts, and absolute power corrupts absolutely. As both the economic and environmental crisis deepen every day, it has become clear that those who hold the most influence over world affairs have made improper choices. It is time for voices of sanity to be heard and for us to take charge of things like our water. To be heard, one must not merely speak—or even shout—but should *take action.*

If local successes can occur in all corners of the globe through the general philosophy of Gandhi's *swadeshi*, while maintaining the prerequisite holistic mindset that it entails, then we will advance through leaps and bounds into a healthier and more productive future.

Chapter Nine

CONTROL OF THE SOUL

Let me admonish you, first of all, to go alone; to refuse the good models, even those which are sacred in the imagination of men, and dare to love God without mediator or veil.
— Ralph Waldo Emerson

Whoever drinks from a well by reason of its being dug by his ancestors, and rejects the holy water of the Ganges, even when placed before him, is an incorrigible simpleton.
—Valmiki, author of *Yoga Vasishtha Maharamayana*, circa 600 BCE

Over the years we have created powerful diversions away from the spiritual truths we've been seeking. Sincere efforts have been made through religion and we cannot discount the true wisdom it has brought forth. Yet history bears out the existence of a dark side to our religious fervor. As far as murdering and butchering other people is concerned, more people have been killed in the name of God than for any other reason. God is and has been the main excuse used by every powerful religion in the world to kill other humans who refuse to believe as they do. An all-loving God would have nothing to do with this. The all-loving God, that really is there, is detached from us so we may have free will and learn lessons on our own—otherwise the lessons will not be learned. The gift of free will does offer freedom, but a huge streak of cruelty follows us in its wake. Before we pay too massive a price, we should examine the big picture and ask ourselves, at what cost must we learn these lessons?

Each religion has what is commonly termed a belief system. Every religion is surrounded by their beliefs and a system of belief. That is the engine of what a religion is; that's the fuel for what a religion is. Everyone is asked, "Do you believe in God? Do you believe in life after death? Do you believe in sin? Do you believe in..." And that's what is composed of our religions. They are not of the pure spirit from above, forming a direct experience to

God—a priest's function, and therefore the religion, is that of your mediator. Religions are formatted and structured by man. Each of us creates our own beliefs just as religions have done, so beliefs are pushed on to us by religions in order to make us conform to their particular standards. On a spiritual level, it works much differently. When we get in touch with that deeper part of ourselves, there are no beliefs being called into question. When something powerful happens on a spiritual level, you either know it or you don't. There is a saying that goes, "You are forced to believe until you get to know." If given a choice, which would you prefer?

An example would be the near-death experience. Our religions tell us that we go to heaven after we die, but only if we're good. So religions tell us that after death there is something out "there," a place that we go to. This is only a belief until, like anything, we experience something to confirm it. The near-death experience (NDE) has people briefly crossing over to the other side, following a white light—in many cases to a destination where they are greeted by loved ones, friends or family, and are often given a choice. Would they like to stay and continue with the incredible peace, joy and bliss they are experiencing, outside of whatever pain their physical body might be having, or do they want to go back and finish some kind of life mission? Those who come back often chose to come back, or have been told that it is not their time yet. But the interesting part of all this is that when someone comes back to this life after having a near-death experience, they are no longer afraid of dying because now they *know* that there is something more and that we live on after we pass from this world. Knowledge has replaced the belief. As a result, fear and uncertainty vanish. Therefore, it becomes clear that religions need fear and uncertainty to survive while direct spiritual knowledge, or *gnosis*, does not. Direct spiritual knowledge dispels fear and uncertainty, while belief systems actually need them to control you.

If we can train ourselves as a culture from an early age to contact the spiritual part of ourselves, then solid spiritual truths will become more self-evident in our culture, and people will act accordingly. They will act more responsibly, more from the spirit than from the materialistic mindset. Our current mindset conditions us to want more, more, and more, and certain elements of greed and the ego take over. Transforming society for the better begins with transforming the self for the better, and preparing ourselves for an individual transformation is the key. It will become a trend for individuals to "transform" and, in time, larger chunks of society will take notice and follow. This transformation is not going to come from a political movement, it's not going to come from a religious movement, and it's not going to come from scientific breakthroughs. We need to stop depending on these outside agencies of "authority" and look within ourselves.

Science has proven that there is a spiritual realm. Quantum physics shows there is a crossover or a meeting point between science and the spirit. As far as progress is concerned, science can point the way, rather brilliantly, but is not going to infuse any transformative power directly into your life. It will not do this for us. We need to do it for ourselves. The spirit is the innermost part of us, and we need to learn how to access that and work with it. It's not going to come from some scientific formula—yet science has been the most positive and supportive area for the spirit in recent years. It has not been found in religion to any degree of importance, and it certainly has not been found in politics.

Science could prove me wrong and develop new ways to access the spirit and allow us to work with it. We cannot discount that, but no matter what breakthroughs might occur it is hard to imagine any of them transcending the use of our own human volition and free will. We must do this for ourselves. If we can actually identify the soul part of us someday and in some way, we still will not be able to substitute a true spiritual experience with the ability to stand there, point to the soul and say, "there it is." The soul must be used.

For example, in a restaurant we look at the menu, find something we like and say, "This looks good." If the menu looks good and sounds appetizing, we do not eat the menu. We must experience the real food to sustain ourselves. We must order the food and actually eat it. This is what we're also doing with television these days. We are, in the proverbial sense, mistaking a cardboard menu for food. We are substituting the real world and the life that we should be living in place of staring at a *box* that is living our lives for us.

Maintaining a True Path

We are cheating ourselves out of so much in this world because we are not being true to the spirit and to the life that we are meant to be living. It's time to wake up and start being true to ourselves and start living a genuine life. Those who do this may find that it is lonely at times, not being able to sit with your family or loved ones and stare blankly at a box, but there is no better feeling than being true to yourself. There is no substitute for that.

Television should not be completely abandoned because, if used correctly, it can be a great learning tool and a window to the world. However, due to the addictive tendencies of the public, the manipulation of advertisers to an often insulting degree, the hypnotic brain-changing waves of the picture and its negative effects, especially on children, and the major role TV plays in the deliberate dumbing down of the population, people should be very discerning. Most aren't.

I once saw a one-frame comic strip showing thousands upon thousands of lemmings that are going over the cliff. These small, mouse-like creatures are blindly committing suicide by the thousands by rushing over the cliff without even looking. And yet, there's one who is going the opposite way saying, "Excuse me. Excuse me. Excuse me." And that's the feeling you get on such a path because it is a very lonely thing—but it's also more genuine and far less self-destructive. Just because you're one of the crowd does not mean that is the most beneficial thing. Being like everyone else is not necessarily the best thing to strive for. Being a sheep and part of the flock simply makes you another number. These types of people just go along to get along. People, in general, are lazy. They do not want to stick their necks out for any reason unless they are *awake* and *aware*, have developed a certain passion for the truth and know that it's worth fighting for.

Looking back at the Revolutionary War at the beginnings of the United States, you'll find that those who stood up to the British and stood up for their rights were the ones who were willing to stick their necks out. It was a huge risk. The vast majority of people—and this is a fact—were completely against them. They thought these freedom fighters were crazy. But these were *revolutionaries*, and that is why it was called the Revolutionary War. It took revolutionary actions to make a change that was to stand the test of time. These people were brilliant. They were visionaries. Thomas Jefferson, Benjamin Franklin, John Adams, and especially Thomas Paine were the most brilliant people of their time. Yet few wanted to listen to what they were saying, including those in the original colonies. Although lesser numbers backed them, they were able to awaken enough people, and just enough people, to make the change. And thank God that change was able to give freedom to a country that so desperately needed it, whereby people could actually come and enjoy freedoms to a degree that they had never even imagined before. The founding of America was an amazing and brilliant piece of work. If any of the founding fathers had been caught, the British would have hanged them and the masses would have allowed it to happen.

Today we do not have such life-threatening dangers for those willing to be catalysts for positive change, at least in most cases; so where are the revolutionaries of today? We need them. What we need these days are spiritual revolutionaries. We need a *Spiritual Revolutionary* slogan in this culture—on tee shirts, etc., used throughout an entire movement by those willing to contribute to a better world, through spiritual means, who will *truly take action*.

But today, just like back then, the general masses have no vision. It's about time that the masses were put in touch with a spiritual part of themselves to give them vision because then, and only then, will the world really start to change in positive ways. Amazing things can happen. Just ask the founding fathers. We have so much potential inside of us and it will never be realized unless we are willing to work for it, dig deep, and get rid of this laziness we have that makes us just "go along to get along," like sheep.

If you want to make a difference with your life, find or expand your purpose, and follow a path you know deep in your heart was meant for you. Then you will be the type of person who needs to step forward and become a catalyst for spiritual change—or an outright leader. Otherwise, everyone is just going to follow the herd, and we're all going to be sheep, or *treated like sheep*, whether we like it or not. It's going to take a grass-roots movement outside of politics, outside of religion, maybe with a little help from science; but it's going to come from the heart, from those who are willing to dig deep enough to make the change within themselves and help it spread to others.

> *Ask questions from the heart and you will be answered from the heart.* —Native American proverb

Otherwise, we're not going to move anywhere, and things are just going to stay as they are and humanity is not going to evolve in any significant way in the near future. We have experienced too many empty answers from our dependence on an economically driven paradigm that has no heart, no soul, or compassion. Clearly, however, when one looks at the big picture, it can be seen that we are evolving in a spiritual way. We are becoming a more compassionate people. We no longer burn people at the stake, throw them to the lions, or lock them in a stockade in the middle of the town square so people can pulverize them with rotten fruit. We are a little more compassionate in our treatment of those we don't like. At the same time, if our passions and angers are aroused, we can still be as vicious as we have been in the past. In spite of this, a certain kind of progress is underway. It's just a matter of how long it will take for us to fulfill our destiny. How long will it take for us to come to our senses and make the changes that need to happen? They are happening; we can see it from an historical perspective, and our increasing awareness can speed things up. There is an awakening that is starting to break through, or least *trying* to occur, but we are shutting it down and trading it off for all the material pursuits and entertainments that are being made available out there. We need to make a choice, so here is a question to consider.

Is it better to be educated or to be entertained?

How do you spend most of your time? Do you prefer to be titillated by reality TV or sitcoms, or do you prefer to challenge yourself by reading philosophy or developing a spiritual practice? Our entire culture is based on entertainments, and that's a huge distraction from what we are truly here for. We are here for a very important reason, and it's not to be entertained by the mindless diversions that we're poisoning ourselves with.

Finding clarity and purpose can actually be easy, but life demands more diversions from within this older paradigm. Everyone is content to let people suffer as long as they can continue to dip their hands into the cookie jar and grab their share of the pot. The system gives us more and more things to do just to stay healthy, try to make a living and keep food on our tables so that we have less and less time to discover how we are being controlled and manipulated. People often say that if we did not want these things, no one would be providing them to us. How convenient for an excuse. Most people buy into it, however, so things fail to change.

For those of us who do have enough leisure time aside from our jobs to investigate things and educate ourselves, there are diversions and entertainments that are created to keep us busy. Alcohol is worse than many prohibited substances, but most governments have legalized it and we can find a liquor store on almost every corner. Mindless computer games and prime time television insure that vast numbers of us accomplish very little toward changing the current paradigm. New reality-substitution computer games are appearing, whereby a computer maps your physical actions on a screen, like bowling for instance, and the result of your throw appears on a screen. Here's an even better idea. If you want to bowl, *go bowling*. Live your life for God's sake, instead of having a damn computer live it for you. Get some exercise. Otherwise, you will have the option of not even bothering with your body any longer. You'll just deposit your head into a steel bucket—for a fee of course—and hook up some electrodes to a computer and live your life that way—in some alternative existence—while you type fantasy-world instructions and cavort around blindly as you play it out, viewing your new life inside of a bucket. People will stampede over each just for the chance to try it. So it turns out that there is a very low percentage of people who are awake and aware enough to see what's really going on. And few of those have the time to actually do something about it.

Things are happening on a cosmic scale here. It is of major importance, what is being played out here. But if you want to sit home and watch prime-time television and drink a few beers and laugh at a few stupid TV shows, well, then, that's your prerogative. Go ahead and waste your life. Be my guest. But at least now, you can't say that you weren't warned. If, after you pass on and it comes time to meet your maker, and you're reviewing your life, and you suddenly realize that you've wasted your life, that you've gotten involved in all of the materialistic acquisitions, and tried to acquire all the material things, and pursued all the entertainments, and not given anything back to the world in a positive sense, but you were just here consuming and enjoying yourself and not trying to better anything or anyone else except yourself in a greedy fashion, and all this suddenly dawns on you, then don't say that you were not warned. You could say, "Oh, yeah. I listened to this Paul Tice guy and it seemed a little interesting, kind of cool, but then after it was over, I went back to sleep. I just fell back to sleep again. Sorry."

Chapter Ten

ASTROLOGICAL AGES

Spiritual struggle seems likely to be the most crucial episode in the next chapter of the history of mankind.
—Arnold Toynbee

The time for an unavoidable change may, in fact, be coming. If we know where to look, there are signs; so let us look at an even bigger and more interesting picture. When we examine the historical pattern of astrological ages, we see that changes are now on the horizon and that something larger than what we normally can conceive of is unfolding. Although what I present is not scientifically solid, the correlations and coincidences are so intriguing that they must be brought out.

The development of astrology predates the Bible, dating to Babylonia and the Chaldeans at least as far back as 1600 BCE, but probably earlier. It is an offshoot of astronomy, which predates all written history and shows evidence of being practiced as early as 15,000 BCE. Instead of clocks or calendars, we used the sky to tell time, predict the seasons, determine when to plant and harvest, and could even foretell eclipses. Entire mythologies sprang up with each great culture, based on the constellations, and were used to teach lessons of wisdom to the people.

When people ask us today what sign we are, it corresponds to twelve separate astrological parts of the year in which we were born, each similar to months in length—for example, Pisces, Gemini, Taurus, or Capricorn. A professional astrologer who does charts will show you a circle with the entire canopy of stars in the sky, broken up into the twelve separate "houses" in a 360-degree astrological map. Your horoscope is cast based on a personal reading from this chart, determined largely in part from your time and place of birth in conjunction with the location of the planets and their expected influence at the time.

From a cosmic level, rather than a personal one, our sun moves through the entire galaxy, through twelve different areas of the sky, astrologically speaking, and it takes about 2160 years for us to move through each of these twelve cycles, separately. It is called the precession of the equinoxes. Western minds credit this discovery to the Greek philosopher Hipparchus in 128 BCE, but most ancient cultures preceding this date still knew about it. They just lacked the ability to accurately measure it, which is what Hipparchus did. The idea originated in ancient Chaldea, and then spread in ancient times to Egypt, where it was clearly understood, and into the holy land. Some scholars present convincing evidence that the precession was accurately known and measured in Egypt long before Hipparchus. These scholars include Sir Norman Lockyer, Maspero, Schwaller de Lubicz, Carl Jung, Graham Hancock, Robert Bauval, and Giorgio de Santinilla, former professor of the history and philosophy of science at MIT and author of *Hamlet's Mill*, among others. The main point, however, is that these ages do occur and this fact alone cannot be disputed.

The lengthy astrological ages that we pass through on earth take the same names as the twelve astrological signs and houses that we acknowledge within a yearly basis. The completion of all twelve cycles composes a "great year" of 25,920 years. Please note that each 2160-year age is a rough estimate. Astrology is not an exact science, as each constellation we pass through varies in size, and God did not draw distinct borders around each one. Different astrologers have differing dates for past ages, sometimes varying within two to three hundred years of each other. They are still fairly close to each other and it must be remembered that we enter into these new ages gradually.

After we finish one age, we move into a new sign. And right now, at the time of this writing, the sign that we are in is Pisces. It is the sign of the fish and, of course, the fish is the universal symbol for Christianity, which has been the dominating religion of this age. Upon looking back in my extensive research and examining each major religion or philosophy that existed in the world at the time of each corresponding astrological sign that we were in, I found a match. After coming to what I thought was a new and exciting conclusion in this respect, I found a section in the great Manly P. Hall's work *The Secret Teachings of All Ages*, where he said, "During these periods or *ages*, religious worship takes the form of the appropriate celestial sign—that which the sun is said to assume as a personality in the same manner that a spirit assumes a body. These twelve signs are the jewel of his breastplate and his light shines forth from them, one after the other.... Thus the sun in its path controls whatever form of worship man offers to the Supreme Deity."

For example, the age of Taurus, the bull, was from about 4220 BCE to about 2160 BCE. Virtually every ancient religion during this time was affiliated with the bull, either as a sacrificial offering to the gods or by being the main object of worship. In Crete, there were sacred bull dances and the legend of the minotaur was born. In India, Parjanya was the bull god of the Vedas but when things transitioned into the age of Aries, a ram figure began to displace him and the populace became divided. Civil war was the result. In fact, the sun gods of most religions were depicted with the head or horns of a bull, but after passing into Aries they were all replaced with ram-headed ones. In Egypt the main solar deity during this time was considered to assume the body of a bull, known as Apis. In Egypt, as in Assyria and elsewhere, the cult of the bull was followed by the cult of the ram and both usage of symbols corresponded with the ages of Taurus and Aries, respectively.

The age of Aries was from about 2160 BCE to about 1 BCE, which was represented astrologically by the ram. In Egypt, we find the priest-kings of the Middle Kingdom to be followers of Amon, the ram-headed god. This was also the age of the Hebrew religion. During the early transitional phase from Taurus, however, the bull was still worshipped by the Hebrews. Before being phased out and replaced by the ram for the remainder of the age, bull shrines existed in Bethel, Gilgal, Schechem and Shiloh. The well-known Old Testament event involving the worship of the golden calf was a reversion back into the old ways of Taurus that was not tolerated, and brought great wrath down upon the people. Abraham was a key Hebrew figure in this age and his original name was Abram—coincidentally containing the English word "ram" within it. It is believed that he lived sometime around 2000 BCE, when Aries was dawning. In a key Biblical moment, Abraham sacrificed a ram instead of his son, Isaac (see Genesis 22:13). A young ram is of course a lamb and lambs were held sacred during this time, often sacrificed, along with sheep and goats, on the altars. The observance of Passover was instituted during this time, when lamb's blood was painted on the doors of Israelites to protect them from a plague. Judaism itself is symbolized by the ram's horn and its' priests were referred to as *shepherds*, whose job it was to tend their "sheep."

The age of Pisces came next and began at about the time of Jesus. In Luke 2:8-17 we find the *shepherds* abandoning their "sheep" in favor of their new savior. We were crossing over from the age of Aries—being partially still in it, but coming into Pisces—so Jesus held aspects of both ages. In his early life, at the end of the age of Aries, he was called "the lamb of God." After he was baptised, he was always associated with fish. Today we are nearing the end of the age of Pisces, represented throughout by the fish, astrologically, which remains the symbol or sign for Christianity. This symbol is seen everywhere in this respect—for example Christians commonly put a small metal version on the backs of their cars. The pope is supposed to be the Earth's representative for Jesus until his return. When worn, the pope's headdress or mitre looks exactly like the head of a fish when viewed sideways instead of at the normal perpendicular angle.

In Luke 2:12, an angel tells the shepherds that their *sign* for the new Messiah would be a baby lying wrapped in a manger, and soon after, in Luke 2:35, Simeon tells mother Mary that, "This child is destined to be a *sign* which men reject." (italics mine) That sign, astrologically, was of course Pisces, the fish. With Jesus representing it at a time of transitioning ages he was, in fact, rejected by the authorities to the point of crucifixion.

In the Jewish Talmud, the coming Messiah is called Dag, meaning "the fish." It was, and is, the sign for divinity. Jesus was referred to as "the fisher of men," and the symbolic Greek name for Christ was *Ichthus*, meaning "the fish." He fed the multitudes with two fish, and many Christians to this day eat fish on Friday. In the Second Century, Clement urged fish to be engraved upon the seals of Christians so they would not be mistaken for pagans, and during the first four centuries of Christianity Jesus was referred to as "the big fish," while Christians were called *Pisiculi*, or "the little fishes." Symbols of Jesus as a fish rather than a man were common—both in household objects and in artistic depictions found on the walls of the Roman catacombs. When it was dangerous to be a Christian and two people met, one would draw a curved line in the sand and the other, if a Christian, would draw the other, forming a fish, letting them know they could trust each other.

Lastly, Jesus himself said he would always be with us, but only until the end of the age.

> ...teaching them to observe all that I have commanded you; and lo, I am with you always, to the close of the age."
> (Matt.28:20, Revised Standard Version)

This has been translated in various ways, including "to the end of the world" and "until the end of time," but it has been shown that "the close of the age" is the most accurate rendering of the original wording. The main word in question comes from the original Greek word, "Aeon," which is most accurately translated as "age" in *Strong's Bible Concordance* or in any good dictionary. The Revised Standard Version of the Bible had, as its mission, to start again with new knowledge and translate everything from scratch as accurately as possible. In its Preface it states, "The King James Version of the New Testament was based upon a Greek text that was marred by mistakes, continuing the accumulated errors of fourteen centuries of manuscript copying.... We now possess many more ancient manuscripts of the New Testament, and are far better equipped to seek to recover the original wording of the Greek text." Which they did. The implications of an accurately translated Matthew 28:20 (above) along with the intentional expunging of other clear astrological references in the Bible, make it no surprise that its original wording had been changed.

Today, the religion of Christianity seems to have weakened and continues to do so as we move closer to the end of this age. All dominant religions have experienced the same fate in relation to the length of a normal age, giving them an expected lifespan of about 2160 years.

The point is that we are at this time beginning to move into something new. That is where we get the term the New Age Movement. To those who remain steadfast in their religious beliefs, this term is used in a derogatory sense, due to the threat of extinction that it brings. Many who place their entire identities with their faith find the idea of a New Age intolerable. Yet, as shown, this is part of a pattern, and this New Age is becoming stronger and more evident as we move closer to the year 2160. Some respected astrologers or researchers expect the arrival of the new Aquarian Age to occur sooner. For example, 2060 is considered the more accurate date by noted astrologers Dane Rudyhar and Robert Hand, separately, as well as by Sir Isaac Newton, Carl Gustov Jung placed its official arrival from between 1997 and 2000.

The appearance of each new age is a gradual event, however. We will not wake up one day and suddenly find the New Age of Aquarius to be here. Its arrival, as with any such age, is moved into gradually. For example, back in the 1960's there was the popular song, "This is the Dawning of the Age of Aquarius." This may well have been the case, representing an initial dawning or glimmer, as opposed to a more obvious presence that will be more evident later.

Today, the entire New Age Movement has grown and is made up, in general, of very perceptive and spiritual people. Many hold opposing viewpoints to standard Christian religion and many other contemporary, modern faiths. They pose a threat to the fundamentalist Christian structure. Christianity feels a clear threat from the possibility of being replaced by something different. Many search the Bible for evidence or clues that could support their continued existence. One event that would clearly insure Christianity's survival would be the return of Jesus Christ; but after more than two thousand years of waiting it seems he is rather late. Despite these larger astrological patterns or ages, numerous places in the Bible warn against astrology and astrologers because it is supposedly evil. Church fathers and leaders have consistently blamed astrology on "demons" over the years, and modern Christians have been trumpeting their warnings more often because time is growing short. A new age will be upon us soon.

Every single time these astrological ages have ended, a new form of religion has stepped in. A number of reputable scholars have pointed out the fact that all of the prophecies that were made regarding the return of Jesus actually happened within the first hundred years after his death. Yet we have continued, for approximately 2000 years, to wait for his return. When will we fully get it? When does it finally sink in that he's not coming back, at least not in the physical form that everyone is expecting? This is like waiting for a bus. You go to the bus station, sit down and wait for the bus. How long do you wait before it finally dawns on you that it's not coming? Are you going to sit there in the terminal and wait for six years for a bus and not find a way to still go about your business and continue your life? In this case we are talking about your *spiritual life*, which grows stagnant when nothing happens.

> *He who waits for God fails to understand that he possesses Him.* —Andre Gide

Jesus remains a symbolic figure and the fact is not disputed that he has shown great value to many people on a spiritual level. I would never say that Christianity has had no value, but its time is running out. It has been part of a natural cycle that is ending. It is time that new symbols come in and refresh the world in a New Age. It's always happened in the past, and it's going to continue to happen in the future. We may not know the reason for it, but our religious and cultural patterns have continued to coincide, at least in a general way, with the successive signs in the precession of the equinoxes. There's a far bigger picture at work here that goes beyond our limited view. We need to step aside from our jingoistic, dogmatic, egotistical, pea-brained point-of-view and look at the bigger picture.

The New Age that's coming is the Age of Aquarius and its symbol is the man with the water pitcher. Its main element or focus of symbolic power is referred to as "the waters of eternal life," coming from the water pitcher that is poured. Well-known researcher Jordan Maxwell points out an interesting astrological passage which comes from the Bible. (Despite the Bible's warnings against astrology, there are a great number of Biblical passages that use it.) In Luke 22:7 through 22:10, the disciples asked Jesus where they should go to prepare a meal for Passover so that they may eat. And Jesus said to them, "Behold, when you have entered the city, a man will meet you carrying a pitcher of water. Follow him into the house which he enters."

This is definitely symbolic. They are preparing for a "Passover" (from one age to the next) and the man with the water pitcher is the symbol for the next age—of Aquarius. It is absolutely not a literal statement because at the time of Jesus, men did not carry water. It was strictly women's work. About this man, Jesus says, "Follow him into the house which he enters." And that is of course the next astrological house, Aquarius, where they will be nourished. This same story can also be found in Mark 14:13. In both cases Jesus tells them that once they pass into that house, they will be shown a large upper room, furnished and prepared, there made ready for us. Notice it says that it is an upper room, meaning it is the next one above us as we continue on through this astrological sequence.

This passage points to the future, where we may find nourishment following an age that does not claim to offer an ultimate answer, but serves more as a stepping stone. Jesus was not saying "follow me." He said to follow the man with the water pitcher. For those who insist on clinging to a fading age and its religion, it might be a good idea to heed these words of Jesus, as far as spiritual growth goes, and to follow the man with the water pitcher so that we do not miss the bus completely.

What can we expect in this New Age based on the Aquarian symbolism? When Jesus was baptised and became "awakened," he was baptised in water. The water is considered by some to be symbolic for eternal life or of mortality. I, however, consider the waters to represent a powerful spiritual rebirth. It represents an awakening for humanity.

Chapter Eleven

PARADIGM LOST

He who rides the tiger is afraid to dismount.
—Chinese Proverb

This world really is a flawed and bizarre place, and the paradigm in which we find ourselves has truly lost its way. If one can look at the world from a more spiritual perspective, then it becomes clear that the economic and material aspects of it are bordering on the brink of insanity. The influences and societal guidelines that we depend on as "authorities" have turned their power into a systematic, mechanistic machine that has hijacked our humanity. We live under the umbrella of a huge mechanistic marketing machine that demands we act as consumers first, rather than caring human beings. Television commercials will go to any absurd length to get people to buy something and they are an absolute insult to the average person's intelligence. Most television programs are as bad as the commercials.

What is it that we use mainly to educate ourselves? It is television. It was supposed to be for entertainment, but due to the hypnotic effects it produces, what we mainly "know" gets reflected back out from us in our behaviour after many hours, and even years, of its hypnotic sessions. The term "television programming" takes on an entirely new meaning. As a culture, we rely on it for the bulk of our knowledge. This is a frightening thing when you truly understand what is happening here. Hours upon hours a day, the average person watches a glimmering box which spews out things that are designed to change your thought patterns and make you obey. What is it going to take for people to stand up and say, "Enough! We've had enough of this ridiculous and insulting treatment!"?

The problem with that happening is that television is so hypnotic, it actually changes your brain waves into a state of submission. Why bother to think if something else can do it for you? The key to approaching this problem is to simply walk away. Saying, "I'm just going to watch this one show and then I'll stay away" doesn't work because by doing that, people end up glued to the television for one more, and one more, and one more. Studies show that the longer someone watches a television screen the more difficult it is for them to leave it because they get pulled deeper and deeper into the alpha state. This is referred to by researchers as the "zombie effect." To many people, alpha waves are addicting. This kind of behaviour is the perfect telltale sign for addictive behaviour—and television out-does any other form of drug, alcohol, or other abusive substance as far as addiction goes. And yet, nobody sees it—or rather, wants to see it.

An alien race from another galaxy, looking down on us and seeing our behaviour, would immediately be stunned at our incredible stupidity. It's a safe bet to say that a number of them are avoiding us until the day finally comes when we wake up. Of course, television is only a small part of the problem here on Earth, but it makes sure to beam the magnitude of our stupidity to every corner of the universe. Our TV signals have been beamed out into the galaxy, traveling at an awesome speed, so that anyone capable of receiving and understanding them light years away will be able to do so. What better way to become the laughing stock of the universe? Have you ever gone to school and seen a shameless goofball kid walking around with the word "idiot" emblazoned on his forehead? That's us.

After 15 years of working in the television industry, I quit. I have witnessed, on the ground-floor level, what is planned behind the scenes when broadcast material is prepared to go out on the air. It's geared mostly toward marketing because, just like radio, the commercials support the station. When you are targeted as a market for television, that means they are attempting to control you. They are attempting to control what you buy, what you think, and how you spend your hard-earned money. It's mostly large corporations that are selling these products and they don't care as much about your personal safety as they do about making a profit.

Profits Over Health

The drug companies are a perfect example. Time after time, we find medicines put on the market prematurely because a patent had been developed for it that allows its complete control in order to reap big profits. The medicine is rushed into production without full testing, people get sick or die, and lawsuits result. But when a foreign company (meaning a competitor) or a natural product that cannot be patented actually works, everything is done to stall or prevent its availability until their own synthetic and controllable version is made. In the meantime, people are forced to suffer or die because corporations would rather make money for themselves instead of helping those who are suffering.

When you look at all the chemicals in the foods we eat, you would not willingly go into a chemical factory and say, "I want to ingest this one, this one, and this one right away, I can't wait" when, in fact, many of these chemicals are proven to cause cancer in the laboratory. They knowingly put this in our products. The sweetener aspartame, also known as Equal, NutraSweet and Spoonful, is known to cause cancer in animals according to the well-respected and peer-reviewed journal, *Environmental Health Perspectives*, among others. Tea, anyone? Sadly, most would say yes. Out of about 100 independent tests on aspartame, over 90% of them show *significant* health risks. It is currently found in many soft drinks and other food items but the FDA refuses to ban it, despite them receiving more complaints about it than any other food related product, ever. Do yourself a favor. Return any products you have that contain it to the store and demand a refund—many consider it poison. The free aspartic acid in aspartame (40% of the product) and the free glutamic acid found in MSG have both been shown to cause endocrine disorders and kill brain cells in laboratory animals. Searle and Company, who first produced aspartame, came out with their own test, known as the Waisman Study, stating that aspartame caused convulsions and death in primates. Many primates share over 99% of our DNA. They never completed this in-house study on their own product because they said the results were "faulty."

Since they do not test on people beforehand, to conclusively prove the dangers, the products are allowed to be sold. Which begs the question, why is the testing and torturing of animals done on these products, if they do not use the data toward human consumption issues? I once bought ice cream that tasted sour and the vendor said he tasted it ahead of time for years, testing each new batch to be sure his customers would be satisfied. He proudly stood by his product and refunded me. Do you think the makers of aspartame or MSG would be willing to eat equal amounts of their product fed to lab animals so their customers can be sure of their safety? Anyone who puts a product out in the marketplace should be willing to stand by it in this way.

Trans fat causes heart disease and is loaded in many baked goods and sweets. Nobody is stupid enough to walk in and order trans fat to ingest it unless of course there is a little cookie on top of it. The cookie is to make you eat it. No one's going to go in and buy these chemicals willingly, but if you disguise it in a cute little cookie, people will eat them by the truckloads. *Except the owners who market it.*

Fluoride, in most toothpaste and now in most of our water supply, was a rat poison during World War II. Sodium laurel sulfate, a known carcinogen, is found in most of our shampoos as its primary foaming agent. Do you wash your hair every day? Do some research and check the labels before you buy because the cheapest manufacturing solutions, that make these companies the most money, are manufactured and sold at the expense of your health and welfare. The general public (us) is supposed to remain ignorant, spend our money, and when we get sick we're supposed to just keep our mouths shut and die quietly. We are being treated like sheep. We have being duped—all in the name of the almighty dollar. What is it going to take for us to wake up? When are we going to come to our senses and start *caring about ourselves?*

To live a spiritual life and to resonate in a pure and spiritual way, we must be free of all of the additives, unnatural sweeteners, chemicals, and all of the things that are not natural as foods. We were not designed to consume this crap and need to function without the encumbrances of a massive machine that is driven by the greed of the almighty dollar. Once again, everything is a vibration. And when you put things in your body that do not resonate with it in a natural way, then all of your healthy, vital signals become disrupted, and all of the electrical firings between the neurons in your body start going haywire—in different sporadic directions, causing disruption and disease as opposed to operating within a smooth and naturally functioning body.

Caring for Ourselves

It's time to start caring for ourselves and treating each other in respectful ways as opposed to ways geared strictly towards making money for those who would sacrifice our health. The consequences grow more critical with each passing day. No matter what business you are in it is time to take careful measure of results and implications for all people who not only respond to your marketing, but for those who don't. We are champions of shortsightedness, so therefore champions of self-destruction.

Currently, economists are debating whether or not we should invest in the prevention of global warming and climate change because it puts our own prosperity at stake. The investment is questioned, with all ethical concerns cast aside, because they forecast a more prosperous future in coming generations so that our children can take care of the problems later—when it potentially reaches epic proportions. How are the coming generations supposed to become so rich that they can handle these growing problems? By continuing the same trend of raping the planet, of course, but in a more exponential way. This is insanity in action—now with scientific backing (at least by some of them). We should have begun to handle these problems years ago, and yet we have people still sitting around creating charts and graphs all day, trying to "figure it out" on paper, so they don't have to *do* anything about it now. We need to take responsibility for what we've done and get busy, for God's sake. The main things we should do about global warming include cutting back on the production of methane from animals immediately, changing our diets, and creating cleaner alternative fuels and forms of transportation. Now. The longer we wait the less likely we will ever achieve a viable solution.

The owners and main stockholders of all the biggest companies (many of whom have a vested financial interest in the things that need to be changed or eliminated), have multiple homes around the world in exclusive spots like the French Riviera, Aspen, Dubai, Rio, or Monte Carlo while virtually everyone else struggles to make ends meet in modest homes at best, or in abject poverty. This would not be such a bad thing, but it happens at the hands of a system that is poisoning or slowly killing us.

Health and Medical Truths
In the medical field, most groundbreaking cures and medical advances are in fact suppressed or stonewalled for years because if we stay sick or in need of medication, the huge medical cartels can continue to grow rich from the world's misery. All it takes is a little time and research to see this for yourself.

The masses, in general, don't get the best doctors. If you get terribly sick they will send you home to die instead of curing you (when it is indeed possible to cure you) because insurance companies aren't about to foot these massive bills and you don't get the million-dollar paychecks. I met a San Diego woman who had liver cancer and they sent her home to die, saying there was nothing more they could do. Despite having just six weeks to live, she researched natural cures, made a tea from all the best anti-cancer agents she could find, drank it all day for months, and became well again. That was two years ago, and she is now marketing the tea that saved her, made from her own research. That is just one example out of millions of a death sentence issued by the medical cartel—but this woman was one of the lucky ones who survived because she refused to accept the verdict without investigating for herself. Her story is not uncommon; thousands have saved themselves with natural cures when traditional avenues had failed.

We are all in this together. There's a huge gap between the people who are actually running this world and owning these huge, multimillion-dollar companies and the vast majority of people who live in poverty or sink deeper into debt, and experience health problems without adequate cures. There is a population problem (based on improper use of resources), so the medical field is not in a big hurry to keep you alive unless you start tossing large amounts of money around.

Most people, if lucky enough to have health insurance, have these things called HMOs—Health Maintenance Organizations. The key word here is "maintenance." The system will do everything it can to maintain your health. Especially if you're sick—they will *maintain* you at that level, but rarely will they do anything to *improve* your health or cure you. An interesting book now out of print called *The Medical Mafia* reveals in detail how the health of patients comes secondary to the medical industry, which needs sickness to thrive. It was written by a French-Canadian medical doctor named Guylaine Lanctot, who apparently lost her medical license as a result of having written it. She cared enough to speak out and was punished for having compassion and a conscience.

It seems that the system in America often does operate in this fashion. For more information I highly recommend you watch Michael Moore's brilliant 2007 film, *Sicko*, which reveals the immense corruption and shortcomings of the current U.S. medical system. Hopefully, as a result of this kind of information being made available, we will stand up—as we rightfully should—and demand proper changes. Free national health care exists in such countries as England, France, Canada, Denmark and many others, while in the U.S. you are left to die—literally die—if you cannot afford an expensive treatment. This is true even if you are insured, because large insurance companies are notorious for finding loopholes and not covering you. A number of health insurance workers have confessed to their past misdeeds, stating that the more insured people they could deny coverage to, and save the company money, the more raises and promotions they would get. People died, and are still dying, as a result—after having begged the insurance companies *for their lives*, but were turned away due to small technicalities in their policies. However, doctors in countries with national health care, like England, are actually rewarded and make more money based on the number of people they *cure*, rather than turn away and don't help. What a concept! People who operate out of true kindness instead of greed and heartless deception.

Most of the medications you are given will not cure you. They will control the *symptoms* and that is what they want—to keep people sick, but with the symptoms under control. God forbid if you should actually get well, which many have done using natural cures that they must seek out on their own. If you don't, however, you have to keep coming back and buying the "system's" medications over and over again. And in many cases this medication is highly addictive. In the long run, it can ruin people's lives. I believe there are known cures for many common diseases and, yet, they are being held back because such cures don't fit the way the system runs.

While alive, your body truly is the temple of the soul. We need to take care of the body, not poison it. We are poisoning both our minds and our bodies at the expense of making those who run certain monopolies rich. We need to start an educational program that will begin to reverse this trend. Programs such as this, however, are always dismantled by those in power. The current system is financially designed to insist that you need these "band-aid" medications and the harmful chemicals and by-products in our foods. They are providing them to us not because we want them, but because they are *telling us* we want them and we in turn believe them. If we became a bit wiser and did not accept these things, they would not be providing them to us. Some

Paradigm Lost 165

companies have seen this void and have stepped up to provide, or attempt to provide, effective alternatives. Of course, their products often end up in foreign countries far earlier than in the U.S., due to the endless red tape or stonewalling tactics of the FDA (Federal Drug Administration).

Natural cures that have proven potency will often run into distribution problems while drug companies scramble to make a patented synthetic version that can be marketed for higher prices despite, in some cases, numerous side effects. For example, tryptophan, a natural relaxant and amino acid found in turkey, almonds and bananas was hugely popular in pill form for many years as an anti-depressant until a batch, or batches, from Japan arrived tainted (some claim it was sabotage, but proof seems lacking). People became sick from it, and it was removed from the American market. The problem was found and corrected, but the FDA refused to allow it back in. Lo and behold, on March 26, 1990, four days after the FDA banned tryptophan, Prozac was introduced on the front cover of Newsweek magazine, heralded as "A Breakthrough Drug for Depression." Because they work in similar ways on serotonin and as an anti-depressant, Prozac, apparently waiting in the wings, immediately replaced tryptophan. Due to the common Prozac horror stories and numerous detrimental side effects, people claim it was rushed into production without adequate testing. Countless murders have been attributed to Prozac, including school shootings, as well as many suicides. Only later, when the FDA could control tryptophan and charge people five times the usual amount for it via prescription, was it allowed back into the U.S. As of this writing, 18 years after its ban, it is starting to be available once again over the counter. The wisdom of nature, and the natural cures she provides, have been and always will be our best medicine.

> *The art of medicine consists of amusing the patient while nature cures the disease.* —Voltaire

Almost never are we given natural remedies by doctors, which can be more effective at *curing* problems, because there is no money to be made in curing people. We are instead given synthetic chemicals and sometimes, only later, do we discover highly negative side effects because these medications were rushed into the market with big advertising campaigns and not tested properly. Various law firms seek victims of these products through late night TV commercials and full-page magazine ads, asking if you have ever taken certain medications that turned out to be dangerous and, if so, to please contact them and join the lawsuit. There have been plenty of them. If you respond and a settlement results, you are usually victimized again with an amazingly paltry check, while the lawyers pay themselves with the spoils like vultures. Do we need all these manipulations in addition to getting sick and/or poisoned by drugs that are supposed to help? No. A more spiritually based society will not be dealing with these issues. Such things would be unheard of.

Eugenics

Those who run the world are banking on the fact that if fewer people control things, then the world stands a better chance of survival. There are negatives to this theory as well. Eugenics could be one of those negatives if allowed to flourish in the wrong hands. Eugenics involves the manipulation of the human gene pool to create more desirable humans and, in some cases, more easily controlled humans. People automatically dismiss the idea and shudder, based on our previous encounter with Nazi Germany's attempt at a "master race" of blond, blue-eyed people along with the planned extermination of the Jews during World War II. Despite this sordid past, eugenics may be a necessary part of our future.

Due to humanity's separation from nature and the advancement of civilization, natural selection in mankind has radically changed. Genetically defective individuals and those with reduced resistance to infection—the sickly among us in general—are not being weeded out of the population early and are therefore allowed to reproduce. Some of these negative genetic traits stay dormant when passed on, some do not, but the bottom line is that at some future point we should expect a noticeable increase in recessive detrimental variants in the gene pool. This means, according to eugenicists, that our hereditary stock is in the process of degenerating. If this is true then eugenics must, out of necessity, be part of our future. When that time comes we should approach this necessity ever so carefully—and with *wisdom*, beyond our scientific knowledge.

John Glad, in his book *Future Human Evolution: Eugenics in the Twenty-First Century*, states that, "The bottom line is that all human social structures are oligarchic in nature, and the implementation of a viable eugenics policy is dependent on a relatively tiny elite." With this in mind, do we want the same mindset or group of people who have gotten us into this worldwide ecological and economic crisis to be making decisions about the human gene pool? Later in this same book Glad mentions John H. Campbell, a biologist at the University of California, who, among others, advocates what is termed as *radical interventionalism*. This is the belief that we should be able to genetically redesign ourselves at will, to, ultimately, create an entirely new species. This idea is based on the fact that our heredity has now been laid open for us like a circuit board by geneticists who are eager to start plugging in new designer genes for the sake of improving our stock. Campbell believes that *Homo sapiens* should be abandoned, to be treated as a "living fossil" or "relic" while we move ahead with genetic technology, possibly creating new genes from scratch with a DNA synthesizer. John Glad, commenting about Campbell on page 102 of his book, states, "Such eugenics would be practiced by elite groups, whose achievements would so quickly and radically outdistance the usual tempo of evolution that within ten generations the new groups will have advanced beyond our current form to the same degree that we transcend apes."

If we were ever to open a "Pandora's box," this would be it. So far, as a species, we have not been able to recognize, identify, or commune with God, so have no right to "play God" by altering the human genome. This would be the height of arrogance—but then, we are good at that.

Much of the focus with a eugenics program is targeted on improving our intelligence. Increasing intelligence, however, does not increase wisdom. They are two different things. *Spiritual growth* will increase our wisdom—we will never get it by tampering with the genetic code. Our moral values and ethical standards (which are wisdom-based) should be improved before we attempt to perform genetically engineered improvements on human intelligence. Time and again, throughout history, highly intelligent people have appeared and acted with no moral character whatsoever—because they were *spiritually bankrupt*. However, the most spiritual (rather than religious) people in history have been the most moral and kind. A better world awaits us from outside of the test tube and from within the human soul. Compassion was not, nor will it ever be, cultivated from inside a laboratory. Increasing intelligence is indeed possible in this way—that is not argued—but it leaves bigger and more pressing needs unanswered.

If we do end up increasing our intelligence in this way, some eugenicists believe we should also create people with limited intelligence to perform our manual labor for us, instead of the traditional hiring of illegal aliens or immigrants. Such a work force would then allow the more genetically enhanced of society to sit on high and look down upon the "workers," like ants, who would be allowed to breed only among themselves (if at all), so that the undesirable forms of work would continue to be done without complaint. Visiting migrant groups are viewed by some as a threat to the viability of any host population, so would no longer be allowed. *Panmixia*, as it is called, may one day threaten the uniqueness of each given race. Some eugenicists fear that racial uniqueness could one day be lost by the continued mixing of races, so would need to be preserved, strengthened and "enhanced" in certain ways.

Although not state owned or sanctioned, a certain type of eugenics program is beginning to be employed in the private sector, through child manufacturing companies that work with, or have, a sperm bank division. Wealthy same sex couples or those unable to parent children are walking in and ordering "designer children" for about $150,000 each. Sperm donors must often have physical exams, genetic tests, and fill out a series of lengthy questionnaires, required to gauge one's intelligence level, income and general health. If the donor makes it through the screening process and meets the standards, the results become part of a "menu" available to interested shoppers. While people gravitate to these "improved" methods, children in desperate need of adoption go unwanted and unloved.

These are just a few things to keep in mind as we draw closer to the day when eugenics will become officially sanctioned by various states or governments in limited forms. We will truly need the technology someday, for health and population related issues, but must have the wisdom in place to use it properly. We can cultivate such wisdom through the four-point plan as outlined in the *Introduction* of this book.

Vegans and Vegetarians

Most people are not vegetarian and will just brush off this section—or at least try to. However, the more spiritually aware one is, the more likely it is that they will be vegan or vegetarian, and more and more people are converting to this type of diet each day. The *Introduction* of this book lists some of the most amazing and gifted people who ever lived, all of whom were vegetarians. Jesus was included as possibly being one of these people. I was reluctant to include him unless there was sufficient evidence, as we know so little of Jesus' life to begin with. It is hard to refute the evidence put forth by Keith Akers, in his book *The Lost Religion of Jesus*. He cites Eusebius, the most well known church historian, who stated that the twelve apostles "embraced and persevered in a laborious and strenuous life, with fasting and abstinence from wine and meat" (*Proof of the Gospel* 3.5). There are numerous references that James, the brother of Jesus, was second in command under Jesus and abstained from eating flesh. Regarding his diet, it is strongly implied by Eusebius that James was brought up this way. "James... was holy from his mother's womb; and he drank no wine nor strong drink, nor did he eat flesh" (Eusebius, *Ecclesiastical History* 2.23.5-6).

These facts, among others, reveal that the twelve apostles, as well as Jesus' brother James, were quite likely vegetarians. Such facts lead to the following questions, as quoted from Akers' work: "Would it not be plausible to assume that James came from the same environment as his brother? If James was raised as a vegetarian and a teetotaler, would it not be plausible to say that his parents raised Jesus in the same way? Why would Jesus' parents raise James one way and Jesus another? Would it not also be logical to say that the lifestyle of the leader of the community sets the tone for the entire community?"

His point is valid. If everyone around Jesus was vegetarian including his own brother, and they were all naturally supposed to be following his lead, how or why could Jesus have been anything else? Otherwise he would have been nothing more than a hypocrite, unworthy of any following at all.

Paradigm Lost 169

In today's world this subject is far more important to the purpose of this book than first suspected, so it must be covered. It took half a century for me to figure this one out and finally change things in my own life. I had insisted on keeping old habits until my own ignorance slapped me so hard I could no longer stand it, so here are the high points. There are three main reasons to become vegetarian or vegan (vegans eat no dairy in addition to no meat):

1) Your health. Most are brought up eating meat from the time we first learn to chew and it's therefore not only acceptable, but a hard habit to break. We are conditioned to eat meat, have learned to love it, but it's not natural. Carnivores have short digestive tracts that pass meat through quickly while we have very long digestive tracts. This means that meat stays in our bodies longer, which allows our bodies to absorb all the unnatural hormones, impurities, chemicals and bacteria that it contains. In addition, we do not have the special enzymes that carnivores have, so meat does not break down very fast but just festers inside of us during its long and difficult digestion process. It actually rots in our bodies instead of fully breaking down, and causes many of the diseases and problems we experience as a result, including heart disease, high blood pressure, and stomach and colon cancer. Also, 80 to 90 percent of the pesticides we eat and 100 percent of the dioxins and dietary hormones we eat come from the consumption of animal products. Study after study has proven that a vegetarian or (even better) vegan diet is far more healthy. Vegetarians have the lowest rates of coronary heart disease of any group in the U.S., 60 percent less cancer, and a fraction of the normal heart attack rate found in others. The risk of heart disease is 50% higher in meat eaters than with vegetarians. Vegetarians and vegans live 6 to 10 years longer, on average, than meat eaters.

Vegans exclude all dairy from their diets like milk, eggs and cheese, which differentiates them from vegetarians. This is harder to do, but more healthy. We are the only species that drinks the milk of another animal, thinking somehow that it is good for us. Get a clue, people. It's for *cows*, not you. It's loaded with fat and cholesterol, designed for a baby animal with four stomachs that will grow to about 1000 pounds by age two. If your baby is going to be a thousand pounds by age two I would highly recommend it. And as adults? We don't even drink *our own species' milk* after we are grown— only a mentally deranged person would even consider it. Cow's milk also contains large amounts of pesticides and hormones, none of which are healthy. It's no wonder that milk has been linked to diabetes, heart disease, and some types of cancer. Also, large amounts of pus are found in cow's milk, because the udders become infected from being continuously hooked up to milking machines. It's become so bad that many people are giving their children chocolate pus instead of chocolate milk!

Eggs are loaded with cholesterol, which clogs arteries, and are a primary source of salmonella poisoning, which kills about 500 people a year in the U.S. alone. If you care about your health, consider veganism. In our society it is not easy to be a complete vegan, but you can start out as vegetarian and work towards it, if desired. There are some great drinks and programs available that can detoxify you from all the poisons we've been fed.

People argue, "I must have my protein," and are convinced that without meat they will be deprived of having enough. Nothing could be further from the truth. In the Western world we eat, on average, twice as much protein as the body needs and by getting it from animals it strains the kidneys, leading to kidney disease. In some cases it can cause osteoporosis from added calcium being consistently excreted through the urine. Additional health problems exist from too much animal protein, but I am sure you get the general idea. Our bodies do not require meat at all—it's a myth. This brings up the question: Is it acceptable to inflict death and suffering on millions of innocent animals for something that isn't even necessary?

Broccoli has more protein in it than some meats, it's a huge source, as well as other vegetables, beans, grains and nuts. It's been shown that a normal and healthy vegetarian diet easily provides enough protein. It should also provide enough nutrients but some vegetarians take supplements to be sure. Depending on where they are grown, some of our fruits, grains and nuts contain about 20 percent less nutrients than in the past due to soil depletion, which should be considered. Regular consumption of legumes, nuts, whole grain foods, green leafy vegetables, and fortified soy products should prevent the need for supplements, but if an imbalanced vegan or vegetarian diet should occur it would most often require the intake of calcium, iron and zinc from other sources, as well as vitamins B-12 and D.

Another concern is the slaughterhouse and factory farm killing process. It operates as an assembly line, with extremely unsanitary results. Most packages of chicken you buy contain feces, based on consistent testing, and food poisoning from salmonella and other forms of bacteria are quite common. As sales of chicken continue to replace beef and we churn out their dead carcasses in increasingly record numbers without much sanitation, all for the sake of profit, we experience more and more sickness from it.

2) *The health of the planet and its people.* The consumption of meat is playing a huge role in the breakdown of our fragile eco-system. More and more rain forest is being stripped away every day to make way for cattle grazing, so we can continue to eat meat. The rain forests are the "lungs of the earth," needed to produce oxygen and stave off the production of greenhouse gases. But meat industry profits come first, so we continue to suffocate our mother earth at the current rate of about seven football fields every minute. Each and every vegetarian, however, saves one acre of trees every year. In the meantime, from virtually every angle of the earth's rain forests, loggers are at work. So far, two-thirds of the world's rain forests are gone, mostly due to cattle ranching. According to *Time Magazine* (Apr. 7, 2008), 750,000 acres were deforested in the Brazilian rain forest alone during the last six months of 2007, equal to the entire state of Rhode Island. Would you smother your own mother at night with a pillow, trying to kill her because you were offered a Big Mac in exchange? The oxygen levels in our air have lessened because we are choking our mother Earth to death, and therefore ourselves, through deforestation for beef. If we continue this trend then plants, animals and human life will soon start dying off from a lack of oxygen, based on the outrageous rate of deforestation. The general public is rarely told about these concerns because there is money to be made from them. We are out of our minds, totally blinded by short-term profits.

Worried about carbon dioxide emissions from cars? That's what they want us to worry about, but according to a number of scientists, and reported by PETA (People for the Ethical Treatment of Animals), methane is 20 times more effective at trapping heat in the atmosphere than carbon dioxide and 23 times more potent according the National Geographic documentary, *Earth: The Biography, Rare Planet*. The feces produced at large animal factory farms is the biggest threat there is to global warming because it is the largest single source of airborne methane in the United States. Added to the rampant and insane levels of deforestation, we are suffocating our mother earth at an alarming and unsustainable rate. Besides creating methane, this same animal excrement has polluted our precious groundwater in 17 U.S. states and 35,000 miles of rivers in 22 states. So far. They're not done yet. The U.S. meat industry creates more water pollution than all other industries combined. In the U.S., 89,000 pounds of feces from animals raised for food is produced every second, *89,000 pounds every second*, and we continue dumping it and spreading the problem. Get out a calculator and figure out how much that is per day. If America is our back yard, this is like having a 150-foot giant living there. We voluntarily feed it, while it excretes huge toxic dumps in our yard every day and there's nothing we can do about it. Except for one thing. *Stop feeding it*. We are living in a cesspool just so a few big industry fat cats can roll in their money. What can we do about it? We can stop eating meat.

Eating meat directly contributes to the starvation of millions of people every year, especially innocent children. They don't get grain to eat because the majority of it is fed to animals that are raised for meat. Innocent children suffer and die terrible deaths just so your child can get a "happy meal" and you a double cheeseburger for 99 cents. That's the food part. What about water? It takes more than 2400 gallons of water to create one pound of beef. Every quarter pound burger eaten causes over 600 gallons of otherwise usable clean water to be flushed away, unable to be used by desperate people who need it. An entire meat-eating diet requires approximately 4000 gallons of water per day to maintain, while a vegetarian diet uses about 300.

More than half of all water used in the United States is used for raising animals for food. But all 80,000 people on the Navajo Indian Reservation in the Southwestern United States have no running water at all. As far as water consumption is concerned, we are treating animals better than the people on Indian reservations. All of these slaughterhouse animals are consuming most of our grains and water, just so we can eat them instead of having far more grains and water for people who need them, plus having a cleaner environment. *Half the world* does not have clean water to drink. For those who do have it, shortages and increasing contamination are everywhere. Water prices will rise while we continue to waste it and diminish the supply. It has been calculated that if the same water were used to produce grain rather than meat, the entire world would be fed and the starvation and suffering would stop.

The structure of the current paradigm is not sustainable and the only real efforts to change it are coming from outside of the greed-based machine—from independent people or groups who care enough to do something. Food and the way we choose to use it is a major key. We all need food, therefore we all have the power for positive change. The paradigm can change or shift in a major positive direction if you and others care enough to change yourself, first. Armed with this knowledge, and not changing how you eat, gives you no right to complain now or in the future. You can actually do something to bring change. According to Sir Paul McCartney, legendary rock star and respected vegan activist, the best thing you can do to help save the planet is to become a vegan or vegetarian, echoing the exact same sentiments of Albert Einstein, the greatest mind of the 20th Century, from decades earlier.

> *Nothing will benefit human health and increase chances of survival for life on earth as much as the evolution to a vegetarian diet.* —Albert Einstein

3) Animal cruelty. Most people view animals as nothing more than items to eat. For example, we are conditioned to think of Thanksgiving every time we see a turkey. Yet people who have parrots or other birds for pets would never consider eating them. Would you eat your own pet? The only difference between that and the chicken on your plate is that you were never afforded a proper introduction to the bird that became your meal. If you were allowed the time to bond with it and create a personal attachment, then you would immediately spare it from your plate and stomach, unless you were starving and it was a matter of survival.

Pigs are actually smarter than dogs and are a joy to be around. Some of them like to play video games. They have fun personalities and intelligence levels equal to a three year-old child. But we brutally slaughter millions of them every day, while they scream in terror because they know exactly what is going on. If you own a dog, would you stand by and allow him to be killed for food like this? Male piglets in factory farms get their testicles pulled out without any painkillers. When a pig is slaughtered it is hung upside-down and its throat is slit. Most would never want to witness this. It is brutally cruel and I for one would never want to watch the equivalent of a three-year-old child die fighting for its life. Would you condone this being done to a three-year-old child? Granted, pigs are different creatures, but their *consciousness* and *intelligence* is the same as a young and otherwise happy child. A number of people who have adopted pigs as pets treat them as members of the family and no longer eat pork. When you choose to eat it, you are "requesting" this cruelty from the demand you create.

Chickens die the same way—strung upside-down with their throats slit. Many remain completely conscious, crying out and kicking while skinned and cut to pieces. On egg farms the male chicks are taken, just days old, and crushed in a mechanical grinder while still alive or gassed because they will never lay eggs.

This is disturbing but please bear with me a little longer. We need to be aware of these things. Another terrible cruelty is the nine million mothers every year who have their babies torn away from them shortly after they are born. I'm referring to female dairy cows. They love their babies as much as we do, and they even baby-sit for each other like we do. But the mothers are used to generate milk *for us*, not for their babies, so the offspring are removed as soon as possible. The male babies are turned into veal—put into tiny crates with a chain around their necks about a week after birth, where they cannot even turn around so their muscles will atrophy to create more tender meat. They are given replacement milk but not from their mothers—milk lacking in nutrients which starves them intentionally—also to make their meat more tender. They never get to grow up or run or play, and never see the light of day again.

The females are artificially inseminated shortly after their first birthday and become "milk machines" thereafter. They all die by about age five when most normal dairy cows would otherwise live to about 20. When workers take their babies, some mothers try to shield their loved ones with their own bodies, some try to fight off the attackers, some withdraw in silent despair or cry pitifully, some frantically chase after the transport trucks. It's heart-wrenching to hear them scream and moan for days afterward; some stop eating and drinking. They are not "dumb animals" that forget all about their babies after a while. Like us, they never forget. Some return to the empty spot where their baby was, searching day after day with broken hearts. For what? So we can drink hormone and pus infested milk instead of the babies, who would otherwise drink it pure? Wake up and *stop drinking it*. When did we lose our humanity and start treating other living beings in such a cruel and heartless way? We will in fact wake up in coming years and begin to care more about these creatures, our health, and the health of the planet.

When I lived in Vermont in the early 1980s, part of that time was with roommates in a four-bedroom house in the country. One of them was Matt, a spontaneous young man who often threw himself into situations without much forethought. He often got into trouble, but was so likable and fun-loving that he could charm his way out of most anything. Because of this I liked him, as did most people, until one day when he noticed a young doe wander into our driveway at dusk on a warm summer night.

Matt excitedly ran in, shouting that there was a deer in the yard. He grabbed his .22 rifle and ran outside while the female roommates and I tried, but failed, to stop him. He was so determined I stayed inside, wanting no part of it and hoping she might run. The young doe was trusting, having never known danger. She was not fully grown, having been born in the spring, and was apparently lost from her mother. Matt walked up and shot her at almost point blank range. She ran out of the yard, across the road, and disappeared into the forest with Matt hot on her trail. I had watched from inside and did not follow. Matt soon returned, having found the poor animal, still alive, which did not get far. I went outside in the yard and Matt, myself, and the two female roommates could hear this animal desperately screaming in the night for help. She was scared, dying and alone. Matt had returned for a bow and arrow because he did not want to take any more shots and get arrested for hunting out of season.

I went to the doe with Matt, but at that point there was no chance for her to live, or for me to help her (which I wanted to do after hearing her cries). I now wish I had stopped Matt from shooting. I will never forget her sounds, which were very human-like. She looked directly at me, pleading with such bright and beautiful—but terrified—eyes that struck me to my soul. What amazed me was something I never expected. We connected. She communicated with me on a level beyond words and shared her emotions and panic with me, through those soulful eyes. She begged me to help her—but I could not. I "talked" back to her and offered comfort, but no comfort could be taken because she knew she was going to die. We were communicating, and the fact that she was so beautiful and intelligent made this event become an introduction to an *equal* form of life rather than something that was supposed to be "less" than me. She was also angry. These were her woods and her home—how dare we do this to her! She was living a magnificent life, loved everything about it and could not have imagined encountering this sudden cruelty. I could not bear to watch what Matt was about to do, so I told her that I loved her and left without seeing it. She screamed for me more loudly as I left, and it crushed me to walk away.

Paradigm Lost   175

This event changed me forever. These creatures are not less than us, they are just different. I, as well as the other two roommates, refused to eat any of the venison after Matt butchered her on the back porch and he could not understand why. I stopped eating red meat altogether. We all went our separate ways within a few weeks, and I barely spoke to Matt during the remaining time. I had hunted deer just a few times in my youth, gladly now without success, and never again did I pick up a gun and intend to harm an animal of any kind—nor will I ever.

Intelligent, beautiful creatures like this—millions of them—go through this type of terror at factory farms and slaughterhouses every day. As of this writing, in the United States one million animals are killed for food every single hour. The way they are killed is horrendous, with the same kind of screaming, and many suffer terribly because the assembly line killers have a daily quota and don't have time to put many out of their misery properly. Your choice to eat meat makes you a party to this action, endorsing it from afar and creating the demand for such death and cruelty. Before they die, these animals live terrible lives. Most of the meat-bearing animals you eat never get the chance to run outside, breath fresh air, know their mother's touch, or feel the ground below their feet because they are stuck in a wire cage or pen that does not allow them to do so much as turn around. Every living creature should have the right to a decent life and each vegetarian saves the lives of over 100 animals every year by choosing to exclude meat.

Holier-than-thou supporters of meat consumption point to instances in the Old Testament Bible, showing where God commanded men to kill animals and eat them, thereby making it okay in their minds because God sanctioned it. This same God threatened multiple times to enforce cannibalism among his people and on at least one occasion (Lam. 4:10-11) it happened, so should we eat each other, too? The God of the Old Testament was a mean, vindictive bully. He murdered many of his own followers for trivial reasons, including innocent women and children. (See Numbers 16:26-35, 2 Samuel 24:15, 2 Kings 2:23-24, Numbers 15:32-36, among others.) This god showed virtually no compassion, but the complete opposite. Having a god without compassion meant that killing and eating animals or murdering *his own followers* was not considered a problem. Those who choose to follow in this mindset should do so with open eyes.

> *The greatness of a nation and its moral progress can be judged by the way its animals are treated... I hold that, the more helpless a creature, the more entitled it is to protection by man from the cruelty of man.* —Mahatma Gandhi

If this is a barometer of our current state of morality, then we are sorely lacking. What accounts for our violent behaviour towards ourselves and animals? As long as we act like carnivores by killing other people and animals, we will eat like carnivores. Does this sound right to you? Most people would tend to believe this, but it actually could be the opposite—those who eat meat like carnivores will act like them. I will explain.

Very few vegetarians are violent people (the claim that Hitler was a vegetarian is a proven fabrication). They are almost always peaceful at heart, meditators, and more conscious and caring, all told, than those who are not. A few of them have told me, and I have since discovered, that when animals are murdered for their meat a rush of adrenaline goes through their bodies out of immense fear. Adrenaline produces the fight or flight response in times of great fear, so is soaked into the meat. "Imprinted" within a dying animal is the violent act of their murder. Then we eat them. When we do this, it is believed that we take on the energy of the animal, including its imprinted fear, its actual adrenaline, and the violence associated with its death. And it has an effect on us. When these same energies get used as a result of the meal, they are directed outward, into the world in a similar way, whether we know it or not.

> *Give them great meals of beef and iron and steel, they will eat like wolves and fight like devils.* —William Shakespeare

In South Korea, millions of dogs and cats are killed for food every year, with an estimated 30 per cent stolen from families who love them. Dog butchers cruelly bludgeon the animals to death to intentionally create this adrenaline rush into the animals' bodies because they claim it "enhances male virility" in those who consume it. Virility is ruled by testosterone, and testosterone, in addition to adrenaline, is linked to *violence*. We are what we eat. Virtually every warm-blooded animal we eat dies a violent death. Any animal that dies a violent death at our hands transfers that violent adrenaline-soaked meat into our bodies. Our bodies process and manifest this violence with a deeper awareness that we are not conscious of. All you have to do is become more fully conscious of this violence in your body to complete your awareness. If you are sensitive and abstain from meat for a number of months, you will actually *feel* this violent energy if you eat it again. It comes through as a "heaviness," however, rather than a violent feeling, and brings your vibrational level down. Don't take my word for it, try it. This may not be the sole reason for humanity's violent tendencies, but it plays a role that needs to be addressed and explored.

Can a higher form of consciousness, coming in our future, put a stop to our violent tendencies? According to www.natural-law.org, there was an extensive five-year study done at Harvard University on the effects of Transcendental Meditation (TM) at a maximum-security prison. Inmates who learned to meditate in this way were able to significantly decrease their aggression, stress and mental disorders. Practitioners of TM claim that if one per cent of those in a city or town practice TM, the crime rate in that area will significantly decrease. This is called the *Maharishi Effect*, named after TM's founder, Maharishi Mahesh Yogi.

Visiting meditation groups, rather than residents, are also known to go into an area and cause crime levels to drop based on their meditation efforts. One such study was published in a peer-reviewed journal, *Social Indicators Research*. Nearly 4000 practitioners of TM from 81 countries meditated with peaceful intent in Washington, D.C. from June 7 to July 30, 1993. It was shown that during this time violent crime rates, including murders, rapes and assaults, had dropped by 23 per cent. Up to the present time, 43 separate studies have verified the field effects of consciousness on some level.

Another study, done by Amy Fitzgerald for the American Sociological Association, reports that communities where slaughterhouses are located have consistently *higher* rates of violent crime than areas that do not have these death factories. It is an interesting juxtaposition, comparing the effects of peaceful meditation in certain areas upon the surrounding levels of crime to areas that practice the brutal and continuous killing of thousands of innocent creatures.

We have not learned to respect other life forms on this planet, but all life deserves to be respected. We have upset the balance of nature because we have failed to live in balance with it and in relative harmony with other life. Other life was not put here to be killed, exploited and used as commodities by us. How would an alien race view our activities? From their perspective it would be clear that we are not that much smarter than the other life forms found on this planet. But because we are, we butcher and kill millions of our fellow creatures every single day. Why would another species, who would observe this, want to drop in and be friends with a bunch of barbarians like us who would likely jump at the chance to snack on a brand new flavor of roasted, fried or marinated flesh from the bones of their exotic bodies? Who knows—they might be tasty to us, but they sure as hell aren't stupid. The truth is, humanity will and does eat anything that moves, as long as it doesn't kill or injure us from eating it. Just throw a little hot sauce on it and we're good to go. If an animal is accessible and not poison, some idiot somewhere in this world is eating one.

We are supposed to have stewardship over the earth—yet we have raped and pillaged it to the point where it is almost unlivable. In certain places it already is unlivable and these areas are spreading quickly. We are violent and uncaring to the planet, its animals and to each other due to our ignorance and lack of spiritual growth. Maybe things could change for the better if we stopped eating as carnivores.

Summary

So there you have it. Eating meat is unhealthy because we are not, nor have we ever been, designed to eat it. It is destroying the planet, and it is viciously cruel. But the vast majority of us still don't get it. More people eat meat now than at any time in the past. Some countries eat cats and dogs regularly, making no distinction between those that are considered as pets (or *are* pets) and those that are not. We are totally out of our minds as a species—like lemmings racing off a cliff. We are at the pivot point, however, whereby things have completely bottomed out and simply *have to* improve. Thank God an awakening is at hand, one that is a complete necessity, and some of us are starting to spread the word and make positive changes. The Internet is exploding with good information in these areas, which the mainstream media will never cover, so get busy and check it out. For example, free vegetarian starter kits are available from PETA (People for the Ethical Treatment of Animals) at www.goveg.com, or from Compassion Over Killing at www.tryveg.com, among others.

Although there are more meat eaters than ever, the numbers of vegetarians are at an all time high and growing tremendously fast. New and delicious vegan foods are becoming available every day and the market trends away from meat, despite the mass media, are beginning to shift. Pay attention to television marketing. The fast food chains and other meat peddlers are becoming increasingly desperate to keep you ignorant of the negative facts relating to your health, the environment and the cruelty involved, in order to keep you eating it.

Education and ethics should be part of this equation, to offset the propaganda and mindless advertising. Millions of people who remain ignorant will demand their steaks and pork for years to come, but quite a number of them, if informed, would change. We must ask ourselves, from an ethical standpoint, if we should allow people to remain ignorant for the sake of vested financial interests, or educate them to prevent the needless suffering of millions of people and animals in the future. School textbooks should explain the dilemma to our children. Young people should be given a choice between becoming vegetarian—or at least limiting their intake of meat, thereby helping others, the environment and improving their overall health—or continuing to contribute to the problem. Although people are beginning to see the problem, it will do us no good to wake up unless action is taken. Do not, under any circumstances, assume that your actions don't count. From your perspective, that is *all* that counts.

Chapter Twelve

NEW WORLD ECONOMICS

It is well that the people of the nation do not understand our banking and monetary system, for if they did, I believe there would be a revolution before tomorrow morning.
—Henry Ford

World events do not occur by accident. They are made to happen, whether it is to do with national issues or commerce; and most of them are staged and managed by those who hold the purse strings. —Former British Defense Minister Denis Healey

Our main purpose in the current system is to consume, and has little to do with thinking for ourselves. As long as the consumer-driven marketing machine controls what we think, we will act in the ways that are planned for us. Such ways include spending our money on what we are told to spend our money on, and to remain in a state of consciousness that makes us willing slaves to the system.

Is this a problem only confined to the Western World? No. China, which remained isolated for centuries, is now diving headlong into this madness. Extreme commercialism has recently landed on their doorstep, and they are welcoming it with open arms. The huge worldwide monetary machine requires more willing slaves to exploit. China, along with India, have opened up to western commercialism and are being primed for the future. Despite the initial reluctance of their banking systems and a "hands-off" policy, limited investments in them are now allowed.

Does it matter than China is a communist country? Only to a point. Take a look at the United States, which is supposed to be "free." The most valuable and important asset a person will have in their lifetime, in most cases, is their home. Yet in the U.S., as of this writing, over 60% of the homes in the U.S. are owned by banks. What is the difference, one might ask, between communism, where most everything is state owned, and the so-called "New

World Order," where the banks own the majority of property? Hard working western consumers are being taken advantage of, being treated as serfs in a more modern type of feudal system that is flawed, unfair and has a limited life span. This system is spreading because it is the only way it can save itself—and the best way to kill it off is through a new conscious awareness and a completely new paradigm.

Communism died in Russia and will eventually be dead in China. A more appealing financial game has rolled into town and communism is as good as gone in China if they allow the central (international) banks more control. The Chinese government owns their main banks, but in doing big business with the outside world, it has become a necessity to let the proverbial fox into the henhouse. The rush is on. Currently, no single foreign entity can buy more than 20 percent of a Chinese bank, and foreigners collectively can own up to 25 percent. In late 2005 their largest state-owned bank, Industrial and Commercial Bank of China (ICBC), sold a ten percent stake to American Express, Goldman Sachs and Germany's Allianz AG. Other foreign investors have poured billions into the Chinese banking sector, including Bank of America, J.P. Morgan Chase, Citigroup, Swiss Bank UBS AG, Royal Bank of Scotland, Merrill Lynch, Morgan Stanley, and Temasek Holdings of Singapore, among others. Some of these companies like Morgan Stanley have been in financial trouble, so where do they get the money? They borrow it from China, using the old IMF trick of agreeing to invest a portion (if not all of it) back into China. If the central banks have any strength left at all, and can continue to gain a larger foothold in China, there will be no point in them bankrolling the state to own things when they can eventually own them directly, through the ingenious takeover debt system that they employ. China, on the other hand, is not planning on this happening at all. They are using the central banks to learn these takeover and control systems for themselves—through expertise and assistance they would not be privy to without granting limited investments. Either way, the official death of communism in China, as it was with Russia, is only a matter of time (and its ultimate demise may be linked to other factors beyond just banking).

This new order of the world and the international banks have most of their attention focused on China and India at the time of this writing. These two countries compose more than 40% of the world's population and both have internally controlled banking systems of their own that must be "cracked" before the international banksters can roll up their sleeves and get busy. Various attempts at entry, through all kinds of chess-like moves will continue for many years to come. These two countries constitute the final phase of world domination and control through financial means, and for it to be thwarted they must fight a *spiritual financial battle*, rather than a purely materialistic one. India has begun to do this on local levels, through people inspired in part by Gandhi and modeled after some of his ideas. China, however, is entrenched in a huge manufacturing explosion that leaves little room for a new spiritually based playing field.

China might one day learn some things from India, as India did from Gandhi, who was one of the greatest spiritual giants the world has ever known. Or they could learn some spiritual lessons from the Dalai Lama, and ultimately afford Tibet, a country they have occupied for decades, a bit more respect or freedom. Tibet is the original home of the Dalai Lama, their spiritual leader who lives in exile. The Dalai Lama advises his people with great wisdom, rather than encouraging violence or revolt. Since they must always live as neighbors with China, he encourages Tibetans not to view them as enemies. If they did, the strife and violence would never end—much like we find in the Middle East. He urges Tibetans to learn the Chinese language so that open communication can be a common occurrence, and encourages them to study Buddhism under certain Chinese teachers whom he trusts. Some would consider these tactics to be a sign of weakness, but they represent true spiritual strength. By creating common ground and a "meeting of the minds," it becomes possible for a level playing field to emerge that fosters mutual respect, rather than opposition and strife. This is our hope for the future.

From a purely economic standpoint, China is playing a more offensive game than India, while the U.S. continues to weaken. Much of North America has already fallen under the control of others, as evidenced by the purchase of U.S. land and assets by many foreign entities. This has outraged many patriotic Americans. Just one interesting development is China's 2007 $5 billion dollar investment in Morgan Stanley, a major U.S. investment bank that recently suffered a $10.9 billion loss. The investment will be converted into stock in the company in the year 2010, which will result in about 10 percent ownership. Gao's China Investment Corp. has invested $3 billion in the U.S. private equity firm called The Blackstone Group, creating a 9.9 percent stake.

The Carlyle Group, a global private equity investment firm located in Washington, D.C., was forced to sell off at least 7.5 percent of itself to Mubadala Development Company from Abu Dhabi for $1.35 billion in late 2007. The U.S. bank, Citicorp, just announced that it has sold 4.9 percent of itself to the Gulf Arab emirate of Abu Dhabi for $7.5 billion. According to the Seattle Times, from a Nov. 7, 2007 article, Borse Dhabi purchased 19.9 percent of Nasdaq in October of that year. Nasdaq is a huge U.S. equities security trading market, with more trading volume per day than any other stock exchange in the world. Almost half of the London Stock Exchange is now owned by The United Arab Emirates and Qatar. And Dubai International Capital, the investment arm of Dubai Holdings, has investments in Tussauds Group, the Carlyle Group, J.P. Morgan Chase, 3i, in addition to a $1 billion investment in DaimlerChrysler, according to its website. Far more is going on than mentioned and this is just the beginning. The west is slowly being taken over financially by the oil nations and others, so a new paradigm, with new self-sustaining energy sources, is needed before it is too late.

The point of listing these various buyouts is to illustrate that this trend is widespread and to stress that if these financial entities did not need to take on outside investors, none of them would have done so. Desperate times bring desperate measures. The system is failing—and its final death throes will one day be upon us, if not on the horizon already. As major western banks and financial institutions flounder and sell out just to stay afloat, more control of their destiny is put into the hands of others. The more adept of the money jugglers, like the Carlyle Group, still turn big profits because of strong governmental ties, especially to the Bush family, coupled with a deep involvement in weapons and defense related deals. Even so, their publicly traded investment fund, Carlyle Capital Corporation, completely collapsed in March of 2008 and they defaulted on at least $16.6 billion of debt. They borrowed twenty times the amount of client money in order to boost their portfolio of bonds, but it was all smoke and mirrors. When banks lend money it does not really exist, except on paper, so when things happen and you get called on the debt (like in poker), your hand is empty, despite your bluffing. Even they are not immune and in general, the western financial world is floundering. Financial experts predict more of the same to come. In a collective sense this is the so-called New World Order at work. They are failing, but don't want you to know about it. Why? Because the financial powerhouses are all engaged in a worldwide game of Monopoly that they think they can still win. This is like the compulsive gambler who runs out of money, so starts borrowing from others just to keep playing. The theme of the game is economic globalization, and they are fighting for a piece of the economic pie that is quickly dwindling away. Financed by others, western financial institutions must pay back their investors if lucky enough to procure any winnings from the continued "Ponzi scheme" of international finance. The lion's share of control holds little chance of falling back into the hands of the originators of the scheme.

Economic globalization is being pursued as the answer while humanitarian globalization, the real key, is largely ignored. An *L.A. Times* newspaper article dated May 8, 2008, entitled "Chinese Firms Bargain Hunting in U.S." reveals how Chinese entrepreneurs are buying and opening many U.S. businesses. It has become more economical for Chinese companies to expand in the U.S. than in their own country and analysts have been advising them of this fact. Everything is cheaper in the U.S. for them except for labor—for example U.S. electricity rates are 75 percent lower than in China, so large plants are relocating.

Businesses are rushing into China in an effort to stay solvent by catering to a new and immense population base. What happened the last time China opened its doors to the West? In 1843 the Port of Shanghai opened to foreign trade. The very first lot in the port was rented to a British company and the opium trade began thriving. Captain Warren Delano from the U.S. appeared on the scene, who was Franklin Delano Roosevelt's grandfather. He made his fortune in the opium trade but when China and England agreed to reduce opium production in 1906, he moved on to other things. He became the first Vice Chairman of the U.S. Federal Reserve Board. In both cases he was instrumental in enormously parasitic operations, one of which was outlawed, and the other should be.

In today's world, one out of every five people are Chinese so the profits and future potential profits to be made in this country are staggering. What will happen once this market is saturated? No one seems to be worrying about that now. The money masters from the west are rushing into China with all of their new marketing strategies. Good luck, China; thanks for opening your doors and welcome to the club. Russia became a member of this club in 1993. Commercialism moved in to "open up Russia," as soon as communism fell because more people are continually needed for this "new order of the world" to work. As the money from China's new form of extreme commercialism rolls in, only some of it fills the coffers of those powerful, behind-the-scenes western organizations that are "opening up China."

What has been the result of China opening its markets to the rest of the world? It has recently flooded the world market with various poisons in animal and human food and in toxic children's toys containing lead. Sixteen of the twenty most polluted cities in the world are in China, as their people and resources are being used at an alarming pace to make profits at any expense. When do we say, "Enough!," and not buy these tainted items? The U.S. government cannot, because it has created a trade deficit of over 150 billion dollars with China (the greatest ever) and China has helped to bankroll payments on the U.S. national debt. Not only that, the U.S. is equally guilty because it started this trend of mass commercialism. The U.S. has now invited the Chinese to set up shop and continue this manufacturing trend within U.S. borders, despite China adding clear emphasis through the outrageous pollution of their own lands that a system such as this is completely self destructive, especially to the environment.

As its people begin to make more money, Las Vegas casinos have rushed in and established themselves in China. The Sands opened in 2004, followed by China's first Las Vegas style mega resort, the 1.2 billion dollar Wynn Macau resort in the Macau province, in late 2006. Early 2007 brought the 1.1 billion dollar MGM Grand and the 2.3 billion dollar Venetian Macau, built by the Las Vegas Sands Corporation. By 2010, Las Vegas gaming companies will have invested a minimum of 20 billion dollars in China while much of the country struggles with major poverty issues. The chairman of the Sands has stated, "We could build ten Las Vegas strips over here, there's so much demand." In just one year after these places open in 2010, Wall Street analysts predict that China's gambling income will exceed the take from Las Vegas. What makes the Chinese so eager to throw their money away by gambling while large numbers of people in their country suffer without clean water or adequate food?

Do you want to get as far away from a spiritual existence as possible? If so, then gamble. From a spiritual standpoint it is the most baseless and empty use of your time there is, whether you are successful at it or not—and in most cases you are not. It is not designed for you to succeed. In general, gambling ruins people's lives who are too weak to resist it. Yet people flock to the casinos, blinded by stupidity or psychological illness, in a mad rush to throw their hard earned money away. Here's an idea: Cancel your trip and give what you would have gambled away to a needy charity. Make a *difference* in the world, for God's sake, and stop acting like morons.

A New Economic Order

Must the U.S. and the rest of the western world side with the floundering New World Order to prevent a massive Chinese/Indian financial world takeover, based on their growing financial strength? Or can we stand up for ourselves and create a completely new paradigm? Only by establishing a completely new paradigm will there ever be adequate answers, for any of us. Our actions or inaction will determine our future, and our freedom.

Astute people behind the scenes in international finance know how to use smoke and mirrors to continue the exploitation of the masses—at our expense. This scenario, and current paradigm, will painfully drag on if we let it. If the insane, economic machine continues to grow unchecked, the only way they will be able to keep track of us is to have a cashless economy, whereby a card, to begin with, or an implanted microchip, will credit and debit each of us as far as our value or resources is concerned. The credit companies might one day be consolidated and merged into a loosely based system if the time grows right and they know they can get away with it. Since the mid 1990's there's been an agreement between many credit card companies called "universal default." If you make a late payment on one card, the other cards are alerted and it affects your credit with all of them. Some people have defaulted on loans that had nothing to do with a late payment made elsewhere. New laws are trying to banish the practice, but even if successful, there will always be something else to replace it. This is the direction that things are going—with us being increasingly victimized, controlled and manipulated, if we allow it.

A worldwide database may eventually control us all if we fail to make conscious changes and allow it to happen. If the west consolidates and can stay financially solvent, a possible compromise could occur with the emerging powers of China, India and others. If we are completely taken over economically, in this fashion, then there would be no other place to turn. It could then be decided whether we, as individuals or communities, will eat or not, and everything else about us, including all our freedoms, would be completely manipulated. The point is that we need to change the paradigm—or at least start doing so—before we are all funneled into a system that will not only enslave us, but continue to operate in a way that will in fact destroy the current ecosystem and ourselves.

The prophetic "mark of the beast" could surface so that those without it would not be able to function very easily. Many have speculated that it will be some kind of identification card with all of our vital information contained on its magnetic strip or, better yet, a microchip inserted under the skin. Many pets are micro-chipped these days to insure against their loss, and a movement has begun to get children micro-chipped to avoid abductions. A few people have done this to their children but the practice holds little hope of being widely accepted, at least for the time being. My prediction is that this program will be started through the prison system. Anyone convicted of a felony might someday be micro-chipped before their release, with the chip being fully trackable through a GPS (global positioning system) satellite that is linked to police agencies. Whenever a crime is committed, police departments or a major law enforcement agency could activate the system and get a readout of the location of all micro-chipped felons at the exact time of the crime in question. If the co-ordinates of a felon match the time and place of a crime scene, they go pick him up. This program might be accepted and laws passed to support it under the premise that a felon loses certain rights from his crimes. Although I have never heard this idea proposed before, it is how I would envision the direct microchip process to begin in humans without complaint.

It seems that people are reluctant to start a mass implant program into children at this time, but in June, 2008, The Middletown School District in Rhode Island announced that it has started a pilot program in partnership with MAP Information Technology Corp., to microchip the schoolbags of children at the Aquidneck School. The American Civil Liberties Union (ACLU) believes this to be an invasion of children's privacy and a potential safety risk due to easily available radio frequency identification (RFID) readers that would allow unauthorized people, perhaps even pedophiles, to access student's private information and monitor their movements. For some reason, this pilot program is being provided at no cost. Because it's free, the program did not require the approval of the Rhode Island ethics commission.

The magnetic strip on the back of your driver's license now contains more information about you than ever before, and serves as a transitionary alternative to micro-chipping you directly. The magnetic strip on your grocery card is another reason for you to shop at the local Farmer's Market or through Community Supported Agriculture. Every single thing you buy is monitored and "interested parties" can access the list, just like your phone records. Do you really want these intrusions? Are you tired of being "tagged" like cattle?

In the United Kingdom, there are so many video monitors watching everything people do in public, there is virtually no escape. The next logical step is a chip. It makes monitoring everyone easier. The purpose of having a card or chip in all of us is not only to monitor, but to control. Our beliefs and many other personal facets of our lives could be eventually dictated with such control in place, and our spiritual freedoms could either flourish greatly or be completely lost, depending on the agenda of those in control. Based on the state of the world, it does not take a genius to understand what that agenda is. Do we continue to follow the hypnotic dictates already in place that are leading us into this stark dead-end? Or do we finally *wake up* and make a conscious, meaningful shift for ourselves away from lives lived in the soulless, empty fashion desired by the manipulative economic puppet-masters who hold the strings from behind hidden walls?

We need to realize that beyond all this material and economic control that already has such a stranglehold on us, lies our most important asset of all. It is our true spiritual essence that connects us to God. It is our true identity, and when realized within an individual it entitles us *not* to be treated like cattle. We hold a part of divinity within us—a divine spark that is not an imaginative or symbolic idea, but an actual part of God that is totally and completely real and *deserves to be free*. Collectively, we, as "God," would never want to imprison ourselves. If we can come to the realization of "God" as our identity, based on a spiritual awakening, then the first forms of action toward each other would not be enslavement or exploitation, but love, compassion and mutual respect.

> *When the power of love replaces the love of power, man will have a new name—God.* —Sri Chinmoy

If you happen to believe that God is separate from us, the same idea holds true—that He would never want us, His children, to be enslaved in any way. History bears out our long spiritual struggle against oppression and enslavement. It's all about freedom and reaching our true potential. If we have lost that, we have lost it all.

Creating a "prison planet" is not what God is about. At the same time, a global government with enough power used wisely, could steer us away from the centuries of warfare and terrible atrocities that we've committed against our fellow man. Let us hope that we can cultivate enough compassion and mutual respect in this coming age to go along with our thirst for profits and power.

One of the main reasons we are here is to learn to live in harmony with the planet and with ourselves. It is an enormous and vital task. If those who continue to take power remain as profiteers and power mongers, then our troubles will deepen. With no change in sight it is up to us, as individuals and small groups, to make more conscious choices. This means *don't listen to the mainstream media*, but follow your heart and stick to your decisions no matter what happens. Use the Internet for information for as long as it can be trusted—legislation is starting to surface that attempts to remove or limit the more intelligent information and freedoms we enjoy. It means following the four-point outline in the *Introduction* of this book. This includes the development of a holistic awareness—but to also the cultivation of strong community ties and to exercise as much control over local resources like food and water that can be comfortably maintained without greed or hoarding. If we all take care of our immediate neighbors, we will limit the likelihood of being exploited or uncomfortable. Getting rid of the dependence on foreign oil should be a primary objective. A teenager was recently on the local San Diego news who converted his car to run on water. A few others have done the same. The point is that if a teenager can do it in his own backyard and still have time to take out the garbage, *what is our problem*? Let's get busy here.

It is entirely possible for us to do away with the oil monopoly and supply most of our own transportation fuels at local levels, using alternative fuels. This includes cheaper and cleaner burning ethanol. For example, Brazil is the fifth largest country in the world and imports no oil. They use just 1% of their land to grow sugarcane, which powers about half of their vehicles. The U.S. has crops more suitable to its own climate that work equally well.

In 1983 David Blume came out with the first edition of his book, *Alcohol Can Be a Gas!* (updated 2007), along with a 10-part television series called "Alcohol as Fuel," which he wrote and hosted for KQED, the San Francisco PBS affiliate. While the first broadcasts of the show were underway to the Bay Area market, big oil heard about the project and, according to the information on alcoholcanbeagas.com, convinced KQED to stop the printing of books and cancel the TV series to the remaining 140 PBS stations nationwide. There were lawsuits, but the oil-funded lawyers kept the information from appearing and the book was shelved for over twenty years. It has now been updated and is available.

The time is right to approach this subject again because we, as consumers, have had enough of big oil. Unstable world events continue to surface and wreak havoc with gas and oil prices, which in turn affects most everything and can cripple our economies. An awakened society will refuse to continue using fossil fuels that harm the environment on multiple levels, and the first steps in that direction are beginning to take place. We deserve a cleaner environment and more control over our economic future. Ethanol can be made from a large number of crops other than corn, which is not very efficient and is the one, so far, most often used. Critics say it takes more energy to produce ethanol from corn than the energy that results from the process. Numerous other crops, by-products or organic matter like algae are better suited, making it possible for thousands of farmers and distilleries to get involved at local levels. Farmers should be able to open their own stations in town or work with local micro-breweries or other such people to do so. Stations selling ethanol, or "E85," are popping up all over the U.S., and maps are available on the Internet to find the ones nearest to you. Automobile conversion kits are becoming widely available to consumers and are reasonably priced.

The only possible deterrent to this is that, right now, large corporations and government agencies are making attempts to jump into the alternative areas and control that, too. Some large corporations hold out hope if we can trust them, and are in a race to perfect the best alternatives. For example, biofuels from algae is tremendously promising and a number of large companies are working on them. We should still try to handle this locally as much as possible, support our farmers, and stand up for the right to do so. If we've learned anything, it's that there's no sense in trading in one monopoly and form of servitude for another. In future years we will look back and see how we beat the oil cartels and their stranglehold on us—hopefully through localized efforts using alternative fuels. It is clear that we will succeed, and how we do this in a local sense should serve as a blueprint for many other economic areas and concerns.

Our lives will grow easier and less costly if we take control of them through our own available resources, including local alternative fuels, community supported agriculture (CSAs), and Gandhi's overall concept of *swadeshi*. Big Brother is a leviathan of spiritual ignorance, too cumbersome to react quickly and efficiently to local needs, but feeding off the sweat of our brows. We only believe him because he masquerades so well as an "authority" and is bigger than us. Roll up your sleeves and get busy on a local level.

A working plan for self-sufficiency should be part of every City Hall or local government, complete with a coordination center that puts it all together and creates local jobs when a void is discovered. Locals care about each other more, and problems do in fact get solved faster due to local familiarity and not having to wait for an overloaded, outside agency to respond. If local funds are not available to fill a void, amazing things are being done with the system of bartering. This form of problem solving should never be dismissed when the choice falls between dependence on a larger system that will either reject or barely fill a need, or bartering between local entities that could solve issues more fully. There is no need, in many cases, to continue being victims, paying huge sums through increased taxes or outright blackmail, or having to beg for assistance.

Corruption is a major problem because the entire system we operate under is flawed. The masses continue to foot the bills, over and over again, while major funds get mishandled or disappear completely. We are not only getting tired of it, but are becoming unable to meet the demands. We are being fleeced and the more we comply, the more freedoms we lose.

Is it crazy to think there really is a "new world order" manipulating things from behind the scenes? Those who influence the world in such major ways certainly do not call themselves that, but it is a loosely knit, yet closely aligned, group of people who are enjoying more and more control over what happens in the world. Yet, few of their actions make it into our major media. One or two underground newspapers have covered the yearly meetings of the Bilderberg Group, the most powerful people in the world who meet, map out and discuss the directions the world is to take in the coming year. Yet most people have never even heard of the Bilderberg Group. Those who really run things are never mentioned on TV or written up in any of the major newspapers worldwide because they own them. It has been rumored that there is a tacit agreement that none of these people's names will appear in any of the media worldwide so that those who are listening will not know who's really in control. Such things are on a need to know basis and as far as they're concerned, the masses do not need to know. Otherwise, it could be an impediment. If you wish to operate in secret at night, the worst thing that can happen is to have a spotlight shining in your face and people asking you questions.

Many I've spoken with have said, "I don't want to read conspiracy related books any more because it's too depressing. You can't do anything about the problem. It's too big and I would rather focus on my own advancement and spirituality rather than something that's not only negative, but too large for me to do anything about." But the point is, something *can* be done. It will not result in an immediate change, but we can start in the right direction.

That leads us back to my four-point outline—the development of our identity, a new educational program, holistic awareness and economic restructuring. The first three are a prerequisite for the fourth, otherwise a *successful* economic restructuring will likely never be achieved. Our current worldwide economic paradigm is continuing to fail, and a lasting answer is needed. Former chief economist of the World Bank and Nobel laureate Joseph Steiglitz admitted that the World Bank has failed to turn most countries around, despite following the proper theories set in place, which are known as the Washington Consensus. The best minds have failed to create prosperity because the very foundation the system rests upon is inept and must be rebuilt.

When we change the way we think and it starts to spread, then and only then will a small wave begin to roll. It will, and it can, grow bigger to the point that sometime in the future, truth will overcome authority as opposed to authority dominating the truth. We cannot rely on authority to make any lasting changes because too much is invested in the existing system, and any sincere attempt at change would disrupt things too much. They might try, which would be a shock, but it is very unlikely. Change should start not at the top, but from a new foundation. We should only rely on ourselves to create it because 1) it is in our best interests and 2) investment in the current greed-based system is not as strong in the masses. This current paradigm has become so compromised that its eventual change is unavoidable. The more positive the changes will be are in direct correlation with how much involvement the masses decide to take, whether it be direct local change or in larger spheres of influence, especially education, found within the first three points. It is time for us to put a stop to our own manipulation, having been worked and taxed and brainwashed almost to death at the expense of the almighty dollar, and to reassess where we truly need to go. By understanding how money and banking truly works, it's now clear—we have done all the work while the banks, in large part, have reaped the rewards.

> *It is only those who are not working in the fields who have time to wonder about grain. It is they, too, who have no right to do so, for they have not tasted it, nor are they working towards the production of flour for the people.* —Indries Shah

It is time to nourish ourselves in new ways and take charge of our nourishment on local levels that we can control. We must want it badly enough—because it is entirely possible to change this paradigm. It is already beginning to happen. It is unlikely that those in control of this paradigm will ever do anything helpful in this respect, unless there are no other options. Hopefully, in time, some of our actions might enlist some key players. We will never know until we try.

Behind Closed Doors

This is not meant to be a book on conspiracy. It's about the evolution of spiritual growth, our human potential, and the evolution of consciousness. There is so much more growth to come and to experience, but there are clear and obvious barriers in the way. The system that operates this world has vested interests in what they do, and they are not targeting any one specific form of political or religious competition. They are targeting them all—communism, socialism, free enterprise systems, capitalism, or whatever form of fundamentalist religion that can cause havoc and trouble on an economic scale. Ronald Reagan was a great advocate of the free enterprise system and the last time this was allowed to work to any degree was during his U.S. presidency. Since then, any form of free enterprise, in its truest sense, has been replaced by what I will term "controlled capitalism." Those who control the world's money supply get each target, no matter who it is, involved in a capitalistic approach, holding out the promise of new found wealth, only to bring them, eventually, to their knees due to debt—making these nations or organizations completely beholden to them and under their control. Key assets must be surrendered, sold off to the banks, just to remain afloat. That is just the way the world is. It is a massive conspiracy, as much of it is not done out in the open. Many important assets are now under the "protection" of vested interests—by those who have risen to the top, and in places of economic power.

Controlled capitalism is winning out because free markets don't rule. The hidden masters rule. They manipulate world markets to the advantage of the international banks—not their clients. The clients are their property, or soon will be. It will take time for China to be completely tamed, but steps have already been taken that will seal the fate of communism in that country. Capitalism on the scale that is coming there is not going to support a communist regime. It will for a while, but just watch it unfold.

In Russia, communism fell like a house of cards. It was not economically viable enough for it to maintain itself, so the system collapsed. They are now building their way up from nothing, with a very weak economy. China, however, is not only maintaining a great economy but building it stronger, in a brilliant effort to save itself from the same economic fate as communist Russia. The communist system doesn't work—it is inherently flawed so must employ forms of capitalism to stay afloat. Managing their money, however, is still done in large part by the state. Most Chinese banks are government owned and they create their own currency. They don't depend as much on central (international) banks, which are common around the world and tied in with the control of international finance. China has always maintained as much internal control of their assets as possible and thereby maintains more control over their own country, and their own fate. The international banks have wedged their foot into China's door, however. They have China sized up in the same way the Las Vegas casinos have done—which China has welcomed with open arms. In both cases, if China plays, the deck is stacked.

The point has been that historically speaking, communism is doomed—and the capitalistic system it has begun to turn to as its only viable option is terribly self-destructive to people and the environment. It is also doomed, and is dooming us. We truly *must* develop and implement an entirely new paradigm to operate from. Times have changed and we must adjust to them, or ultimately perish.

As we move forward we should understand that the entire worldwide capitalistic, economic system has proven itself to be the best system that we have available to us. At the same time, no system is perfect. All economic and political systems the world has ever known have a limited life span. We have reached a point where things have to be constantly manipulated and readjusted on a number of complex levels, beyond the basic ones we know about, just to keep things going. Most people know nothing of the particulars due to the multiple levels that these adjustments occur on.

Many countries should have gone bankrupt a long time ago—completely and totally bankrupt. But things get readjusted and these countries go into debt to the international banks. These countries basically become the "property" of these worldwide banks. The almighty dollar is in control; not politicians, not separate governments, as we are led to believe—but underneath the surface of it all there is a worldwide monetary and banking web that has ensnared virtually everyone. This is not a subject that is openly discussed in the media, although anyone who is willing to look can find out about it. We are given the illusion that each government controls its country, but they are just puppets, all dancing to the economic tune that is being played by the ones who really own you and control the money. It's the golden rule—he who has the gold, makes the rules.

For those who fear the so-called New World Order that is supposed to be coming, here's some news. A one world economic system that controls virtually everything is already in place, at least in the western world. This has been a long process. It has taken a couple of centuries for it to reach this point. There are still a few areas that are not totally within their grasp, but for the most part it's done. Its power base affects every single economic, monetary structure on at least some level. The New World Order is not an outrageous fantasy or a paranoid delusion. It's already here. Take out a dollar bill. Turn it over. It's right there on the seal: "Novus Ordo Seclorum," which means "the new order of the world." They "officially" announced their appearance in 1933 when the dollar was redesigned. This was when the international banks took over the United States. It was bankrupt after the stock market crash of 1928 followed by the great depression, and was being bailed out on the bankers' terms. From that point forward they have managed to take control of every major facet of the U.S. economic structure that presented itself, including corporations, banking institutions, and the stock market. This is not to say that they are evil, *per se*. It has served well as an economic system, but is now outdated and needs to be overhauled or replaced. Surprised as you might be to discover the existence of the "New World Order," it's even more surprising to know that it's gotten so old and inept, it needs to be thrown out and trashed. Evidence of severe mismanagement by shady manipulators and power mongers abound, simply because they have managed to operate in the shadows all these years. It's not perfect, even if run correctly, but it kept America going for a while and was the best we had at the time.

What we have to be worried about are the people who run it, and what is being slowly taken from us—meaning our freedoms. This equally applies to the United Kingdom, Australia, Europe and the entire Western world. We also need to examine what they are feeding our minds, and our bodies, in exchange for us turning over our power and freedoms to them. Much of our power is gone, *but from only within this older, outdated paradigm*. We do have some power, and can use it in immense ways. We just don't know how to use it. We are being told things that are preventing us from using it so that the economic world machine can keep rolling right over us and manipulating us for their own means. What can we do? Avoid television for our information—if we can snap out of its "programming" long enough, and use the Internet instead. Avoid processed foods and eat less meat to become far healthier, and put the chemical/poison-makers that inject them into our foods out of business. Each person should go through the four-point new paradigm plan of identity, education, and holistic awareness, followed by a personal restructuring of whatever they can, economically, by spending their money wisely as a result of making an *educated choice*. If this happens on a large enough scale it could force the U.S. government into issuing its own money, instead of depending on that dinosaur called the Federal Reserve, thereby breathing new life into what will otherwise be its own financial corpse.

If the U.S. fails to step up and control its own destiny, then the loss of their financial power will be complete—the price to pay for a world government to come into power. The U.S. is on schedule to lose more of its economic clout so that it will not be able to stand on its own. Instead, it will continue to be propped up and fully dependent upon outside controlling interests.

In addition, if international finance completes its world takeover then our own humanity is lost through exploitation of each other and the environment. When the final pieces of this puzzle fall into place, our fate will be sealed. The only thing that will save us is the collapse of this house of cards, because the international banking scheme is not a strong answer in itself. It will prey upon us and the other nations of the world in order to survive, and force us into playing host to its parasitic needs. The vast majority of loans that individuals, companies and nations have received, which they thought would save them, have turned out to be nothing more than a Trojan horse.

International banks operate on the "impossible contract" problem. Over 99% of their money is borrowed into existence through loans. In 14 years, a debt of ten dollars at 5% interest becomes a twenty-dollar debt. This is not sustainable for long periods when huge sums are involved. Every 14 years the money supply must double just to pay the interest on these loans. The creation of new goods and services helps to siphon off some of this demand, but it's a pace of growth that cannot be maintained. The only thing saving the system, for the moment, is the huge new third world market, especially China. When that becomes saturated there will be no place left to go. In the meantime we shuffle loans and goods back and forth under a ticking clock, while the pace in which the banking system operates continues to quicken.

Private commercial banking has become obsolete, but they don't want us to know this. Many of these banks are insolvent, but are leeching off of us and weakening our economies at our expense—not theirs. It has become too burdensome and we should not have to put up with it. Congress or the leaders of any nation in this position should note how strong the economies are right now in both India and China due to their own internal banking institutions and the ability to create their own money. We should put the insolvent banks into receivership—take them over. This also means dumping the Federal Reserve, which is not federal at all but a private company, owned by a consortium of banks that control U.S. money. Begun in 1913, it is considered by many politicians to have been one of the worst mistakes we ever made. One of the original founding banks of the Federal Reserve and still active today is the J.P. Morgan Chase Company (which Dubai International Capital now has holdings in). I do not claim to be an expert in economics, but it seems to me that if the U.S. government printed its own money like other countries do that are experiencing great economic activity, it would lessen the problem of national debt and eliminate the necessity of having outside entities like Dubai International Capital having part ownership in the actual creation of U.S. money.

Due to new eminent domain laws, our own government has, in recent years, just walked in and seized the homes and businesses of hard working people to build malls and for private development purposes, because it was "needed to improve the economy," which is an outrage. Taking the insolvent banks in this same way would be far more practical "to improve the economy," and could help put victimized people, as just mentioned, back into business. We are all being victimized by this outmoded financial system and unless we do something it will continue to get worse.

In the Western world our quality of life is still better than other parts of the world. Those who have not traveled have no idea how well we have it here in the West. The current world economic system supports this higher standard of living, but it is being terribly depleted. Much of it, including our more successful industries, continue to be transferred overseas—to places like India and China. Although I am not a financial expert, it seems that a more enlightened society would not hesitate to generate a more viable system. If we can set off on a more spiritual and fulfilling path, we will design an economy that will better serve our higher and more developed spiritual needs.

To help in the transitional phase, I believe we should have in place a simple bartering system that could act as a safety net. It would not be powerful enough to support an entirely new economic structure, but could help maintain basic needs as we cross into a new way of doing things. Bartering is already popular in many areas but not officially accepted, mainly because revenue is not involved so it takes away from the government's tax base. Due to the historical greed factor and corruption found in governmental bodies, I hold no hope for any official bartering system, simple as it might be, to be endorsed or created by government. This falls entirely upon us.

As a more enlightened society continues to grow, so will a system of bartering. The huge war machine, which demands billions of dollars to function, will become slowly diffused. As it does, the huge tax base needed to fuel it will no longer be necessary, opening the door to a free exchange of goods and services. A new field will open up for economists who can also operate as social engineers, in devising and then integrating a large scale bartering structure into the new paradigm. Some people are currently involved in the foundational groundwork of bartering at local levels, but without the science involved to create long-term benefits.

The Wall Street Disaster of 2008
As this book was going to press, Wall Street experienced its worst financial disaster since the stock market crash of 1929. A last minute mention is inserted here to reiterate how flawed the system is. In addition to the list of failed banks and financial institutions a news story was released about the FBI investigating twenty-six different companies for financial wrongdoings. The story completely vanished at the same time a proposal surfaced for a 700 billion-dollar taxpayer-provided bailout for such companies as a reward for their mismanagement and, in some cases, outright criminal activities. Congress first voted against the bailout but, out of desperation, a few minor points were added to the bill (along with all kinds of unrelated special interest "pork,"), intense lobbying took place and it was voted through on a second attempt. These are private, non-governmental businesses that have failed and taxpayers should have no legal obligation to bail them out. If the government would take over the banks and run them (and print its own money), as we see being done so successfully in other parts of the world, we should then have a vested interest in supporting government programs. But without such direct control and/or having *proper regulations* over businesses that would prevent corruption, mismanagement and outright criminal activities,

we are doing nothing more than rewarding the worst elements of this flawed system with billions of dollars, so they can continue with business as usual. At the same time, average middle-class homeowners who are struggling to adhere to the payment policies demanded of them and, in some cases, who are out on the streets with no home because of them, are offered nothing. The victims are left with nothing—except the bill. This defeats the entire purpose of government, which is supposed to serve its people instead of exploiting them or allowing others to do so.

One thing is clear—it will take many years for the economy to recover. Its failure has been proven and at the time of this writing, its negative repercussions are spreading throughout Europe and will be felt for years to come. It is time to reassess the entire economic structure and build from scratch a better world through identity, education, and a holistic world-view, so that the basic operating structure of the western economy can eventually be run successfully, from outside of its current mindset.

> *No great improvements in the lot of mankind are possible until a great change takes place in their mode of thought.*
> —John Stuart Mill

A New Direction

We have been speaking economically, but what's missing from the equation is the spiritual and religious dimensions. A shift in this area, on par with economics, is beginning to move us into the New Age. It has always been the case with each new cycle in the past, and it will be the case again in the future. What's going to be different this time, however, is the world is larger and more complex than it has been during the ends of previous ages that we know of. The world has always had a variety of religious beliefs, but in past ages there was usually a single, more dominant one at the time. Today, with such diversity in religious power throughout the world, the beginnings of the next age are going to prove interesting. Because of this, the overall transition may not be a smooth one. We are already beginning to see the strain through the greatest telltale earmark of spiritual ignorance—terrorism.

A shift is clearly beginning to occur in the way we think and perceive on spiritual and religious levels. It comes as a precursor to the economic changes that are needed, and is therefore easier to accomplish. Just as the fish symbolized the Age of Pisces, we have water being poured out as the symbol for the Aquarian Age. Water is not solid, but is the purist definition of fluidity and is a highly spiritual symbol. When you pour it out, water covers all areas and naturally seeks the *lowest ground* first. What we must do, and are clearly already doing, is develop a mutual respect and compassion toward all faiths and beliefs. Many of the more mature faiths have come to an understanding that theirs' will not take over the entire world and no faith will ever succeed in doing so.

Religion is such a volatile and passionate part of life that we would self-destruct in a number of different scenarios before any one religion could successfully *force* the people of the world to obey them. You cannot, nor will you ever, succeed in controlling people's beliefs. We must seek out the very lowest, poorest and most destitute people and spiritually nurture them, help them, and show them respect for who they are instead of rushing in with missionaries to force change at the same time help is being delivered (as was common in the Age of Pisces). We will not have a dominant religion in the coming age, but a dominant and respectful *mindset* among them that connects us all.

Jesus taught compassion and mutual respect, but Christianity changed as it grew. It corrupted and added to his original teachings to the point where they became ineffective. The men involved in spreading the faith became worldly, cruel and arrogant power seekers, thereby causing the ultimate failure of this faith during its efforts to change the world. From the perspective of the new Aquarian consciousness, the dominant Piscean fish of this fading age was just one creature that lives in the water. It did succeed to an acceptable and predictable level in the Piscean Age, but that water is starting to be poured out as spiritual nourishment for all of the different peoples and faiths who seek it. It is time to start anew, and on a larger, more meaningful scale (no pun intended). The "answer" cannot be found in just one religion—it must be shared among them all.

Chapter Thirteen

MUTUAL RESPECT AND RELIGION

For all things proceed out of the same spirit, which is differently named love, justice, temperance, in its different applications, just as the ocean receives different names on the several shores which it washes.
—Ralph Waldo Emerson

Truth, crushed to earth, shall rise again;
The eternal years of God are here:
But Error, wounded, writhes in pain,
And dies among its worshippers.
—William Cullen Bryant

Any one world economic system that would come to full fruition based on the outmoded path that we travel is not going to bring together the different religious factions that have been fighting for centuries throughout the world. People get passionate about their religions, and fundamentalist factions will stop at nothing to keep their religious goals alive. This mindset creates war. Religion has been fought over for centuries and if this world is ever going to be controlled in a manageable fashion, all of the different religions have either got to come together in some way or be eliminated and replaced with something new. This is something that will materialize more clearly as this New Age comes more into focus because, once again, every time we have emerged into a New Age, a different, dominating religion has come into the world and replaced the old one. Since the world today has become more complex than in past ages, this creates a tremendous hurdle for us in getting into the next age. However, there is a solution: mutual respect. This is where the individual comes in. We still have our own personal power. In the same way that we can make a personal choice as to what we eat and consume, and what we spend our money on, we also have the ability to choose mutual respect among all faiths. As we educate ourselves in a more spiritual fashion and develop our holistic awareness, the natural consequence will be more compassion and mutual respect. It is this mindset that will bind us all together. Surely there will continue to be fundamentalist factions that will insist on remaining faithful, and therefore blind, but their survival will be limited by the immense strength of a "wave" of higher consciousness that will sweep across the planet. People of different faiths will overlook our differences when providing essential items to one another that cannot be had from within one's own religious group. We will learn that differences in belief matter less when we can reach out and share our humanity and love towards one another without having dogmatic prerequisites in the way that cause nothing but suffering. What is the point of that?

Due to its emotional volatility, religion remains a powerful tool to control the masses and boost flagging economies. Secret government agencies from countries the world over have a habit of manipulating religious emotions in an effort to create war. There's nothing like a good old-fashioned war to create jobs, bombs and merchandise that can be sold to both sides of a conflict. For example, since the end of World War II to the time this book was written, the United States has sold weapons of war to over 100 different countries. Dozens of other nations peddle planes, tanks and ingenious killing machines to whoever happens to be at odds with another country—it's big business. Manipulating religious climates plays a huge role in getting these conflicts started; more people have been killed in the name of God than for any other reason. But if God is truly a *loving God*, then what is the point? This form of behaviour is the complete opposite of mutual respect, which we are only now beginning to cultivate. Instead, we have been promoting hatred and murder among the brotherhood of man, just for sake of profits. It is true that we are born with violent tendencies, but to turn them into a commodity for profit, and make a business out of it, is sick. It is deranged behaviour. We are saying, "Go out and kill people. We will not only provide the weapons you need, but our operatives will also supply a worthy excuse, or we will manufacture the stage for the conflict, just so I can have your business. How's that for customer service?"

There are experts on world affairs who will argue to the contrary that it's not religion that has been fought over and caused so many wars throughout history, but territory. Territory plays a role at times, but in general it is secondary. When territorial conflicts do arise, the fighting does not last very long unless religion is an issue. For example in Israel, especially Jerusalem, there are three different religions that have been vying for control of one small area for over half a century, with no end in sight. Northern Ireland has experienced a similar passion and problem.

As soon as the religious passions of a people in a certain area are subdued, then territory is no longer a problem. Issues of ownership and borders get resolved swiftly and clearly. Get religious passions and a demanding "god" out of the way, and there's usually no problem handling the disputed territory between rational people. Mutual respect between religions would accomplish the same ends.

In past ages, religion was always the dominating force in the world, with the economics falling under its dominion. In today's world, it is the banking cartels and economics that control everything first rather than religions, governments or elected officials. It may not be far from the truth to say that money has now become our God. What we must learn is that we can never replace our spiritual nourishment or any form of its expression with a materialistic counterfeit.

It was Karl Marx who said, "Religion is the opium of the people." In Marxism he wanted workers to keep things moving, and not be distracted by religion. But when you stifle the only spiritual expression that a people have, they become nothing more than automatons. It is no wonder that Marxism failed—and from an economic and spiritual point of view it was an extremely swift demise, leaving no doubt whatsoever that people cannot operate in this way. What those in power today have learned is that it is best to manipulate religion rather than do away with it completely. Religion is currently used to the advantage of those in power to reach economic gain. It has become an art form—but like Marxism, will not last. We are evolving and becoming more respectful.

Our Awakening

As we spiritually evolve and get closer to this New Age, we are starting to wake up. We really *want* to wake up, but the jury is still out as to whether or not we actually will. Yes, it seems there is a wave that has started to cast itself across the planet, but we are at a crossroads and must determine whether or not the obstacles in our path will be allowed to defeat us. People are starting to read more, and investigate more in this direction. Will it be enough? Many want to understand more about who they are and where they are going—and as that continues to happen, people are questioning religion.

With this probing, deeper questions about ourselves are being addressed. The basic tenets of our religions only scratch the surface because we have become more intellectually sophisticated than people from the more primitive past, when these religions were first formed. Many are finding that their religious beliefs are outdated and based on centuries-old concepts that no longer apply to the modern world, and to the many things that we have learned scientifically and intuitively about ourselves.

Spirituality and religion are two completely different things. As one starts to awaken to the spirit, it becomes clear that man-made religion does not hold as solid an answer toward what many of us are seeking. For some people it suits them fine, but for a vast and growing population, that's not the case any more. Something is happening. It's on an intuitive level, so is hard to put into words. It is something we just "know," something that is beyond words. As we grow more and more in this intuitive way and start to develop in this direction more strongly, we find that religion does not supply what we need. The more dogmatic a religion is, the more offensive it becomes to a spiritually based person. Too many rules about what one must believe as a prerequisite to be part of the flock turns followers into cookie-cutter automatons.

There's a bumper sticker that says, "Religions are just cults with more members." If you think about it, it's true—there's not much difference in how each one operates. Certain things must be believed if you're going to be a member, and it's the same with both groups. Religions are more accepted only because they've been around longer and more people joined. You could go down the list of what a cult desires of people and what it is that religion desires of people, and they are virtually the same things. Yet people in major religions do not feel like they're involved in a cult because they have so many members and they're not so alone. Small cults get all the attention because they're so unique. They stand out because they walk a different path. Cults, in general, can be more extreme than religions, but you cannot forget the fundamentalist factions of modern day religions, which are just as cultish in their deeds to observing outsiders.

Cults are notorious for brainwashing. Yet the level found in fundamentalist beliefs is equal to any smaller cult you would find throughout the world. There is no possible way that you would find an open-minded fundamentalist person in any religion. They simply will not listen to an alternative view under any circumstance—because of *brainwashing*. In fact, they have been known to become quite angry, violent or belligerent when one requests to share an alternative view of things in an open and peaceful way. That's the way cults operate, as well. There is nothing you can say to cause them to even *consider* an alternative view, no matter how much it can be backed up with factually relevant material, either scientifically, archaeologically, or through simple common sense.

From a spiritual perspective, from those who are opening up in a spiritual way, there is complete tolerance toward other views. There is an understanding that each person is equally respected as a human being and has the right to believe anything they want as long as it does not harm someone else. When you experience cult members or fundamentalists who are trying to cram their ideas down your throat, things can get very heated if you decline to convert or you disagree with the mindset. Mutual respect is more easily obtained by the spiritually awakened than by those who have been indoctrinated.

Just take a look at history. You will find by searching throughout history, groups of people who were peaceful but who always fell victim to domineering, violent groups. Most of these peaceful religions or philosophies had high spiritual values and intentions. And the ones who stamped them out—the ones who performed the violence—clearly had little spirituality involved in their actions. In each case, it was simply a domineering, callous attack, often backed by money. The control of people's minds, through religion, and the control of economies are intimately connected. Those in power always have two main concerns—economic and religious—that go hand in hand. The economies of the time will always flourish if you can control what people think.

Religion once played the major role in creating people's perceptions, but now we have television influencing our thoughts rather than the local pulpit. TV truly has stepped in and taken religion's place. Not only are we told directly what to think and buy, we are also *prevented* from thinking too much with all of the entertainments being thrown at us to dumb us down. The Internet, if used correctly, is the antidote for people seeking relevant information that will inspire positive thought and action. Even more effective than this is inner exploration, within ourselves. That is where *everything* of relevance truly is, whether one can discern it or not.

One of the most notorious achievements of the past, yet brilliant in its own right, was the selling of indulgences by the church. The control of people's thoughts and solving the economic concerns of the church were both taken care of in one fell swoop. The selling of indulgences involved the church telling the people, who did not have much money to begin with, that if they contributed a certain amount of money to the church they would spend less time in purgatory. And if the donation was big enough, they could, in effect, buy a free ticket into heaven. The church filled their coffers and took care of their economic concerns, while reinforcing a belief that one would be truly saved if they coughed up enough money to satisfy the church. If the church was "convinced" with a big enough donation, it took the time to become a special, direct intermediary to God on your behalf and put in a good word for you. Thousands believed they were going straight to heaven.

In the early 1400s in Bohemia, a man named John Hus had had just about enough of all this and exposed the whole sham. The Pope didn't like that; but at the time, there were actually three different people all claiming to be Pope. So all three Popes didn't like it. They fought among themselves for prominence while still trying to solve the problem of Hus. They also did not allow people to read the Bible in their own language. John Hus stood up and (I will paraphrase) said, "We want to translate the Bible into our native language so we can understand what our beliefs are supposed to be. We want to learn more about our faith. We should have the right to read and understand our own Bible instead of listening to it in Latin and wondering what was said." And the church basically said, "No, no, no! *We* control the religion, not you. It's a business. Get out your purses. Get out your wallets, cough up enough money and we'll tell you what to believe. That's how it's done. And if you have anything more to say about it, there's the stake right over there. We will burn you to a crisp if you create trouble for us, and that will be the end of that." And that's exactly what happened to Hus. They burned him at the stake in 1415. Groups of people called Hussites revolted and battled church forces for decades as a result, raising people's consciousness and creating a constant reminder for spiritual freedom that few people ever forgot. Luther's Reformation soon followed, and prominent historians credit Hus for its initial foundation, stating that without his work the Reformation may never have come to pass.

Let others have their truth and the truth will prevail. —John Hus

We no longer have indulgences, but other forms of religious manipulation have taken its place. At some point in our spiritual evolution, we're going to say enough is enough, and we're not going to fall for the manipulations of man-made religions any longer. I believe we are nearing that point in our spiritual evolution. It's time we recognize our own spiritual freedom and dignity, and stop depending on religions that dictate what we're supposed to believe. As spiritual beings, we're perfectly capable of determining that for ourselves.

We have been learning and evolving, in a spiritual sense, away from outside "authorities," while our inner worlds become more accessible. Another example of what we have left behind is the historical intolerance of the Inquisition. This began about 1489 with the publication of the book *Malleus Maleficarum*, which means "the hammer of witches." It was the guidebook for the detaining, torturing and sometimes killing of "witches." Witches, in general, were thought to be women, and many of them were engaged in using natural remedies for healing. Such information was passed down through generations and many women were very good at it.

If someone turned in a so-called witch to the authorities, then the possessions of that witch would be given over to the church, and about ten percent of their estate would go to the person who turned them in. What a great incentive to turn all your friends and neighbors in! Research this subject closely and you will find that those at the very highest levels of power knew there was no such thing as witches. They wanted to increase their wealth and confiscate property at a desperate time. Using accusations of "witchcraft" was a convenient way to do it. They preyed upon the ignorance of the masses to achieve their ends, including the majority of church lackeys who did all the dirty work, killing and torture, and it worked.

Today, the game has remained much the same, but operates on a more sophisticated level. Instead of coming in and grabbing your possessions based on imaginary "witches," which we don't fall for any more, imaginary money that does not really exist is created in the form of bank loans. Both people and nations are unable to pay them back. Even paying on the interest is difficult, and we become beholden to those who loan us the "money"—to the point of becoming their property. These days it is better to keep the serfs alive who can produce for you and make their monthly payments. If certain countries are so poverty stricken that they are deemed never able to do this, then tragic events do befall certain parts of the world that result in the mass deaths (genocide) of "useless eaters," through disease, starvation or brutal warfare. Strangely enough, nobody rushes in to help or save these starving masses in time, despite the resources being available. The events in Darfur are a recent example.

In a spiritually based paradigm, none of this would be happening. Most everyone would be healthy and there would be no shortage of resources because they would be maintained far more responsibly. The idea of exploitation would be almost non-existent. You may think I am dreaming of an unreachable utopia with such ideas, but practical steps over a number of years can make this dream a reality. Although we do not know exactly what the future holds, we have a general idea as to the direction we need to travel in order to reverse some negative human traits and their resulting trends.

> *There are some people who live in a dream world, and there are some who face reality, and then there are those who turn one into the other.* —Douglas H. Everett

The next chapter in the human story is about to unfold.

The goal of religion could finally be realized if its similarities were celebrated rather than its differences attacked. Mahatma Gandhi said, "I came to the conclusion long ago… that all religions were true, and also that all had some error in them." We have been focusing on the errors and not the common truths. A few thousand masterful books focusing on the errors of religion were written during what was called the "Freethought Movement" between the Civil War and World War I, from such writers as Robert Ingersoll, H.L. Mencken, D.M. Bennett, Mark Twain, and numerous others. We knew something was not quite right with religion, but were not as spiritually mature as we are today so knew only to attack it without building on the positives. It worked well and became such a threat that for a time it became unlawful to send such materials through the mail. D.M. Bennett, founder of the Truth Seeker Company, spent time in jail for doing this. The foundations of religious belief began to erode during this era, but the only clear answer as to where to turn as an alternative was atheism. Atheism began to flourish; but was soon followed by a glimpse of more spiritual ideas. Spiritualism was one of these—a movement devoted to the idea that we survive death in another conscious form and can, at times, communicate with the living. But then World War I came along. There's nothing like a major war to create a distraction away from spiritual truth.

Religion was also threatened at the outset of this war, but a war always turns that completely around—religion becomes a rallying point. God is beseeched to step in on each side claiming to have Him as their ally, expecting victory as a result. The God or gods, and the religions they represent, have always been rationalized as benevolent agents in warfare going back for centuries. Each side claims Him; only one ultimately benefits.

War breeds contempt and hatred but it is only through mutual respect and compassion that we will transcend our petty religious attitudes and reach the ultimate goal of religion. What is the ultimate goal of religion? It is not to make war and kill people, although it is used in that respect. Despite what the politicians say, asking for His help to kill thousands of other people will not bring an all-loving God running to our doorsteps. The goal of religion is to achieve a renewed connection with God and fighting wars *does not* achieve this end.

Changing Historical Patterns

To effectively change the world we must change the historical pattern. In the past, we were able to do this with geography by discovering proper knowledge. Not long ago, historically speaking, most people believed that the world was flat. Different "sects" existed, corresponding to our religious ones. Some believed that it was supported on the back of a turtle, others that it was supported by Atlas (before artists showed him with a round Earth), others claimed angels supported it and others believed its support was "a necessary mystery." We eventually changed history by discovering true knowledge about the nature of the Earth. With religion and its different forms, we have the same situation today. Science will one day identify clearly the "field" in which the God-force resides and we will use this information to better tap into the same field within ourselves. We will one day strip away the veil of ignorance that creates our separate religious viewpoints and will change history once again, relegating the "crutch" of holy books and dogmatic belief systems to a secondary position. Spirituality will return, but will be recognized for its *inherent importance* this time, rather than being stamped out, in some cases, as "heresy."

History bears out the fact that the most spiritual of groups have always been the most peaceful, and were not the ones who were marauding around spreading aggression. Very few if any of these spiritual movements ever launched a physical attack against the dominant religions of the time. It has always been the other way around. Spiritual groups like the Essenes, Marcionites, Bogomils, Waldenses, Cathars, Sufis, Tibetan monks, Unitarians, or other similar groups did not rape, pillage or try to forcibly cram their beliefs down the throats of anyone. Nor did they try—let alone succeed—to kill as many religious followers as they could. Dominant religions, however, commonly used these tactics to get their point across. Religions are focused primarily outward, while spiritual practice involves an inner quest. Spirituality is more interested in the development of personal power, used to control and master one's self; while religions are focused more on power structures that are used to control and master others. With spirituality, the only enemy is you—or a certain part of you—but with religion everyone who happens to disagree with you is the enemy. As a result, spiritual groups of any consequence always fell victim to the religious institutions of the time and were stamped out. This includes the Cathars of France, the Bogomils of the Bulgarian area, and the Waldenses of Italy and southern Europe, among others. These groups began to flourish peacefully because people realized important spiritual values in their teachings. But as the teachings spread, persecutions and large numbers of killings followed. These three groups were competing Christian sects so they were religious— but were expressing things in a more spiritual way. For example, they believed in inner truths and followed the original teachings of Jesus, but did not buy into the outer trappings of the church that were added later— such as the worship of the cross and other images, indulgences, the idea of holy water, the adoration of saints, purgatory, and everybody's favorite—church music. They ignored these things because none of it is in the Bible. The Waldenses also believed in what Acts 18:24 says: that God does not live in shrines made by men. They were right. God cannot be found within an enclosure of four stone walls, but only within yourself. Therefore, churches were not required for worship, but a group of people willing to look within, were.

The Waldenses still survive to this very day, having persevered through centuries of attack. A few of their churches exist in the United States and elsewhere. They are just one example of how a peaceful group can be persecuted by a stronger religious authority even if that more peaceful group is more accurate in its beliefs than the one that is in power. It seems that the more power a religion has, the more intolerant it can become.

If we can educate ourselves enough to see the difference between power structures and spiritual freedom, then we will be on the right path for the breakthrough that we need. This is what the Age of Aquarius is all about, and what its symbol—the man with the water pitcher—is trying to tell us. We are moving into a time that will allow more tolerance and understanding, which is something that has continued to grow over the centuries. This trend will greatly accelerate if we work toward these ends.

Chapter Fourteen

THE GOD PACT

Improve Your Life and the World

The vast majority of people are good at heart and believe in an all-loving God. Honoring such a God in one's life should lead to the same type of existence – one filled with love. Is that so hard? There is a way to bring this into being and it's called The God Pact. It does not promise to eliminate hatred or cruelty because they are part of life, but it has the potential to lessen them. Evil touches our lives in terrible ways and seems to be growing in this world of ours. This gives incentive for each person to take control of their choices and beliefs – and to do something. The God Pact allows you, as an individual, to take a stand and recognize a God of love. It allows you to make a living statement against random violence and terror by bringing the principles of a loving and compassionate God directly into your life.

One of the most daunting tasks facing governments in the world today is trying to prevent random violence or terrorism. This pact is not limited to individuals, or by borders, so it could help larger groups or nations as well. Beyond improving people's lives on a personal level, it could one day have an impact on violence throughout the world. Here is The God Pact in its personal form, meant for individuals.

THE GOD PACT

1) I believe in just one God, who is all-loving and prefers peace over war.
YES or NO

2) I believe that we, as human beings, are all God's children.
YES or NO

3) I believe that an all-loving God is not biased or exclusive to any single belief system or religion, no matter what it might be.
YES or NO

4) If my religion or form of worship never existed, but all others did, I would still believe in God.
YES or NO

I HAVE MARKED "YES" AND AGREE WITH ALL THE ABOVE
I therefore bind myself with God by my signature below and from this day forward, pledge to conduct myself with love, compassion and mutual respect toward my fellow man, avoiding harm toward others unless engaged in the protective action of myself or others.

_____

DATE _____

5) Provisionary section: I have answered "No" to at least one of the above points so cannot sign this pact. But aside from my own views about God, I believe it is possible that adoption of this agreement between others could bring more peace to the world. Therefore, I extend support in this limited way by voting in favor of its adoption.
YES or NO

I HAVE AGREED WITH THE LAST PROVISION ONLY, WITHOUT COMPROMISING MY PERSONAL BELIEFS

_____

DATE _____

Must we wait for some far off date in the future for us to become much wiser, and respect all faiths? Or should we start doing it now? As individuals. Science has found evidence for God. In the distant future, governing bodies may enter into agreements involving a mutual respect for God. But it hasn't happened yet – which might explain much of the world's problems today. Not once have we ever created a pact of any kind that shared the one true God among its signers. It is this that is being proposed. Today, some would say this is insane, to forget about it, and it will never happen. So far, this pact has not spread. I've tried. Is it really that far-fetched? Is this idea crazy? The God Pact is not insane and is meant to reduce the *real* insanity and cruelty that we inflict on each other today.

Terrorism will not go away but will likely increase – unless we do something. Fighting violence with violence often escalates into more violence, which is what has been happening today. However, peaceful means have been shown to work better and produce more lasting effects. Such proof remains from the work of great men like Mahatma Gandhi and Dr. Martin Luther King, Jr. The world is a better place as a direct result of these people and others like them. The God Pact follows in the same spirit found in the work of these men.

History proves that great things can happen if people would only try. The movements that achieved the best results have often come from individuals or small groups who were so passionate about their goals that their ideas caught on and spread. The Internet and other grass roots avenues make such things possible today. Collective action by individuals rather than governments is becoming the best way to achieve positive change. Governments have grown cumbersome and any new changes moving through their channels develop complexities that often short-circuit the original goals. And they are divisive by design. This is why collective action in simple grass-roots form often works better.

Achieving world peace through government has never worked. World leaders and their governments have failed to achieve world peace because it is virtually impossible to satisfy so many complex goals of so many different cultures and religions worldwide. When our differences are the focus, peace is never possible. Peaceful coexistence becomes possible when the focus is moved from our obvious differences to the most positive things we have in common. The God Pact operates from within this positive realm. It's worth a try.

Signing The God Pact makes our loving and compassionate God more accessible to people and puts the behavior in motion. Non-violent lifestyles can be adopted by people everywhere to create more safety in their communities. It could then spread. No one will argue that creating a small peaceful group is more than possible which, from its interactions with other groups, could spread the same conduct. Eventually, cities or societies with violent tendencies would be forced to engage in more non-violent actions whenever these peaceful coalitions reach a critical mass. It would work gradually, but it would work.

Governments try to enforce peaceful conduct between countries today, through sanctions against rogue nations, but this system is flawed. In the long run it rarely works and violence continues. Peace cannot be forced upon others – it must be voluntary. The God Pact agreement, if recognized, includes *directly engaged people*, thereby creating better results. Any government that truly represents their people would be more inclined to act on their behalf. Although world peace is a monumental task and seemingly insurmountable, first steps should be taken through something like The God Pact.

It should start with individuals and when enough interest is generated, communities or nations may wish to acknowledge it. Before politicians become involved, the *people* should be allowed to sign it or not sign it on a community level or ballot. Politicians must know how God is acknowledged and perceived before any representation can be made. Many say God is Love. An all-loving God clearly wants peace in the world rather than violence and if recognized as such – and honored as such – then more peaceful behavior should follow.

Each and every person has a right to make a meaningful choice about their God in a direct way that matters. It should not be up to vested interests to speak for you before you can voice – and vote – on how you perceive God. After all, we have often found weapons manufacturers, politicians, bankers, investors, international financiers, and nations with barbaric fundamentalist leaders who still live in the dark ages, that have all claimed to support the view of a loving God, but have done nothing but spread hate and greed to achieve their own personal aims. The voices of all the people (and not their representatives) should be heard as a foundational basis. We have the RIGHT to express this and vote on it. So far, this has not been done. Let it be done now. If you have not reviewed or filled out the form, please do so.

The Definition of God

The "God" referred to in this pact is based on modern knowledge and equates to something that goes beyond religion – so is inclusive to them all. The true and authentic God can be viewed scientifically, as an all-pervading connective force, or mystically, as the underlying cause for existence, but does not and should not take on the name of any supreme being designated by a single religion. Despite various dogmatic claims, no single religion holds exclusive ownership to the true and authentic God (which is the purpose of point number four in the Pact). So far, all that religions have done is to grope clumsily for God's true essence. The God Pact can bring this essence closer to us. The pact itself can enhance our religions, but it should not necessarily operate from within them.

Why God Transcends Religion and Churches

The most devout fundamentalists should understand that their form of belief does not have a monopoly on God. Every religion has human founders and were created by men, despite what some may claim. God is not the founder of any church or belief system. People are – *inspired people, and great people*, but people nonetheless. If God were to found a belief system, He would have come down to earth and created one singular church, making sure to leave no doubt in the minds of men everywhere as to what it was, and there would be only one true religion to match the one true God. This has not happened. Despite this fact, the true God remains available to all people and all religions that seek Him. No one is "wrong" in their sincere effort to find God and most countries rightly honor freedom of religion as a result of this fact.

God is already recognized by the U.S. government and many governments worldwide – found on coins, mentioned in slogans, etc. This offends very few because no specific religion is promoted by the government, due to the separation of church and state. The United States honors God by putting "In God We Trust" on its coins and currency. As a result, people from any religion can agree with the statement "In God we Trust," and not be offended. In this act alone, it is acknowledged that God transcends religion. Presidents often end important speeches with the words, "God bless America" or "God bless our troops," without mentioning a religion – because an all-encompassing God is being referred to. We already *acknowledge* the one true God and *know* that He is there. Let us, for God's sake, embrace Him! Collectively. He is *not* a construct of any religion and, despite what atheists might tell you, He is more than an "idea." God is there; we must stop ignoring Him on a personal level because of our limited views.

The limited, biased and proprietary view many have of God is most always a construct of religion. This view, in effect, relegates Him to nothing more than an idea. Only the followers of the religion are willing to accept this "version" or idea of God. God is not limited in this way. We created our religions based on limited views. These limits are now being expanded. It is time to grow up. For example, we are learning to respect all faiths and belief systems as long as they do not harm other people or beings. Mankind is diverse and there are good people everywhere who love and respect God. Your religion, whatever it might be, does not own Him.

Originally, we made God a religious instrument by inserting Him into small separate movements – movements that were eager to claim God for themselves in an attempt to gain converts and self-justification. We have since grown wiser and have begun to understand that we are all God's children.

The term "God" should not automatically make this a religious issue. It is first and foremost a social issue – one that uses the universal term of "God" for everyone's benefit. The true God or unifying force throughout the universe is sometimes observed in religion, but operates apart from it in many ways. God is within us and within nature, and should be expressed in social, scientific and spiritual ways rather than exclusively through religion. Religions tend to separate people due to differing beliefs, but The God Pact asks for a powerful recognition of the one unifying force, entity, consciousness, essence or being that binds us all together. We are being asked to look beyond religion in the execution of this pact. Doing so may allow us to transcend our current understanding of God – and ourselves.

You are invited to sign this yourself as a personal pact with God, honoring Him in a promise to live in peace. It's your own *personal recognition of God* and, if you wish, send or post a blank form to others to consider signing. Embrace each other in a peaceful "community" of your own. Eventually, signed forms might reach local representatives – or send a collection of names in petition form of those who have signed it and wish it to be recognized on a political level. If it should ever appear on any kind of ballot, it should be explained on the ballot that if one true God is recognized by the majority of people, the governing bodies in their jurisdictions are then obligated to represent the following points:

If agreement to the aforementioned points is made by a majority vote, the following agenda must be carried out by the representative governmental bodies:
1) Each governmental or ruling body agrees not to ban any form of religion or spiritual belief whatsoever unless such religion or belief system allows, performs or intends physical harm to others or, outside of this, infringes upon a person's God-given right to believe as they wish.

2) Each signing nation, community or person agrees never to attack another signing entity unless they are attacked first, and agrees to never exceed a cer-

tain pre-determined limit of offensive and defensive weapons. If a signing party is attacked by any entity whatsoever, all other signers agree to come to its aid in every capable non-violent way, with violence being permitted for the purpose of self-preservation or to end on-going, severe attacks.

3) It is agreed that non-signing nations that engage in continued aggressive weapons accumulation, unwarranted violent actions, or domiciled terrorist bases or training centers would experience trade and financial sanctions by all signing nations collectively until weapons are eliminated or cut back to agreed amounts, violence is ceased, and religious or spiritual beliefs can be freely chosen as a God-given right. A limited level of humanitarian aid, when deemed necessary, may occur as a gesture of good will and compassion.

Why it is Time for The God Pact

Some may argue that violence will always be a part of the world and we must learn to live with it. But each of us has a *choice*. We can accept that it exists – but we do not have to embrace it. Or support it. We do not have to go along with the crowd like sheep and choose to accept the violence around us just because it is there. We might not be able to eliminate it completely, but we can lessen its presence through our own actions and choices.

Before peace can exist among nations you must make it part of your *own* existence – personally, then locally, then internationally. That is what The God Pact is all about. This simple process can create peace in any jurisdiction, county, state, province or nation where people are allowed to make choices for themselves and are willing to work at it. It starts with your own personal connection to God – something we each have. The pact allows you to claim for yourself an all-encompassing God of love. This God is shared among all religions, but in different forms. It is time to share God actively among all people, and not just among religions as a distant and dogmatic figurehead.

No one, up to now, has ever created a clearly written pact between people and the one true God they happen to acknowledge. And never have people collectively gotten together, from different places or belief systems, and agreed to conduct themselves in accordance with God's most obvious wishes, common to all faiths, which could be outlined in such a pact. A positive, loving, compassionate God can be the criteria for peace, which could be shared among its signers. It can begin with as little as two people, or between two island nations.

Discovering the Larger God

God no longer belongs strictly to religion, but exists within every part of our lives. Our understanding of God has increased. Quantum physics and advanced science reveals that we are actually *part* of God, which means we each have a God-given right to determine how we operate within the whole. God remains a collective outer concept, but we are becoming more conscious of Him, directly. We have a bigger version of God on our hands, which goes far beyond the conception of a great all-seeing man with a beard sitting on a throne in the sky, looking down upon us and judging us. Our newfound understanding, although less than complete, requires more thoughtful actions than we have previously exhibited in order to reach God or commune with Him peacefully. That is yet another purpose of The God Pact.

Most of us would agree that we all have a connection to God, whether it be through our souls, our religions or by simply being alive and part of nature. The highest God that encompasses all of creation is common to us all, and binds us together. It is the one special thing that we have, as individuals. Therefore, each of us has the God-given right to express this connection in a powerful, meaningful way that goes beyond our religious differences in a way that can be shared harmoniously, among us all. We have the right to live the way we want to live, based on our connection to God. Collectively, why should we *not* decide to live in peace once and for all, and to take steps to insure it? Our view of God, collectively, should be our guiding light.

Correcting the Misuse of God
God has been used to justify war for centuries. If The God Pact should become enacted among us, God would *prevent* war rather than cause it. Complete respect would be maintained for every peaceful, moral religion or form of worship no matter what it might be; all are equally respected. No individual is in any way coerced into giving up their faith – they are simply taught respect toward others, which everyone deserves.

The true God transcends all religions, yet is part of them all. No religion can logically lay claim to a monopoly on an agreed upon, all-loving, non-exclusive God. This overall view is briefly addressed in the U.S. Pledge of Allegiance, where it states "one nation, under God,..." The God Pact would go one step further and place "all nations under God" (that sign the Pact), whose people wish to live in harmony. It also puts in place a shared conduct agreement toward world peace, including compassion and mutual respect.

Mankind has been moving toward this conduct, trying to find a clear path. We have been learning. Immature children have a hard time showing compassion or mutual respect and can be quite cruel to their peers. Many adults have retained these shortcomings – sometimes in devastating ways. If, however, we can gain a better understanding of God, we may well improve our behavior.

We are all children in a vast kindergarten trying to spell God's name with the wrong alphabet blocks. —Tennessee Williams

There's been nothing wrong with God all this time. It's what's wrong with us that has been causing all the problems. To solve these problems, we need to acknowledge God, *together*. We need to acknowledge our shortcomings in observing Him, and begin to do so properly and respectfully, through formal agreement. Slowly, over time, world affairs would become less brutal.

How long will grown men and women in this world keep drawing in their coloring books an image of God that makes them sad? —Meister Eckhart

The true God is a God of love, not sadness. Why have we insisted on the negative? We have warped His image and connected Him to causes of sadness that shift the blame over to God and away from us. War and violence have made mankind sad – *through our own doing*. It is not God's fault that we kill each other and it is time we grew up. We really *are* God's children and because parents always love their children we are, as a result, slowly learning that God does not hate us or wish to be appeased with our blood. We have begun to understand that God is not responsible for war. It is, and has always been, us. We must take responsibility for our actions and put in place something that will express the love of God rather than the vengeance of men. Our ignorance has caused damage but we are learning how to correct it.

Slowly, over the centuries, we have become less barbaric. We no longer throw people to the lions in arenas or burn them at the stake. Certain groups still perform barbaric deeds, often magnified by the Internet, but in a collective sense we are evolving and growing closer to God. There is still further to go, but from a larger historical perspective, one can see that we have indeed progressed. Great people like Mahatma Gandhi and Dr. Martin Luther King, Jr. have raised the consciousness of millions and made tremendous progress through non-violent means, while remaining close to their guidance from God. Today, we have reached the realization that the more collective an effort is made to stop violence, the more positive the results will be. Without a collective effort, progress will stall. The God Pact could be the most collective effort ever made. It could result in more acts of love and less acts of violence in both nations and individuals.

God as the Primary Example of Love

There is no shortage of teachings that reflect the love of God. Religious texts showing God as cruel and violent would be recognized as needing revision, based on the fact that early religious ideas required violent thoughts and actions in a world more barbaric and ignorant than what we have today. We now know that violent beliefs and wars only propagate more pain and violence. Far less is gained than what was originally envisioned by some of the early religious founders and their followers. History bears this out, and it is a lesson we should have learned by now. *A nation, religious system or person is not capable of finding God by using violent actions*. Violence is sometimes needed for self-preservation, through self-defense, but should never be done in the name of God or purport to be a reflection on the true nature of God. All great spiritual masters who have experienced God have said that the closest thing to describe It is *Love*.

The Genesis of The God Pact

It is hoped that The God Pact will one day be presented to a few nations that would consider it. As little as two island nations could draw it up between themselves and sign it, making sure the wording will stand the test of time and allow for future signers to join the alliance. Or the wording could be altered to accommodate individuals who could first sign it on a *personal level*, anywhere in the world. Being aligned with God – the true God – feels good! One can treat friends and neighbors accordingly, as the pact suggests. Did you sign The God Pact? Yes, I did. Maybe it will spread. With governing bodies, the agreement should include a clause allowing it to be integrated with one or more larger, similar alliances at a later time. Who will take these first steps? Two island nations? A meaningful movement must start somewhere. Why not with you?

The Vatican represents the Catholic people and it is a nation unto itself – recognized as a national territory under international law. It has borders, coins its own money and maintains formal diplomatic relations with 174 different countries. Since they are supposed to be closest to God and serve as a representative in this respect, promoting such a pact would seem like a good opportunity for them. The word Catholic means "universal," or "all-inclusive." Such a pact would seem fitting for an organization that could then live up to its name and promote a new era of peace. Such a pact is not meant to "belong" to any one religion. It just asks acknowledgment of God as our universal, loving father among all people. The God Pact may still be too "radical" for them, but if the movement grows, there could one day come a time for more serious consideration by them and among all representative bodies of religion.

Importance of The God Pact

Quantum physics and advanced sciences have proven that there is a God-force that connects all things. It exists. God really *is* connected to each of us, but we have failed to acknowledge it. In recognizing this truth it may be wise that we, as humans, make a *unified effort* to connect to this *unifying* God-force. This one step, officially connecting to God via The God Pact, is a practical way to accomplish this. It offers a clear way to begin the unifying process by involving virtually everyone. The God Pact is not only an effort to achieve more peace in the world – it is an effort to realize the ultimate goal of religion, which is, by definition, to connect us (and you) back to God.

The word religion means to "rebind." "Ligio" means "to bind," and "re" means to "do again." We cannot *rebind* something unless we were actually bound to it before, in the first place. For example, to retie a shoe means it was once properly tied. Somehow we have lost our connection to God, and we are trying to rebind ourselves back to God through various forms of "re-ligion." Based on the state of the world, with its violence, misery and degradation of the things that support life, we have clearly failed to gain back our connection to God. We cannot do it by going into a physical church, by reading out of physical books, or by binding ourselves with other church members, because all of that exists "out there." Our connection to God is not "out there." The kingdom of God is within you. It is one thing to teach that concept – it is another to find ways to realize it, to actualize it. Attempting to *live it* in a setting of peace, with help from The God Pact, may one day rebind us back to God. Relying on concepts, faith or prayer to accomplish this has *failed*. It is time to live it.

The world is in a mess and we need to get to the root of its problems. There are a million different ideas on how to proceed, with no real consensus. The God Pact can provide a consensus. Peace should be a natural state of affairs for nations. If all nations would agree to be peaceful, you are left with only radical sub-groups, which are more easily controlled. Building armies and having weapons are necessary for defensive purposes, so should certainly not be banned. Realities dictate preparedness against violence that will always exist – but the Pact could allow us more control over unprovoked violence and terror.

Your Connection to God

What does The God Pact means to you, personally? From a spiritual level, this could be the most meaningful thing you ever do. If you do have part of God within you – this having been experienced by some and borne out by science – then what could possibly be more important on a personal level than to make a focused effort to align with it?

This approach to alignment and proper conduct, and then agreeing to abide by it on a social level, has been *missing* from the history of mankind. Doubters may ask, "How could such a thing really be enforced?" It can't. "Enforced" is a bad word, because it includes the word "force." In large part, The God Pact is not something that can be "forced" in any way on an individual. By agreeing to it, you are reflecting your very *essence*, which is connected to a loving God. You cannot force something that naturally occurs. You merely have to recognize it and abide by it. The vast majority of people have good hearts and this general goodness will be put into the public consciousness even more so, with the spreading of The God Pact. The only "forcing" that would result would be that violent, war-mongering groups or people would, over time, have to align themselves more with the vast majority of mankind. Who will have found God.

A Call for Action

Pacts are the same as contracts, and contracts are *binding instruments*. The God Pact, when signed, can "bind you back to God" through your own conscious choice. It can, at least to a certain point, accomplish for you what religions have been trying to do for centuries. It can also start what could be a process for world peace. Do you want to change the world and live in peace – or at least help create such a climate for your children? The God Pact is here.

If no groups or governments adopt it, at least *you* can. Sign it if you wish. Send, post or share copies to those you think would be interested. Pledging yourself to peace and aligning with God can't be a bad thing. Former songwriter John Lennon once said, "Give peace a chance." Maybe it's time to give God a chance. Then more peace may result. Please spread the word and give The God Pact a chance.

Chapter Fifteen

SHIFTING THE PARADIGM

An invasion of armies can be resisted, but not an idea whose time has come. —Victor Hugo

Truth never yet fell dead in the streets; it has such affinity with the soul of man, the seed, however broadcast, will catch somewhere and produce a hundredfold. —Theodore Parker

Humankind is clearly changing. Our consciousness is beginning to shift into a more cooperative mode while the ravaging effects of competition become more clear. The questions is whether or not we can stem the tide of past mistakes and prevent it from destroying us. We are on a slide toward self-destruction and despite our sudden awakening and subsequent efforts, it may be too little too late. Although our greed has so far gotten the best of us, I personally have faith in the spiritual power of mankind—if we are ready to tap into it.

Other cultures have failed at this in the past. It's a hard lesson that other cultures learned, at tremendous cost. Some were smaller and more isolated than what we face today, but the lesson is still there. For example, there is nothing left today of the ancient Mayan culture of Central America. They had magnificent pyramids and great cities hundreds of years ago and, for the longest time, archaeologists were completely baffled as to what happened to this culture. These people often cut the hearts out of sacrificial victims on top of their pyramids, believing the sun would nourish itself from their blood and create healthy crops in return. Other victims were sacrificed by being thrown into the cenote, which was a deep well that many of these communities had. The idea was that they would receive rains by throwing sacrificial victims into the waters. Most times, very young people were sacrificed—usually virgins. They died needlessly out of a superstition that the deaths of innocent, unblemished children would bring the needed rains and crops to the people.

The entire Mayan culture was not only violent to themselves, but to all other tribes within the surrounding areas. Archaeologists have since learned that the downfall of this entire civilization was largely attributed to the fact that they were completely violent and at war with one another to such a degree that they self-destructed. They drove themselves out of existence because they were constantly at war—killing and taking prisoners of other tribes, sacrificing or murdering them, but often experiencing revenge and retribution as a result. Finally the violence was just too much and they were unable to sustain themselves as a culture. It is believed that they abandoned their cities and the few who were left melted into the surrounding jungles to live a more agrarian existence, in tune with nature and the land.

> *Those who cannot remember the past are condemned to repeat it.* —George Santayana

What we are leaning today is the same lesson but on a larger scale. We should certainly not abandon our cities and all become farmers, but we must learn how to live in ways more balanced with nature. According to the World Resources Institute, about 100 species go extinct each day from tropical deforestation alone, with up to 150 being lost every day, in total. The current extinction rate runs between 18,000 and 55,000 species per year, *three or four every hour*, due to our greed and ignorance. Many cures for our worst afflictions could be lost forever. More importantly, how long can we expect to continue at this pace without experiencing drastic repercussions?

Natural weather disasters are much nastier and more common due to the climate changes we have caused from CO^2 emissions, ozone depletion and global warming. We've lost so much protective ozone with the hole in the south pole region that school children in southern Australia have been told by a 2006/07 "government initiative" not to venture outside unless they are wearing large-sized protective hats to shield them from the high levels of solar radiation.

As for global warming, a few scientists have been paid off to act as political stooges and present "legitimate" studies showing how global warming is simply a natural occurrence and the result of normal cycles. This is an effort to delay the depletion of profits of vested interests. Most people are not buying into it—the writing is on the wall and only a fool would refuse to see it. Some politicians and business lobbyists are now claiming that the entire green movement is a conspiracy designed to destroy the economy and wrest political power from them. They are so blind that they are only capable of viewing things from within a limited political "box." The green movement is not playing a political game; it is addressing a legitimate concern of *survival* and unfortunately must deal with narrow minded, egotistical, power hungry politicians who refuse to see anything beyond the four walls of power politics in the process. The survival game is a bigger game that, if recognized as such, tends to disrupt the way politicians like to play their game. If lobbyists' money and political control get diverted from the political sandbox for bigger reasons and more legitimate concerns, the children will throw tantrums and lie about what is happening. Whenever attention gets diverted outside of the sandbox, all kinds of theatrics will result.

A maturing process is beginning to take hold. We are starting to understand our interdependence within a holistic world view. Instead of an "us against them" mentality, we are just barely beginning to nurture each other on a larger scale, looking beyond our separate "tribes" or countries. We have learned to nurture and care for each other, mostly from within our own groups. On a larger worldwide scale, we're still fighting amongst each other as far as countries go—between nations, states, and political and religious factions. It seems, however, that the overall message is starting to sink in. We no longer treat people closest to us in the brutal sacrificial fashion of the Mayans, although we still treat other people that we are not quite so close to in very inappropriate ways.

We continue to have it in our minds that someone has to be the enemy—yet the only real enemy is that particular idea in itself. The only enemies we create come from within our own minds. Many times, from personal experience, we have been in situations where we believe there is someone who is an enemy, but then the situation arises where we have to actually sit down and get to know them better. When this happens we often realize that there is not that much difference between us and good friendships are known to develop. This happens on an individual level many times—perhaps it has happened to you. If we can find ways to achieve this same "bridging of the gaps" on a more global scale, among groups of all sizes in addition to individuals, then we will continue to make progress in this area.

It is spiritual growth and maturity that brings this kind of breakthrough. It has nothing to do with religion. Religions divide us and make us different, whereby a recognition of the spirit allows us to see the goodness that is held in common. That is precisely why spirituality transcends religion, and why a spiritual path is the next step for humanity rather than a religious one. Religions have spawned violence over and over again, due to our focus on their differences and the insistence that others change their ways and convert to ours. Spirituality accepts our differences, fosters mutual respect and focuses on our most common spiritual roots. It is time for us to stop acting like animals and to start acting like *human beings*. It is time for us to graduate to the next level—or to at least continue learning how to get there.

Religious paths are separate; spiritual paths are the same. When it comes right down to it, there are many different spiritual methods and many different religious paths, but it is the spiritual methods that will bridge us as opposed to focusing on religious differences. A deep spirituality allows us to be tolerant; whereby a deep religious conviction breeds intolerance. Religions are dogmatic. They tell you that "this is the way, and it is the only way to God." Everyone from outside the faith is expected to not be with you in the afterlife because they did not follow your religious path; whereby the spirit and true spiritual paths join us as one and we share and celebrate in what we know, deep down, to be our common spiritual traits and the connection that we share with God. Like Gandhi once said, "God does not have a religion."

It will be difficult to transcend our religious convictions because they have become so ingrained within each separate culture the world over. When we visit a different country, we expect to see the richness of the religious motifs and symbols that have become the trademarks of that culture. Growing into a more spiritual path rather than a purely religious one could be interpreted as a threat to many of these cultures, but that should not be the case. Many religious symbols represent deep spiritual truths, which should be celebrated and treasured, not done away with. Only repressive, fundamentalist regimes (or atheistic ones) try to destroy meaningful religious icons, but that would be frowned upon in a climate of mutual respect. A more spiritual and open trend would still represent change in a proud culture and could be viewed in a negative way rather than a positive one. This is the major hurdle that we face in trying to reach this next paradigm—one that will involve a more elevated spiritual awareness than what we've been experiencing so far.

The Importance of Education

If one is concerned about bringing more compassion, balance and sanity into the world, it can best be done through education. Our educational systems need to be instilled with more spiritual values rather than the simple memorization of facts or the adding up of numbers. There is a deeper dimension to us that our educational systems have not yet accessed. The political and economic support systems for our schools do not care as much about spirituality as they do about creating people who will put money into the economy. They are more concerned about creating workers. If the system itself is not willing to offer deeper forms of education, then we must employ an alternative educational system of our own that will fill this empty void. The Waldorf and Oak Grove systems are proven, excellent alternatives that need to be seriously examined and expanded upon. Certain facets of the educational programs of both Mahatma Gandhi and Daisaku Ikeda must also be considered and studied from a purely spiritual, non-religious standpoint.

A revamped educational system will not happen overnight in a huge revolution or upheaval. It's a slow, gradual process of awareness. As people become more spiritually aware through this type of education, more jobs will, in fact, be created by a caring population. New forms of outreach will appear, designed to help others in need throughout the world. Gearing our young people for strict, profit making ventures has begun to run out of speed, and it's time to start gearing and training our young people to care more about others and the planet rather than themselves.

In the current system of things there are a huge number of people throughout the world who are in need, but the current profit-making mindset will not even approach these issues or attempt to help them. There's massive starvation on the planet and the majority of humans live in squalor. Less than half the people in the world have clean water to drink, more than half do not. Great problems exist worldwide with disease, famine, and warfare. This current paradigm stands by and allows massive suffering, doing little to alleviate it unless a great disaster occurs to elevate the attention level. If we can start approaching these problems from a different perspective, it may improve our lot and make things more profitable for everyone involved. That, of course, is a long-term view of things, but it can, in fact, happen with time. We have already come a long way, but there's much further to go.

The religions of the world will be around for a long time to come, despite their shortcomings and our growing spiritual awareness. It is important to develop more spiritual awareness within them, which is what will be happening. It is equally important to explore other spiritual avenues outside of traditional religions, which can open the spirit in ways that the religious structures have not done. Alternative methods of spiritual growth are not of the devil. Despite what various religious organizations will be telling you and have been telling you, it is not true. It is a desperate attempt on their part to maintain the control they have over the their followers. Period. That's the bottom line. We are growing up and out of the ancient, archaic belief systems that have insisted on ignorance, over the centuries, to maintain their base of power. If we want to grow and make this world a better place, and also make ourselves better people, then we must put aside the biases of religious powers that the more strictly closed-minded adherents still cling to from centuries past. Times are changing. People are waking up and finding out that many of the beliefs of the major religions no longer match up well with how we define ourselves, and understand ourselves, as spiritual beings.

There is goodness in every religion, and we must still use the goodness and wisdom that they offer. We would be fools not to. We should certainly not throw out religion completely, as some would be willing to do. Religions have very redeeming values for people if not taken to an extreme. But if we are to grow, we must also follow our hearts. In responding to the modern world, our hearts sometimes lead us in different directions than what an outdated religious concept might be dictating, demanding or suggesting. What we must remember and what we have lost touch with is that we are first and foremost spiritual beings. Almost all of us lose touch with that from a very early age. Part of the new education that we should be focusing on requires that we not lose touch with that spiritual part of ourselves.

There have been many cases of young children talking about where they came from before they were here, sometimes discussing past lives in great detail. What most parents and educators do, however, is train us from a very young age not to look back at all because we are in the here and now—we are in this material world that needs our full attention. The focus is simply on that alone, without regard for anything that might exist on a deeper, unseen level. We simply do not understand who we really are and where we were before we came here, and that frightens people. We are afraid of the unknown. So instead of teaching our young children to hold on to some of that important spiritual knowledge, we instead train them to ignore it and not confront it. That is, in fact, what most adults are doing with this spiritual part of themselves. From a young age we are not taught to look back or inward, while we still have the means to do it. Instead, we are taught to look straight ahead with blinders on and move as fast as we can away from that true part of ourselves that we, as children, are more closely in contact with. Soon, we forget completely. As we grow, an occasional feeling or event will point us inward and although we may sense that our intuition is right and that we should listen, it gets repressed.

There is a simple exercise for young children that maintains contact with that most important part of ourselves, which is, in fact, who we really are. They simply have to close their eyes and focus on a very deep, inward part of themselves. They just need to know it is there—after that, it's not so much of a problem to access. Children are fascinated with everything in the outside world at a young age—all kinds of toys and things are put in front of them, but they are never given the chance to look inward.

If we can cultivate inward spiritual awareness, we may have a higher number of wiser and enlightened people as adults. Although already covered earlier, it is important to reiterate the importance of a more complete educational experience for our children. From a personal standpoint, I would "daydream" a lot in kindergarten and first grade. Of course, that meant I was not paying attention. It could be argued, however, that I really was paying attention and, in fact, paying more attention on a deeper level than anyone else in that room at that particular time. But inner awareness is considered to be a defect in the desired product, and any display of it shows that something is "wrong." There should, however, be a time set aside for this. If educators or parents could create the right time for inner exploration, then children would develop a better focus in normal consciousness. They would accomplish things more successfully and thoroughly when focusing on outer things, as long as they have time to do inner work. It would create more balanced individuals. Of course, there will be hyperactive children who will not want anything to do with that. But from a very young age the vast majority of them would be able to keep intact, as they grow older, their intuitive abilities and a connection to the inner part of one's self that is truly there. This is never taught to any of us unless it is self-taught—or maybe found in a rare college-level class when we're older and have been desensitized to much of what is within ourselves. If, instead, it is nurtured up through childhood from a young age, there could be adequate spiritual growth involved.

This is not asking for a major upheaval in education; it is requesting a small portion of time in the areas of inner development because everything is so intensely focused on the outer world. There's fear of the unknown that keeps us from allowing children to focus in a different way. It would be beneficial for young children to confront the awareness of where they were before they came here. After all, they're more closely connected to that, time-wise, than we are. This could be the first philosophical exercise given to children, of which none others seem to exist. It has the ability to put them (or keep them) in touch with that spiritual part of themselves, or to create conceptual, spiritual thinking which is otherwise never cultivated. To allow a child to think about where, in fact, they were before they came here is something that few children are asked to do. Reporting on it, should they experience anything, should not be mandatory, but voluntary. At times, children have come forward on their own to share such information when it has occurred quite strongly and spontaneously. Because of the level of detail that we hear from these children, there can be no doubt that there is something valid to these reports.

What would happen if we nurtured this? Yet when such cases do occur, the children are most always redirected away from it and back into the outer physical world. An outer, material focus takes precedence, and should still take precedence, but we should not try to bury our children's heads completely in the sand based on our own ignorance and fear of the unknown. Many times, parents or teachers just write off such reports as fantasy, but there is usually a gnawing doubt within them about what's really going on. Once children are allowed to maintain the deeper connection as to who they are, then adolescent years can be spent exploring things that will develop their abilities in a spiritual sense, as opposed to continuing to shut them down. I cannot outline an entire spiritual curriculum nor do I claim to be qualified to do so; but what I am suggesting is that such a thing be seriously explored, developed, modified or adopted.

The existing Waldorf educational method and Oak Grove School are the most likely candidates since both are proven prototypes with amazing results. One imperative point, shared by both of these programs, is that the curriculum not be connected to any particular religion whatsoever. Doing so would otherwise put children into a position of being "programmed" with an agenda by adults, and expected biases and responses could surface that might not otherwise be there.

If we can develop and nurture that spiritual part of our children, then the world cannot help but to be a better place in the future. For those of us today that will not be able to develop those skills that our children will have, we can at least be aware as best we can of our own spiritual selves.

The Future of Consciousness

When the first wave of spiritually based people complete their formal education process, they will be prepared to live a fuller and more accurate life based on a more accurate definition of themselves. Finding and following one's personal path in life will not be as difficult. Today, many grope around in the dark, trying to find their way, while some never find it at all. This will be a thing of the past. As individuals achieve self-realization, so will our society. As a result, I am proposing what I call the SVQ, or *Spiritual Value Quotient*.

The SVQ will reflect a social value based on its worth in a compassionate, spiritually grounded society. It will reflect proper compensation based on what one's work contributes to society in terms of spiritual value. For example, teachers would be paid more than they currently are now, and professional athletes would be paid less. It would be unrealistic to expect teachers' salaries to surpass those of professional athletes', but the gap could and should be shortened. In general, educational work will reflect more value than entertainment. On a sliding scale, those whose professions contribute to our spiritual well-being or advancement will command a better salary than those who don't. This alone will contribute more interest and demand for such services, and to our continued moral growth rather than its breakdown. A higher quality of people will result—meaning fewer robberies, and less cheating, stealing and crime in general. People will be more conscientious and care more about their neighbors than we do today. There will also be an increase in enlightened human beings. I do not claim that the SVQ will be the answer to all these things; it is merely meant as something that will help us put things in their proper perspective.

In today's world there are a number of people who are considered to be enlightened. They have reached an amazing level of spiritual development. It is something that is very real. Advanced spirituality is barely recognized in our society. We view such enlightened people as outcasts—as ones who do not fit in. But in the future, as more people reach this level of consciousness, there will be places in our society for such individuals to fit in. It is my opinion that these enlightened people have become more 'fully human" than the average person on the street. This should be our natural state and someday it will be; yet trying to function as a fully developed spiritual human in today's world is an extremely difficult task. Our first step, in order for us to become a "true human," or enlightened human, is to become a truly "socialized human." We all cannot become enlightened overnight, it is too far to go in so short a time; so becoming what is termed a "socialized human" will allow us to at least work in this direction. It is a realistic path because we have not yet had the educational training that has been proposed for our children.

To be a truly socialized human, there are four things necessary. These four points are things that we can attempt to teach ourselves. If we focus enough, these things are within our grasp and achievable. We cannot develop the higher states of awareness and functionality that our children will have, but these things are still important and will help us to set an example.

The first trait of a fully socialized human is humbleness—to put the ego aside with all its greed, envy, and status seeking. The second is compassion—to be aware of what others truly need, especially those less fortunate and in true need of essentials. Number three is generosity—to act on our compassion. And number four, to be a fully socialized human would be to have financial stability. This does not mean to have wealth. It is to be financially stable to the point of self-sufficiency. To operate on a social level, you must be able to function with a fair amount of resources. Self-sufficiency allows you to employ a certain degree of action. When you have financial stability, you can make choices about what to do with your free time with whatever money is left over after paying for living expenses.

We must have humbleness, compassion, generosity, and financial stability to be a truly socialized human. To be *fully human* is something entirely different, and that will come when later generations come. Today there are an extremely small number of people whom we can consider to be fully human in every aspect—especially the spiritual aspect.

These four areas are important for people to work on because they do form the basic core of a strong, spiritual framework for society. It is something we can build on. These things can easily be worked on by virtually everyone and results can be achieved. Nothing is out of reach by working on these four different aspects. Why? Because social aspects are the outward results of spiritual work. If we focus on the results of spiritual work rather than the spiritual work itself, it allows an older generation to bypass the needed time for spiritual growth. It is less perfect, but attainable by approaching it from the other direction. It requires more effort, which is different from operating within our current state of being, developed after years of standard conditioning.

Young people staying in stronger touch with the spiritual part of themselves would develop highly evolved ethics more naturally. With this kind of progress being made, the future could hold more promise. The current paradigm has long functioned on its material, economic and religiously based focus. But without the spirit, people are bankrupt in what they are attempting to accomplish because the entire groundwork, the entire foundation for all of this, is based on who we really are. And we are, first and foremost, spiritual beings—ones who are living in total darkness regarding this truth and are completely out of touch with who we really are. Therefore, we act and function improperly toward the planet and each other.

The material, economic and religious areas of focus are dead ends without us knowing who we really are because without knowing that, we cannot possibly know where we're going. A zebra that does not know he is a zebra can gallop into a modern city and be completely confused without ever knowing why. Yet tell him he is a zebra so that he knows it and identifies with it, and he will immediately head for the freedom of the African plains. So if we discover who we are and we know where we're going, or *should* be going, then things will become much easier.

While we remain primarily materialistic and wait for a higher spiritual awareness to integrate itself into our lives with the help of a new educational focus, we need to turn our attentions away from our current political structures and religious institutions. These organizations have caused us more trouble than good—and history clearly bears this out. We instead need to focus more on the economic structure of things on world and local levels. Taking control of whatever we can on a local level will put our fate, and a certain degree of control, back into our own hands.

From a larger economic perspective, if we took away our advanced technologies and energy sources, which drive the world's economies, we would have a complete economic collapse, with resulting worldwide panic, starvation and wars. However, if we took away all of our political and religious leaders and kept the economy intact, we would get along just fine without them. Things would probably be better, without all of the warfare and trouble that normally goes along with their activities.

Political organizations and politicians in large part are just riding on the coattails of the big economic power structures of the world, dancing to the tune that is played for them while trying to extract whatever they can for their own advantage on the side. Political "power" is nothing more than a parasitical power, and politicians feed off whatever bones get thrown to them by the power elite—the unseen masters who control the world's economic fate.

Governmental groups often hold power in exchange for operating like a "hit man" in the larger scheme of things, attacking with their armies whatever might appear to be an economic threat to those holding the purse strings. Even more so, they work to create perceived threats as a context for the military/industrial complex to produce and sell their wares, thereby keeping the world economy healthy. War, and killing our fellow man, is big money.

A new paradigm is needed to destroy this vicious cycle, and this will never be accomplished until we learn, from experience, that world peace will never be achieved through brute force and dishonest manipulation.

Except for the Vatican, religions control very little in an economic sense. Those days expired long ago and, in general, they were not something desirable. People need something to believe in, however, so religion is useful. It keeps the masses occupied and out of the affairs of large economic concerns. Those who believe God will punish them for being dishonest or doing something wrong actually open the door widely for those who manipulate world economies in sometimes less than ethical ways. It makes the banksters' jobs easier, with fewer questions being asked and less competition to deal with.

Only when a belief system or faction becomes fanatical does it become a concern. Fanatics are not afraid of being punished by God—they turn things around and believe they will be rewarded. They think they are chosen by God to mete out His punishments on others, thereby making everyone a target who happens to disagree with them. If a terrorist target turns out to be large, economies can be affected. Therefore, economic powers prepare against such things, using governments as enforcing agents.

The key for humanity's future is to upgrade our social and economic awareness, with less dependence on the restrictive mindset put forth and shared by all political and religious groups that have held sway during the past few centuries. We have grown and learned to the degree that we are capable, but our spiritual freedom is now stagnant and diminished. At the same time we must nurture ourselves with a new educational approach as previously described, which will give us new strength.

Why Change Must Come

Sooner or later change must come. The more we look at the way the world truly operates, the more clear it becomes as to how corrupt things are. Many times the news media don't report the things that are going on behind the scenes, but there is tremendous corruption. As a general rule, if people can get away with it (or even think they can), they will do it. There are so many being hurt by others for the personal gain of those who can get away with things that there is very little integrity or honesty involved in the key positions that need ethical behaviour the most. Those who hold the most wealth and have achieved the most success in this world, in general, are not the nicest and most trustworthy people that you could ever want to meet. It's not philosophical or political ideals like socialism or communism that is the enemy, it's pure greed. Capitalism is not the enemy, either, because the capitalistic system would work better with the right people in place, operating from a different mindset. More could be accomplished with a capitalistic structure using people who are spiritually aware. But from a materialistic point of view, rather than a spiritual one, capitalism operates in an exclusionary way whereby those who are in power are the only ones who have the resources and the riches. Very little of it gets disbursed for positive means—nowhere near what could happen with a different paradigm in place. A spiritual mindset with the same resources would make a world of difference.

With individuals, many believe that material wealth is the most worthy and secure path to pursue. Yet some of the most unhappy people in the world have been very wealthy. Riches do not cure those whose lives have been shattered or whose hearts have been broken, but those who are spiritually strong can survive material hardship. Therefore, it makes more sense for us, individually and collectively, to focus more on our inner resources rather than outer ones.

Some philosophers have put forth the idea that life itself is a school, and we are here to learn. If we fail to learn the right things, then we have to keep coming back until we get it right. So from a philosophical point of view, we should create a school *within the school*, one that provides methods of teaching and learning that are more philosophical and spiritual than we have had in the past. By doing so, we can begin to treat each other better and learn the lessons that we are here to learn more easily. We could then be able to share those lessons and pass them on to future generations.

This world is full of warfare, strife and starvation, which goes on and on and on. It is appalling to see the incredible wealth that some have while so many others spend lives of pure suffering. In most cases we turn a blind eye and cannot be bothered—but we are truly all connected. We are God's children, and there is something that does, indeed, bind us all together. And when we turn a blind eye to our collective suffering, we are turning a blind eye on ourselves in a very big way. And when we turn a blind eye on ourselves, that means that we are depriving ourselves of things that we should be having. It has nothing to do with money or wealth or comfort, but it has everything to do with our spiritual growth, with who we really are, and why we're really here. And if we turn and walk away from what we should be doing here, then that God force that links us all together is defused, short-circuited and no longer in harmony with us.

A world order that commits planetary suicide in the search for profit while driving the majority of human beings into despair and poverty is a killing/producing machine without spiritual center. —Joel Kovel, History and Spirit: An Inquiry into the Philosophy of Liberation

Without knowing it, we are collectively connected in spirit. We show clear differences from other people through various religious and spiritual practices, but we are all connected together on a very deep level. What each of us is doing on this level is important and has implications that go far deeper than our own *personal* salvation due to the connection that we share. The obvious implication is that those who control things like industry, government or our food supplies and act without considering the greater good are going against our purpose for being here. And again, it has nothing to do with socialism or any political philosophy of any kind. It has to do with being fully human and cultivating the expression of spiritual strength, spiritual power, and spiritual abundance—all of which should define us more accurately and come naturally to us. In later generations, it will. For now we have to work at it, learn more about ourselves and start applying what we learn in the world. Future generations will look back and see that politics and religion were both used as "crutches" while we engaged in the early stages of our own self-discovery, healed ourselves more fully from our rift with God, and became spiritually strong. We could say that we did the best we could with what we had, and learned the needed lessons along the way.

Internal Evolution

The physical evolution of all species, including mankind, is a fact of nature and occurs at a very slow rate. Unlike other species, mankind is experiencing a spiritual evolution in addition to a physical one. This internal evolution moves at a faster rate than the physical version, and is reflected in our outer actions—especially in the way we treat each other.

My previous book, *Triumph of the Human Spirit: The Greatest Achievements of the Human Soul and How Its Power can Change Your Life*, historically maps out, in chronological fashion, the high points in the evolution of the soul up to modern times. This current book picks up from there, revealing the next steps that will be taken in this collective, spiritual journey of the human race.

What is it that we can look forward to in this coming age? We can expect a more holistic world view from both environmental and religious frameworks, as previously outlined. The Aquarian astrological symbol, the man with the water pitcher, distributes what is necessary for the corresponding symbol of the previous age to function—water. Water is a spiritual symbol.

The dominant religion of this ending age, which was personified by the Piscean fish symbol, is being replaced by the very life-blood of every religion, which is spirituality. What we will learn is that water supports the life of fish; fish do not make possible the existence of water. A larger spiritual vision is unfolding among all faiths as opposed to any singular religion being dominant.

Also, water is the major component of the human body. We are composed of at least 70 percent water—so an age that is represented by water will clearly bring a potential wholeness and completeness to the understanding of who we are. We will experience a great age of spirituality where a more collective awareness will become part of the religions of the world. A spiritual awakening will slowly happen within each of the separate religions, bringing us all together as water itself does with life. There would be no life without water, and we are flowing into an age where there will be water, in a spiritual sense, for us all to be nourished from.

The vast majority of the world's people will learn important spiritual lessons from within their own religions because most have yet to accomplish this. There is a deeper, more meaningful message within each of the religions of the world that most people have not yet accessed. Again, it has been more of an outer worship than an inner journey. In the end, however, the spirit will bring us all together because despite the differences in religion, we all share the same spiritual source and the same spiritual makeup. It is religions that have divided us; it's the spirit that is going to bring us together. Once we start understanding, once we start educating ourselves in ways that will bring us onto this common ground, then we will know that we are in the New Age.

The world has grown too complex for one single religion to come in and, with its strength, take over the world. A few religions may still think this is possible, but it is totally and completely impossible. As we move further and further into the future, it will become increasingly clear to everyone that a strict, dogmatic religious path of any kind is not the path that is meant for us. That path is a dead end, and an entirely new way of seeing things will open up to us.

This is what happens when a new paradigm develops. The way people see things changes, a shift in consciousness happens. Sometimes it is a quick and major shift; more often it is slow and gradual. But it does, indeed, happen. A paradigm shift does not happen with people thinking in the same fashion that both created and then supported the previous paradigm's existence. It was Einstein who said, in effect, that the same form of thinking that creates a problem cannot be used to solve it. It's just not possible.

We have outlined ways in which we can begin seeing things in a new and productive way and it is hoped that they may, in fact, be helpful as this paradigm continues to unfold. This shift seems to be gradual, but at certain times in the ancient past paradigms have shifted from the result of cataclysmic events. Anyone researching this area will see that there have been cataclysmic events on a major scale in this world, and that does not preclude us from having such things happen again. If a major disaster should hit the planet or a large portion of it, local or state governments would not have the money or resources to handle it. Many of our governmental institutions are either too financially depleted, short on manpower, flat broke, or simply incapable of handling such things. The U.S. federal government is very slow in responding to isolated disasters, and if something were to happen on a large scale, it would be a total, unmanageable disaster. Most other countries in the world are less prepared than the United States, so there would be big trouble.

At any given time, the economic structure that supports this older paradigm could be instantly pulled out from under our feet. At that point we would have to start all over again and piece everything back together. Such events themselves, as traumatic as they can be, can cause a negative shift in consciousness. For example, Immanuel Velikovsky, in his book *Mankind In Amnesia*, describes how massive disasters have taken place in the past and we have collectively blocked them out as a species due to the trauma involved. Such events create a negative shift in consciousness rather than a positive one, and have set us back and prevented our spiritual advancement. By training and educating ourselves in more spiritual ways, we would create better coping mechanisms should such events happen again in the future. A higher and better form of consciousness will clearly allow us to handle situations like that far better than we would today.

For those who think the idea of changing our form of consciousness is just pure fantasy, there are a number of good books that support this. For example, *The Origin of Consciousness in the Breakdown of the Bicameral Mind*, by Princeton University psychologist Julian Jaynes, postulates how, back around the time of the Trojan War, we were more right-brained in our thinking. We were more creative and poetic in the past than we are today. Today we are more left-brained; more scientific and logical in our thinking. In the future, with more spiritual awareness likely, we may, in fact, connect *both sides of the brain* to become more full and complete human beings. This is entirely possible. I highly recommend this book by Jaynes for those who doubt that a change in consciousness can happen and thereby create an entirely new way of thinking. Not only is such a change possible, it is coming again.

Our way of viewing things has continually changed. It has happened over long periods of time, and our cultures have changed as a result of it, over and over again. We have evolved from cavemen up through the ages and created all kinds of new and exciting changes to improve ourselves—including the advent of farming crops, the creation of cities; we developed major technologies, cured diseases, walked on the moon, and much more. It is all the result of our consciousness changing, and it will continue to change. We have advanced enough to afford ourselves a better view of what's coming. We should be able to prepare ourselves for it so that we can continue to evolve for the better, and make this world a better place.

We have over 12,000 *million* brain cells, making us so intellectually complex that we hold an almost infinite variation of new abilities and insights, just waiting to be tapped into. With the power of our minds we can continue to produce new combinations of abilities and act on them. In this way, we have always made new leaps, through sudden insight, rather than slow progress. The results we have achieved have often been completely unpredictable, but incredibly positive and revolutionary. Our spiritual maturity has always lagged behind these amazing insights and advances. Reaching a new level of spiritual maturity could well be the next step on our path—part of the next tier of abilities that will unfold—because now is the time that we need them. What we have learned (or should have learned) in this technological, materialistic age is that great knowledge can fail without wisdom.

The most vexing question of all, that continues to come up concerning this world and its increasingly problematic state of affairs is, "Is it fixable?" Is it *really* fixable? Or is this place specifically designed as an imperfect arena, never to be "fixed" at all, but for us to individually work out our own stubborn imperfections? After all, if we were perfect, we would not need to be here. Whether we know it or not, every single one of us—all of us—have a few broken, imperfect parts. So how can broken people fix a broken world? As long as people remain spiritually and morally incomplete, it cannot happen.

What can happen, however, is for *you*, as an individual, to diligently work out your own imperfections, your own "karma," and ultimately, your own spiritual and moral advancement while here. We can do this as individuals by staying focused on the various ways we need to better ourselves. Out of the four points I espouse as a guide for the new paradigm, the first three must be approached initially as individuals—identity, education, and a holistic worldview—but can also take place within larger supportive groups. Only when enough of us "get it" can the economic structure of the commercial system be positively altered. Under such conditions, with the success of numerous *individuals*, followed by stronger and larger supporting groups, would the world economic structure be *forced* to comply, and that is the only way it will change in a lasting way.

When we learn this lesson, so that we are all trying to better ourselves as opposed to pointing fingers and casting blame on others, insisting that "they should do this," or "they should do that"—when this lesson is learned and we are all on the same page with it, only then will the world improve as a whole.

The natural result of this individual work is the realization that it's not an individual journey at all.

For those who would say, "I am just one person. How could I possibly make a difference?" You must remember that what the rest of the world does should be of lesser concern than what *you* choose to do. As long as you are alive, the only view of the world that counts is yours. The universe is *your* universe and others should not be allowed to control it. You have the power to change yourself far more than anyone else. You have *complete power*—over you. And that is where it counts. Don't waste it by worrying about what everyone else is doing. Yes, it's true that one person cannot change the world and you are not expected to do that. But you can change *your own world*, rather than everyone else's. Do not waste the opportunity, because it is the most important one you have.

Life is performance art. If you want to leave a lasting message for the world, or to convey one right now, you need to *perform* it. Talking about change will not *make* the change. Talking is, at best, an effort at inspiration and without action, is a waste of breath. Don't waste your breath and hope others will act from your "golden words." No words are golden unless results prove their worth, and you cannot count on others to be as passionate or as successful as you could be.

Life is also a learning process. We learn by truly living life, by acting, and by doing—not by merely observing. Creativity and compassionate action are the two most God-like attributes that we possess. They are meant to be used, not hidden away. So our challenge is to be directly involved with life using our God-given attributes. I love quotes and have collected them all my life. In collecting and sharing them, I have learned much, and have created a few of my own. The one I offer in this book serves well to sum up my views.

> *When mankind becomes willing to help each other, help for himself will appear.*

It is my hope that this book has served as a spark toward your awakening, and in igniting a future awakening for all. Now that you have completed this book, will you fall back asleep or make a conscious choice to awaken? It starts, and ends, with you.

Bibliography and Recommended Reading

Akers, Keith, *The Lost Religion of Jesus: Simple Living and Nonviolence in Early Christianity*, Lantern Books, New York, NY, 2000.

Andreas, Joel, *Addicted to War: Why the U.S. Can't Kick Militarism*, AK Press, Oakland, CA, 2004.

Blume, David (Foreword by R. Buckminster Fuller), *Alcohol Can Be A Gas!*, International Institute for Ecological Agriculture, Santa Cruz, CA, updated edition, 2008.

Brown, Ellen, *The Web of Debt: The Shocking Truth About Our Money System — The Sleight of Hand that has Trapped Us in Debt and How We can Break Free*; Third Millennium Press, Baton Rouge, LA, 2007.

Burnett, Thom and Games, Alex, *Who Really Runs the World?: The War Between Globablization and Democracy*, Conspiracy Books/The Disinformation Company, Ltd., New York, NY, 2007.

Clouder, C., and Rawson, M., *Waldorf Education*, Floris Books, Edinburgh, 1995.

Constable, Trevor James, *The Cosmic Pulse of Life*, Updated Fourth Edition, The Book Tree, San Diego, CA, 2008.

Cremo, Michael, *Forbidden Archaeology: The Hidden History of the Human Race*, Torchlight Publishing, Imperial Beach, CA, 1998.

De Santinilla, Giorgio, and Von Dechend, Hertha, *Hamlet's Mill: An Essay Investigating the Origins of Human Knowledge And Its Transmission Through Myth*, David R. Godine, Publisher, Jaffrey, NH, 1992.

Estulin, Daniel, *The True Story of the Bilderberg Group*, TrineDay, LLC, Walterville, OR, updated 2007.

Feuerstein, Georg, *Holy Madness: The Shock Tactics and Radical Teachings of Crazy-Wise Adepts, Holy Fools, and Rascal Gurus*, Paragon House, New York, NY, 1991.

Fischer, Louis, editor, *The Essential Gandhi: An Anthology of His Writings on His Life, Work and Ideas*, Random House, New York, NY, 1962 (later editions available).

Fort, Charles, *The Book of the Damned*, Boni and Liveright, Inc., New York, NY, 1919; reprinted by The Book Tree, San Diego, CA, 2006.

Fort, Charles, *The Complete Books of Charles Fort*, Dover Publications, New York, NY, 1975.

Fuller, R. Buckminster, *Critical Path*, St. Martin's Press, New York, NY, 1981.

Gandhi, Mahatma, *True Education*, Navajivan Publishing House, Ahmedabad, India, 1962.

Gandhi, Mahatma, *Vows and Observances*, Berkeley Hills Books, Berkeley, CA, 1999.

Gerson, Charlotte, with Bishop, Beata, *Healing the Gerson Way: Defeating Cancer and Other Chronic Diseases*, Totality Books, Carmel, California, 2007.

Gerson, Max, M.D., *A Cancer Therapy: Results of Fifty Cases and The Cure of Advanced Cancer by Diet Therapy, A Summary of Thirty Years of Clinical Experimentation*, Sixth Edition, The Gerson Institute, San Diego, California, 2002.

Glad, John, *Future Human Evolution: Eugenics in the Twenty-First Century*, Hermitage Publishers, Schuylkill Haven, PA, 2006, full text also available as free download at www.whatwemaybe.org.

Goswami, Amit, Ph.D., *The Self-Aware Universe: How Consciousness Creates the Material World*, Jeremy P. Tarcher/Putnam Books, New York, NY, 1993.

Grof, Stanislav, *Beyond the Brain: Birth, Death and Transcendence in Psychotherapy*, State University of New York Press (SUNY), Albany, NY, 1986.

Grof, Stanislav, with Valier, Marjorie (Editors), various contributors, *Human Survival and Consciousness Evolution*, State University of New York Press (SUNY), Albany, NY, 1988.

Hai, Suma Ching, *The Key of Immediate Enlightenment*, Suma Ching Hai International Association Publishing Co., Formosa, Republic of China, 26th edition, 1996.

Hall, Manly P., *The Secret Teachings of All Ages*, Philosophical Research Society, Los Angeles, CA, 1975 edition.

Hawken, Paul, *Blessed Unrest: How the Largest Movement in the World Came into Being and Why No One Saw It Coming*, Viking Penguin, New York, NY, 2007.

Huxley, Aldous, *The Perennial Philosophy*, Harper and Brothers, New York and London, 1945, reprinted Harper Perennial Modern Classics, New York, NY, 2004.

Jaynes, Julian, *The Origin of Consciousness in the Breakdown of the Bicameral Mind*, Houghton Mifflin/Mariner Books, New York, NY, 2000.

Kauffman, Stuart A., *Reinventing the Sacred: A New View of Science, Reason and Religion*, Basic Books, New York, NY, 2008.

Kazantzakis, Nikos, *The Saviors of God*, Renaissance Magazine, Athens, Greece, 1927, trans. and reprinted in English, Touchstone Books, New York, NY, 1960.

Keel, John, *Disneyland of the Gods*, IllumiNet Press, Lilburn, GA, 1995.

Keel, John, *Our Haunted Planet*, Fawcett Publications, Inc., New York, NY, 1971; reprinted by Galde Press, Lakeville, MN, 2002.

Kovel, Joel, *History and Spirit: An Inquiry into the Philosophy of Liberation*, Beacon Press, Boston, MA, 1991.

Krishna, Gopi, *Kundalini: The Evolutionary Energy in Man*, Shambala Books, Berkeley, CA, 1971, reprinted 1997.

Krishnamurti, Jiddu, *Education and the Significance of Life*, HarperOne, New York, NY, 1985.

Krishnamurti, Jiddu, *Krishnamurti on Education*, Harper & Row, New York, NY, 1974.

Laszlo, Ervin; Grof, Stanislav and Russell, Peter, *The Consciousness Revolution*, Elf Rock Books, London, 2003.

Lanctot, Guylaine, *The Medical Mafia: How to Get Out of It Alive and Take Back Our Health & Wealth*, Here's the Key, Inc., Quebec, Canada, 1995.

Mander, Jerry, *Four Arguments for the Elimination of Television*, Harper Perennial, New York, NY, 1978.

Mead, G.R.S., *The Hymn of the Robe of Glory*, Theosophical Publishing Society, London, 1908, reprinted by The Book Tree, San Diego, CA, 2005.

Miller, George David, *Peace, Value and Wisdom: The Educational Philosophy of Daisaku Ikeda*, Rodopi Books, Amersterdam & New York, 2002.

Muses, Charles, and Young, Arthur M., editors, *Consciousness and Reality: The Human Pivot Point*, Avon Books, New York, NY, 1974.

Rensch, Bernhard, *Homo Sapiens: From Man to Demigod*, Columbia University Press, New York, NY, 1972.

Robbins, John, *Diet for a New America*, HJ Kramer, 2nd edition, Tiburon, CA, 1998.

Russell, Peter, *The Global Brain: Speculations on the Evolutionary Leap to Global Consciousness*, Jeremy P. Tarcher, Inc., Los Angeles, 1983; reprinted with new subtitle, *The Awakening Earth in a New Century*, Floris Books, Edinburgh, U.K., 2008.

Sannella, Lee, M.D., *The Kundalini Experience,* Integral Publishing, Lower Lake, CA, 1987.

Steiner, Rudolf, *The Child's Changing Consciousness and Waldorf Education*, Anthroposophic Press & Rudolf Steiner Press, New York & London, 1988.

Tice, Paul, *Triumph of the Human Spirit: The Greatest Acheivements of the Human Soul and How Its Power can Change Your Life*, The Book Tree, San Diego, CA, 1999.

Velikovsky, Immanuel, *Mankind in Amnesia*, Doubleday & Company, Inc., Garden City, NY, 1982.

Watts, Alan, *The Book On the Taboo Against Knowing Who You Are*, Vintage Books edition/Random House, 1989.

Wells, H.G., *The Open Conspiracy*, C.A. Watt & Co., London, 1935, reprinted 2006, The Book Tree, San Diego, CA.

Wilbur, Ken, *The Spectrum of Consciousness*, Quest Books, Wheaton, IL, 2nd edition, 1993.

Wilson, Colin, *Mysteries*, Perigree Trade Books, 1980; reprinted 2006, Watkins Books, London.

Winn, Marie, *The Plug-In Drug: Television, Computers, and Family Life*, Penguin Books, New York & London, updated edition, 2002.

Wolf, Fred Alan, *The Spiritual Universe: One Physicist's Vision of Spirit, Soul, Matter and Self*, Moment Point Press, Needham, MA, 1999.

Yatri, *Unknown Man: The Mysterious Birth of a New Species*, Simon and Schuster/Fireside Books, New York, NY, 1988.

Index

A
Abraham 153
Abu Dhabi 181
Alcohol Can Be a Gas 187, 237
American Express 180
animal cruelty 172
Aquarian Age 155, 157, 196, 231
Aquarius 155-156, 208
aspartame 161
astrological ages 5, 151-157
astrology 151-157
Aurobindo, Sri 7
awakening 7, 9, 11, 22, 59-60, 102, 149, 157, 178, 186, 201, 219, 232, 235

B
balance of nature 23, 177
Bank of America 180
banking 80, 87, 166, 179-180, 190, 192-194, 201
banks 84, 92, 111, 179-182, 191-192, 194-195
Bible 36, 52, 54, 86, 127, 133, 151, 154-156, 175, 203-204, 207
Bilderberg Group 83, 87-88, 112, 189, 237
Blume, David 187
Borse Dhabi 181
brainwashing 103, 202
Brown, Ellen Hodgson 88, 237
Buddhism 68, 122, 181
bull 152-153

C
capitalism 191, 230
Carlyle Group 181-182
Catholic 120, 217
cattle 16, 98, 170-171, 186
CFR 87, 112
chemicals, in food 143-144, 161-162, 164-165, 169
China 17, 81, 179-185, 191, 194, 238
Christianity 32, 51-53, 91, 119, 121-122, 133, 152-156, 197, 237
Christians 12, 32, 39, 51, 153-155
church 36, 51-52, 54, 96, 120-121, 124, 131, 133-134, 137, 155, 168, 203-205, 207-208, 212, 217
commercialism 96, 179, 183

communism 17, 142, 179-180, 183, 187, 191, 230
Community Supported Agriculture (CSAs) 142-143, 186, 188
compassion 9, 11, 15, 33, 53, 55-56, 60, 64, 79, 82, 85-86, 89, 105, 110, 124, 130-131, 135-136, 139, 141, 149, 164, 167, 175, 178, 186-187, 197, 200, 206, 210, 214, 215, 222, 226-227, 235
Compassion Over Killing 178
consciousness 3, 7-9, 11, 23-26, 30, 33, 37, 46, 48-49, 51, 56, 58-59, 61, 64, 72, 76, 82, 85-86, 89-90, 98, 100-102, 110, 112, 115, 119, 122-124, 126-132, 138-139, 173, 176-177, 179, 190, 197, 200, 204, 213, 216, 218, 225-227, 232-234, 238-239
constellations 151
cooperative 17, 142, 219
Council on Foreign Relations 87
creation 7, 17, 41, 65, 94, 108, 117, 123, 126, 128, 132, 139, 142, 194, 215, 233
creativity 27, 41, 48, 56-57, 66, 69, 129, 235
crime 177, 185, 226
CSA farming 142-143, 186, 188

D
dairy 169, 173
Dalai Lama 85, 181
dark ages 7, 37, 124, 140, 212
deforestation 171, 220
devil 36, 135, 176, 223
dogma 10, 91, 111, 127, 133
dogmatic 13-14, 34-35, 37, 39, 54-55, 118-119, 121-122, 124, 130, 134, 156, 200, 202, 207, 212, 214, 222, 232
dualistic 10, 24, 26-27, 32, 58, 65, 73, 106, 110, 127-128, 130
duality 10, 23-24, 26-27, 66, 73, 130
Dubai 168, 187, 194
Dyer, Dr. Wayne 136

E
economic 9, 12, 14-17, 20, 21, 30, 60, 81, 87, 89, 104, 141-142, 144, 149, 159, 166, 179, 181-182, 184-186, 188-189, 191-196, 199, 201, 203, 222, 228-229, 233-234

240

economic restructuring 9, 14, 189, 234
education 5, 9, 11-13, 29-30, 35, 37-44, 48-49, 51, 56-58, 61, 89-91, 112, 141, 143, 164, 178, 189-190, 193, 196, 208, 222-229, 234
Einstein, Albert 16, 107, 113, 172, 232
Emerson, Ralph Waldo 16, 29, 115, 145, 199
enlightenment 38, 54, 88, 90, 92, 94, 98, 119, 121, 127-128, 131
ethanol 16, 187-188
eugenics 166-168
European Economic Community 81
Eusebius 168

F
factory farms 171, 173, 175
FDA (Federal Drug Administration) 161, 165
Federal Reserve Bank/Board 87, 111, 183, 193-194
First Law of Thermodynamics 30
fish 73, 75, 93, 152-154, 196-197, 232
Fort, Charles 73-75
free will 117, 139, 145, 147
fundamentalist 12, 13, 35, 39, 52-55, 90-91, 124, 133-134, 155, 191, 199-200, 202, 211, 212, 222

G
gambling 68, 184
Gandhi, Mahatma 16, 17, 40, 69, 90, 100, 105, 108, 142, 144, 175, 181, 188, 205, 210, 216, 222
global warming 162, 171, 220
globalization 60, 182
Gnosticism 122
Gnostic(s) 32, 51-52, 121-122, 132-133, 138-139
God 14, 19, 27, 36, 49, 51-52, 55, 66, 72, 81, 86, 90-92, 94, 98, 104, 115-139, 145-146, 148, 146, 150, 152-153, 156, 162, 164, 167, 175, 178, 184, 186, 199-201, 203, 206-207, 209-218, 222, 229-231, 235
God Pact, The 209-218
Goethe 71
Goswami, Amit, Ph.D. 128

greed 61, 68, 79-80, 87, 106, 120, 130, 141, 146, 150, 162, 164, 172, 183, 187, 190, 195, 212, 219-220, 227, 230
Grof, Stanislav 124, 238
Gurdjieff 9, 46

H
healing 204, 237
health care 164
higher consciousness 59, 100-101, 200
higher self 26-27, 47, 101, 128, 130
holistic 7-9, 13-14, 17, 38, 40, 60, 113, 115, 117, 119, 122, 128, 142, 144, 187, 189, 193, 196, 200, 221, 231, 234
human nature 69, 79, 109
Hus, John 203-204

I
identity 7-10, 19, 30, 49, 60, 100, 124, 128, 130, 135, 182, 186, 193, 196, 234
ignorance 25, 43, 58, 76, 88, 91, 120, 169, 177, 188, 196, 205, 207, 216, 220, 223, 225
Ikeda, Daisaku 13, 41, 222, 239
India 17, 29, 38, 40, 153, 179-181, 184-185, 194
Industrial and Commercial Bank of China (ICBC) 180
internal evolution 231-235
international banks 15, 88, 180, 191-193
International Monetary Fund (IMF) 79-80, 87-88, 111-112, 180

J
J. P. Morgan Chase 180-181, 194
Jaynes, Julian 233
Jesus 10, 16, 51, 53, 54, 60, 105, 120, 133, 130, 153-157, 168, 197, 207, 237
Judaism 153
Jung, Carl 92, 133, 152, 155

K
Kauffman, Stuart 116, 129, 238
Keel, John 73-75, 238
Kennedy, John F. 69, 123
King, Jr., Dr. Martin Luther 69, 105, 108, 113, 123, 210, 216

Krishnamurti, Jiddu 12-13, 35, 38-39, 42, 238

L

lamb 153
livestock 15-16
London Stock Exchange 181

M

Mankind In Amnesia 233, 239
materialism 87, 97, 103
materialistic 9, 11, 14, 20-21, 30, 80, 82, 85-86, 89, 97-98, 104, 112, 116, 130, 141, 146, 150, 180, 201, 228, 230, 234
Maxwell, Jordan 4, 156
meaning of life 22, 79, 84-87
media 8, 80, 82-83, 102, 112, 178, 187, 189, 192, 229
medical 163-164, 239
meditation 11, 20, 33-34, 42, 49, 98-101, 104, 177
Merrill Lynch 180
methane 162, 171
milk 169, 173
money 11, 15, 20, 47, 55-56, 67, 80-84, 103, 106, 108-111, 135-136, 141, 143, 160, 162-165, 171, 179-180, 182-184, 190-195, 199, 201, 203-205, 217, 221, 222, 216, 227, 229-230, 233, 237
Moore, Michael 164
Morgan Stanley 180, 181
mutual respect 9, 11, 55-56, 90, 124, 141, 181, 186, 197, 199-202, 206, 210, 215, 221-222
my God can beat up your God 14, 36, 91

N

Nature 10, 14, 17, 20, 23, 26, 64, 66, 76, 97, 102, 116, 129, 165, 166, 177, 213, 215, 216, 220, 231
near-death experience 118, 146
New Age 12, 39, 61, 102, 116, 128, 134, 152, 155-157, 196, 199, 201, 232
new paradigm 7, 9, 14, 17, 89-90, 180, 182, 184, 192-193, 195, 229, 232, 234
New World Order 88, 142, 179-180, 182, 184, 192

O

Oak Grove School 12, 13, 35, 38, 41, 226
oil 16, 21, 83, 143, 182, 187-188
Oneness 49, 59, 117, 124, 129, 130
Origin of Consciousness in the Breakdown of the Bicameral Mind, The 233, 238

P

paradigm 7, 9, 14, 16-17, 21, 30, 50, 61, 63, 80, 82, 83-84, 88-90, 105, 112, 141-142, 149-150, 159, 172, 180, 182, 184-185, 189-190, 192-193, 195, 205, 219, 222-223, 228-234
paradigm shift 142, 232
Passover 153, 156
peace 13, 23, 41, 56, 107-108, 146, 209-211, 213-215, 217-218, 229, 239
pesticides 143-144, 169
PETA (People for the Ethical Treatment of Animals) 171, 178
philosophy 13, 41, 43-44, 110, 111, 144, 149-150, 231, 238
Piscean Age 197, 232
Pisces 151-154, 196-197
politics 107-113, 147, 149, 221, 231
pollution 171, 183
Pope 91, 153, 203
population 17, 25, 63, 82, 88, 109, 111-112, 147, 163, 166-168, 180, 183, 202, 223
precession of the equinoxes 152, 156
protein 170
prozac 165

Q

quantum physics 10, 23, 49, 59, 74, 89, 115, 128, 139, 146, 214, 217

R

rain forest 15, 170-171
ram 153
reincarnation 25
religion 10-14, 19, 21, 34, 35-37, 39, 41, 52-55, 68, 90-91, 96, 98, 105, 115, 117-125, 130, 132-134, 137, 145-147, 149, 152-153, 155, 157, 168, 191, 197, 199-208, 209, 211-215, 217-218, 221-224, 226, 229, 231-232, 237, 238
"robot," the 45-50, 53, 58

Index 243

Royal Bank of Scotland 180
Russia/Soviet Union 81, 142, 170, 183, 191
S
Schopenhauer, Arthur 85, 115
Self-Aware Universe, The 128, 238
self-awareness 64, 128
Shaw, George Bernard 65
shepherds 151
slaughterhouse 166, 167
socialized human 227
soul, the 10, 14, 19-21, 25-27, 29-32, 37, 44, 46-50, 53, 59, 66, 68-69, 72-73, 85-87, 90, 91, 94, 100, 104, 115, 117, 125-126, 129, 131, 134, 137, 145, 147, 149, 164, 167, 174, 215, 219, 231, 239
spirit, the 71-73, 100
spirits 19, 66, 71-73
spiritual evolution 130, 204, 231
spiritual freedom 52, 98, 122, 186, 204, 208, 229
spiritual growth 33, 42, 88, 118, 123, 134, 136, 157, 167, 178, 190, 221, 223, 225, 227, 230
Spiritual Value Quotient (SVQ) 226
spiritual values 17, 142, 203, 207, 222, 226
spirituality 14, 16, 37, 53-55, 90, 121, 124, 134, 142, 189, 201, 203, 207, 221-222, 226, 232
Sri Chinmoy 186
starvation 15, 109, 112, 171-172, 205, 223, 228, 230
Steiner, Rudolf 12-13, 39-40, 239
swadeshi 17, 40, 142, 144, 188
Swiss Bank UBS AG 180
T
television/TV 20, 32, 43, 45, 47, 56, 67, 68, 81, 83-85, 92, 93-97, 102-103, 105, 136, 140, 147, 149-150, 159-160, 165, 176, 187, 189, 193, 203, 239
Temasek Holdings of Singapore 180
Tibet 181, 207
tolerance 55-56, 202, 208
Toynbee, Arnold 151
Transcendental Meditation (TM) 177
Trilateral Commission 83, 87-88, 112

true self 27, 43, 46, 135
tryptophan 165
Twain, Mark 206
U
UNESCO 13, 39
United Nations 16, 56, 80, 87, 201
V
Vatican 217, 229
vegan 16, 168-170, 172, 178
vegetarian 16, 168-170, 172, 175-176, 178
Velikovsky, Immanuel 233, 239
Vivekenanda 55-56
W
Waldenses 207-208
Waldorf 12-13, 38, 41-42, 222, 226, 237, 239
Wall Street 184, 195
war/warfare 8, 21, 23, 30, 54-56, 82, 84, 87, 107-109, 112, 123, 148, 153, 161, 166, 187, 195, 199-200, 205-206, 209, 215-216, 218, 220, 223, 228-230, 233, 237
water 8, 16, 65, 79, 88, 101, 112, 143-144, 145, 156-157, 161, 171-172, 184, 187, 196-197, 207-208, 219, 223, 231-232
Web of Debt, The 88, 237
Wilson, Colin 45
Wilson, Robert Anton 96
Winfrey, Oprah 136
wisdom 8, 11-13, 21, 22, 26, 35, 41, 43, 51, 87, 89, 91, 99, 101-102, 104, 110, 117-119, 127, 131, 145, 151, 165, 166-168, 181, 223, 234, 239
witchcraft 204-205
World Bank 79-80, 87, 112, 189
world peace 107-108, 209, 211, 215, 218, 229
World Resources Institute 220

www.ingramcontent.com/pod-product-compliance
Lightning Source LLC
Chambersburg PA
CBHW070532170426
43200CB00011B/2399